A Half Century of Super B

MW00581233

In 2016, the Super Bowl, the climactic spectacle of American professional football, celebrated its 50th anniversary. The Super Bowl stands as the broadest 'shared experience' in American culture. As television ratings, cultural practices, and scholarly tomes reveal, more people participate in watching the Super Bowl than in any other common endeavor in the United States. The Super Bowl has become a new national holiday dedicated to the celebration of consumption—the driving force underneath modern culture.

Beyond the borders of the United States, the Super Bowl does not rank as highly as a global phenomenon, though it increasingly draws larger audiences in a few nations around the globe. Some watch as curious students of American habits, and others seem to be developing affinity for American-style football. The global dynamics of the consumption of football reveal much about the parameters of American 'soft power' and cultural influence in the new globalized social networks that are emerging as consumption increasingly powers not only the United States but also the world economy.

A Half Century of Super Bowls: National and Global Perspectives on America's Grandest Spectacle analyzes the Super Bowl in shaping American and global communities and identities. It was originally published as a special issue of the *International Journal of the History of Sport*.

Peter M. Hopsicker is an Associate Professor of Kinesiology and Head of the Division of Education, Human Development, and Social Sciences at Pennsylvania State University, Altoona, USA. He is also a member of the Graduate Faculty of the Department of Kinesiology and a member of the Executive Committee of the Center for the Study of Sports in Society at Pennsylvania State University.

Mark Dyreson is a Professor of Kinesiology and History at Pennsylvania State University, State College, USA; the Director of Research and Educational Programs at the Penn State Center for the Study of Sports in Society; the Managing Editor of the *International Journal of the History of Sport*; a former President of the North American Society for Sport History; a Fellow of the National Academy of Kinesiology; and the author of several books and numerous articles on the history of sport.

Sport in the Global Society: Historical Perspectives
Series Editors: Mark Dyreson, Thierry Terret and Rob Hess

For more information about this series, please visit: https://www.routledge.com/Sport-in-the-Global-Society---Historical-perspectives/book-series/SGSH

A Half Century of Super Bowls

National and Global Perspectives on America's
Grandest Spectacle

Edited by
Peter M. Hopsicker and Mark Dyreson

LONDON AND NEW YORK

First published 2018 by Routledge

2 Park Square, Milton Park, Abingdon, Oxfordshire OX14 4RN
52 Vanderbilt Avenue, New York, NY 10017

Routledge is an imprint of the Taylor & Francis Group, an informa business

First issued in paperback 2020

British Library Cataloguing-in-Publication Data
A catalogue record for this book is available from the British Library

ISBN13: 978-1-138-59142-4 (hbk)
ISBN13: 978-0-367-59025-3 (pbk)

Typeset in Minion Pro
by codeMantra

Publisher's Note
The publisher accepts responsibility for any inconsistencies that may have arisen
during the conversion of this book from journal articles to book chapters, namely the
possible inclusion of journal terminology.

Disclaimer
Every effort has been made to contact copyright holders for their permission to reprint
material in this book. The publishers would be grateful to hear from any copyright
holder who is not here acknowledged and will undertake to rectify any errors or
omissions in future editions of this book.

Contents

CONTENTS

Citation Information

The chapters in this book were originally published in *The International Journal of the History of Sport*, volume 34, issues 1–2 (January 2017). When citing this material, please use the original page numbering for each article, as follows:

Introduction

Chapter 1

Chapter 2

Chapter 3

Chapter 4

Chapter 5

Amerika: *The Super Bowl and German Imagination*
Lars Dzikus
The International Journal of the History of Sport, volume 34, issues 1–2 (January 2017)
pp. 81–100

Chapter 6

A Century of British Readings of America through American Football: From the Fin de Siècle *to the Super Bowl*
Iain Adams
The International Journal of the History of Sport, volume 34, issues 1–2 (January 2017)
pp. 101–120

Chapter 7

'We Will Try Again, Again, Again to Make It Bigger': Japan, American Football, and the Super Bowl in the Past, Present, and Future*
Kohei Kawashima
The International Journal of the History of Sport, volume 34, issues 1–2 (January 2017)
pp. 121–138

Chapter 8

The Super Bowl as a Television Spectacle: Global Designs, Glocal Niches, and Parochial Patterns
Mark Dyreson
The International Journal of the History of Sport, volume 34, issues 1–2 (January 2017)
pp. 139–156

For any permission-related enquiries please visit:
http://www.tandfonline.com/page/help/permissions

Notes on Contributors

Iain Adams is the Principal Lecturer at the International Football Institute, UK, a research partnership between the University of Central Lancashire and the National Football Museum.

Richard C. Crepeau is Professor Emeritus of History at the University of Central Florida in Orlando, USA. His research interests include American professional football, intercollegiate athletics and baseball.

Mark Dyreson is a Professor of Kinesiology and History at the Pennsylvania State University, USA; and the Director of Research and Educational Programs at the Penn State Center for the Study of Sports in Society.

Lars Dzikus is an Associate Professor in Sport Studies at the University of Tennessee, Knoxville, USA. He received his PhD in cultural studies in sport from The Ohio State University, Columbus, USA.

Elysia Galindo-Ramirez is a PhD student in the College of Communications at Pennsylvania State University, State College, USA. She also has a Masters in Cultural Studies from Claremont Graduate University. Her research interests include the representation of gender and sexuality in sports media, feminized sports, and e-sports.

Craig G. Greenham is an Assistant Professor in the Department of Kinesiology at the University of Windsor, Canada. He holds a PhD in history from the University of Western Ontario, London, Canada and is a former journalist. The author's research interests include the relationship between media and professional athletics.

Peter M. Hopsicker serves as an Associate Professor of Kinesiology at Pennsylvania State University, Altoona, USA. Hopsicker earned his doctorate from Pennsylvania State University.

Kohei Kawashima received a PhD in American History from Brown University, Providence, USA (1992) and currently teaches at the Faculty of Humanities, Musashi University, Tokyo, Japan.

Matthew P. McAllister is a Professor of Communications at Pennsylvania State University, State College, USA. He is the coeditor (with Emily West) of *The Routledge Companion to Advertising and Promotional Culture*. His research focuses on political economy of media and critiques of commercial and promotional culture.

Series Editors' Foreword

Sport in the Global Society: Historical Perspectives explores the role of sport in cultures both around the world and across the timeframes of human history. In the world we currently inhabit, sport spans the globe. It captivates vast audiences. It defines, alters, and reinforces identities for individuals, communities, nations, empires, and the world. Sport organises memories and perceptions, arouses passions and tensions, and reveals harmonies and cleavages. It builds and blurs social boundaries—animating discourses about class, gender, race, and ethnicity. Sport opens new vistas on the history of human cultures, intersecting with politics and economics, ideologies and theologies. It reveals aesthetic tastes and energises consumer markets.

Our challenge is to explain how sport has developed into a global phenomenon. The series continues the tradition established by the original incarnation of *Sport in the Global Society* (and in 2010 divided into *Historical Perspectives and Contemporary Perspectives*) by promoting the academic study of one of the most significant and dynamic forces in shaping the historical landscapes of human cultures.

In the twenty-first century, a critical mass of scholars recognises the importance of sport in their analyses of human experiences. *Sport in the Global Society: Historical Perspectives* provides an international outlet for the leading investigators on these subjects. Building on previous work and excavating new terrain, our series remains a consistent and coherent response to the attention the academic community demands for the serious study of sport.

Mark Dyreson
Thierry Terret
Rob Hess

Super Bowl Sunday: A National Holiday and a Global Curiosity

Peter Hopsicker and Mark Dyreson

On 15 January 1967, the National Football League (NFL) and the American Football League (AFL) staged the first AFL-NFL World Championship Game, a contest that would soon become known in common parlance as the Super Bowl. Held in the mammoth Los Angeles Memorial Coliseum that seated more than 90,000 spectators, the game featured the NFL's Green Bay Packers against the AFL's Kansas City Chiefs in a spectacle that celebrated the recently engineered merger between the two rival leagues – a deal that would spawn over the next half century the most powerful sporting corporation in American culture. The new conglomerate, which kept the moniker 'NFL' to identify itself, reigns in the twenty-first century as the most influential and lucrative entertainment behemoth in the national landscape, a multi-billion dollar industrial giant that dominates US television broadcasting and aspires to global mega-event status.[1]

Ticket prices for the original Super Bowl ranged between a reasonable $6 and $12, but more than 35,000 seats remained empty on game day as the Packers dismantled the Chiefs, 35–10. For the only time in Super Bowl history two major television networks, the Columbia Broadcasting System (CBS) and the National Broadcasting System (NBC) broadcast the game to a relatively modest national viewership of 60 million, a much smaller audience than future Super Bowls would command. Neither pregame shows nor special commercials designed to debut during the broadcast accompanied Super Bowl I. When NBC failed to return from a commercial in time for the second-half kickoff, league officials had the teams re-kick. The half-time show featured standard football fare, performances by Grambling College, the University of Michigan, and the University of Arizona marching bands. Those same musicians rather than a world-famous pop star performed the 'Star Spangled Banner' before the game commenced. From many perspectives, the inaugural Super Bowl fell short of achieving its 'super' superlative. The game was hardly the cultural touchstone it would later become in American society. Indeed, it was just another game. As journalist Fred Clair, who chronicled Super Bowl I for the *Pomona* (California) *Progress Bulletin*, recalled a half-century afterwards: 'Could anybody have predicted where it would be (nearly) 50 years later? Certainly not.'[2]

On 7 February 2016, fifty-one years after Super Bowl I, a sell-out crowd of more than 70,000 packed NRG Stadium in Houston, Texas, for Super Bowl LI. Country music star Luke Bryan crooned the national anthem; pop music icon Lady Gaga performed the half-time extravaganza; and pregame television shows ran for hours before kickoff. More than 111 million American television viewers tuned in–a conservative estimate based on a ratings system that only measures televisions in private homes and does not account for the 20–25% of viewers who watch in public settings such as bars, churches, and restaurants. A thirty-second commercial slot cost more than $5 million; and Fox network managed to get back from its lucrative advertising schedule so the NFL did not have to redo the second half kickoff.[3]

A half-century after the NFL's first attempt at adorning its season-culminating championship football game with a spectacular atmosphere, Super Bowl LI demonstrated that the venture has become more than just a game. The Super Bowl is now an American institution, producing an experience that exudes the qualities of a quintessential American holiday – a holiday that, paradoxically, frequently seems to treat the NFL's championship game as an ancillary to the festivities. In the five decades between Super Bowl I and Super Bowl LI, the popularity of Super Bowl Sunday has exploded. It has become the largest shared experience within the national culture. More Americans watch the Super Bowl than vote in elections, attend religious services, or commemorate patriotic sacrifices. Indeed, those who express disinterest in the Super Bowl can swiftly incur accusations that they are un-American.[4]

After several episodes in which it remained just another football game, the Super Bowl became an American mega-event by the mid-1970s and Americans increasingly viewed it as the nation's newest holiday. Since the 1970s, succeeding Super Bowl instalments have pushed the boundaries of nationalistic and patriotic displays, tested the scope of the metaphors describing conspicuously consumptive practices, and branded the event as a national holiday. So powerful has the appeal of this annual sporting festival become that the normal activities of an American Sunday are frequently reorganized to accommodate the game. Corporations spend millions of dollars on television commercials designed specifically for the Super Bowl. Some of them only air once, at the Super Bowl, during this competitive parade of advertising spots that has come to be known as the 'Ad Bowl'. Superstar celebrities of all genera vie to sing the national anthem or headline the half-time extravaganza on a stage viewed by over two-thirds of Americans. Politicians seek to associate themselves with the all-American nature of the production – the ostentatious displays of red, white, and blue, the fly-overs of military aircraft, and the scenes of armed forces service men and women participating in the day from foreign lands.[5]

In the United States, the holiday nature of Super Bowl Sunday reveals itself in a variety of ways. Like other holidays, the Super Bowl leads Americans to alter their daily routines. Businesses close while celebrants meticulously plan profligate parties. People gather for a common purpose – to participate in the shared rituals that have developed to celebrate the spectacle. Similar in many ways to Thanksgiving, Super Bowl Sunday gatherings include feasts of specific food and drink – chicken wings and crudités, chips and guacamole, fried finger foods and pizza, soda and beer, Bloody Marys and other football-themed cocktails. Super Bowl Sunday also evokes overt displays of nationalism that rival the Fourth of July, Veterans Day, and other patriotic holidays. Super Bowl commemorations have included not only the singing of the national anthem in front of a football-field-sized flag held by American service men and women, but also pregame recitations of the Pledge of Allegiance and the Declaration of Independence. The Super Bowl has included brazenly nationalistic elements since its inception and has served as an official kick-off to the nation's bicentennial in 1976, a pep rally for the Gulf War in 1991, as well as a memorial to the victims of the 9/11 terrorist attacks in 2002. Furthermore, Super Bowl Sunday stands as the day when Americans celebrate conspicuous consumption – a public demonstration of the American ability to buy things – that rivals Christmas and other gift-buying holidays. Marketers spend billions of dollars on television advertising to take advantage of the huge captive audience ensconced in front of television sets to hawk everything from beer and avocados to computers and automobiles. Indeed, the Super Bowl's dedication to the celebration of consumption makes it a part of the driving force underneath modern American culture.[6]

In 2017, the Super Bowl's focus on consumption and advertising connected the nation's newest holiday to highly charged political dialogues in the United States. With debates over immigrants, borders, race, and gender issues raging through the American political landscape, major corporations entered the fray with Super Bowl spots that challenged the positions staked out by the recently elected presidential administration of Donald J. Trump. The automaker Audi aired an advertisement promoting equal pay for equal work that evoked the debates about gender equity that had roiled the 2016 presidential election. Coca-Cola resurrected a 2014 spot that featured a multi-ethnic cast singing 'America the Beautiful', evoking an image of racial harmony in stark contrast to the racial and ethnic tensions surrounding the Trump administration. Google ran an advertisement with a similar theme that showcased American diversity and featured a 'welcome home' cake at the end of the video collage. Anheuser-Busch In Bev, the enormous US-based global brewery chain, aired a Budweiser beer advertisement that chronicled the anti-immigrant challenges faced by founder Adolphus Busch as he migrated from Germany to the United States in the 1850s, providing a historical spin on the quest for the 'American dream' and twenty-first century perspectives on the merits of immigration. Airbnb sponsored a spot that challenged the Trump administration's 'travel ban'.[7]

In the most provocative of the corporate assaults on Trumpian ideology, the building supplies and home improvement chain 84 Lumber produced a spot chronicling the quest of a Latina mother and daughter to migrate from Mexico to the promised land of the United States. The advertisement that ran on television ended there, after Fox television, which broadcast Super Bowl LI and also owns the Fox News network that has been consistently supportive of the early days of the Trump administration, refused to air the rest of the spot. 84 Lumber directed viewers who wanted to see the rest of the ad to their company website. So many people sought to watch it that the site crashed repeatedly. When it did work, viewers saw the mother and daughter make it to the United States, only to be confronted by President Trump's 'great wall'. A construction worker using 84 Lumber supplies had conveniently carved a door in the fortress, however, beckoning the refugees to the other side. The advertisement ended with a blunt rejection of anti-immigration sentiment: 'The will to succeed is always welcome here'.[8]

The role of the US in the world, and the world in the US, has historically wafted around Super Bowls. The American variant of football showcased at the Super Bowl remains a remarkably parochial spectacle while association football (soccer in US parlance) has become the 'world's game'. The NFL has long harboured designs of transforming the Super Bowl into a global mega-event that would rival World Cups and Olympic games. League officials have for the past several decades touted potential audiences of more than a billion tuning into global telecasts of the game. In spite of the NFL's expansionist rhetoric, however,

Super Bowl Sunday certainly does not hold the day-altering power in the rest of the world that it that wields in the US.[9]

Still, the Super Bowl has made beachheads in other nations, especially across the border where President Trump plans his massive wall in Mexico, as well across the US border to the north in Canada. Indeed, Mexican and Canadian telecasts started with Super Bowl I in 1967 and have built substantial audiences in both nations. In addition, from the early history of the Super Bowl, the American Forces Network (AFN) has beamed the game to foreign outposts for American military personnel. AFN signals have bled from US bases into the local airwaves where some of the locals who view themselves as curious students of American habits seem to be developing affinity for American-style football. Pockets of interest in the Super Bowl have sprouted in a variety of nations, particularly in Great Britain, Germany, Japan, and Australia. However, the recent annual statements in NFL press releases that claim global Super Bowl audiences of more than a billion viewers in as many as 200 nations should be read with tremendous scepticism. Still, the Super Bowl has become a growing global curiosity, and the global dynamics of the consumption of football reveal much about the international dynamics of American 'soft power' and cultural influence in the new globalized social networks that are emerging as consumption increasingly powers not only the US but also the world economy.

This collection of essays investigates the historical transformation of Super Bowl Sunday from a mere professional football championship game to a much-anticipated annual event of shared experience firmly fixed to the American holiday calendar as well as a growing and influential worldwide curiosity. With an assemblage of distinguished scholars from the United States, Canada, Germany, Great Britain, and Japan, these analyses of the first half-century of Super Bowl history provide insight into the political, cultural, and economic development of this relatively young social phenomenon.

Several scholars from the United States provide local perspective. Richard Crepeau from the University of Central Florida examines the historic and rapid development of the day – a day that quickly included all of the tenets of a holiday festival in the United States – by focusing on its explicit displays of and connections to excess. Penn State Altoona's Peter Hopsicker uses the prominent sport critic Robert Lipsyte's concept of 'Superbowling' to provide a historical narrative of the commentary surrounding each Super Bowl. Three predominant threads emerge from this examination that peg Super Bowl Sunday as a day of conspicuous consumption, shared experience, and national holiday. Matthew McAllister and Elysia Galindo-Ramirez, also from Penn State (University Park), focus on the conspicuous consumption aspects of the day through an analysis of Super Bowl commercials – an aspect of the day that took on a life of its own in the 1980s. Utilizing the concepts of 'spectacular consumption' and 'commodity audience', the authors identify Super Bowl commercials as a model for contemporary advertising – one viewed as a legitimate form of entertainment culture.

Moving beyond the borders of the United States, four other scholars provide insight into the worldview of Super Bowl Sunday. To the north, Craig Greenham of the University of Windsor (Canada) compares the Grey Cup to the Super Bowl through the lenses of the Canadian media. He finds that while the Super Bowl garners a significant presence on the Canadian calendar, Canadian sports pundits continue to promote the Grey Cup as the anti-Super Bowl – a tactic that rebukes American cultural imperialism and excess. Across the Atlantic, Ian Adams of the University of Central Lancashire (UK) provides a history of American football and the Super Bowl in the British imagination. After a look into the history of American football's development in the United Kingdom, Adams suggests that Britons regard watching the Super Bowl in the same way they view taking a one-day holiday to another land. Lars Dzikus (University of Tennessee) explores the German imagination and the Super Bowl. Using accounts from Germans who established American football leagues in Germany as well as other media accounts, Dzikus discovers that the Super Bowl was one way that Germans constructed the images, ideas, and symbols that they associated with the US. Kohei Kawashima of Musashi University, Japan, situates the growth of American football within Japanese history, society, and culture. After a discussion of the past and present status of American football in Japan, Kawashima offers his assessments of the future of the game and the Super Bowl in the Far East.

In the collection's final essay, Mark Dyreson of Penn State University (University Park) assesses American perceptions of how the world views the US through the Super Bowl. Dyreson investigates the growing globalization of Super Bowl Sunday and discovers that most international interest exists in Canada and Mexico. Beyond that, fascination with the Super Bowl is confined to a few unique 'glocal' markets scattered around the world. The widespread and intense worldwide interest imagined by the NFL simply does exist. Still, Dyreson notes that in some parts of the world, especially where fascinated locals strive to establish an American football culture, the Super Bowl has become a burgeoning curiosity.

In its first fifty years the Super Bowl has evolved in the United States from just another championship football game to the largest and in some ways the most significant shared experience in American culture. As the NFL and the US television networks that stage the spectacle seek to globalize their product, they have met more indifference than resistance. For American audiences, the halcyon days of the Super Bowl were not in the 1960s when the game first sprang to life. The 'golden age' began in the last two decades of the twentieth century and has continued into the twenty-first century, a period in which the Super Bowl became an indelible component of the nation's culture. Whether over the next half-century the NFL and US television corporations can create a global interest in American football remains to be seen.

Notes

1. For insights into the history of the Super Bowl see Richard C. Crepeau, *NFL Football: A History of America's New National Pastime* (Urbana: University of Illinois Press, 2010); Don Weiss with Chuck Day, *The Making of the Super Bowl: The Inside Story of the World's Greatest Sporting Event* (Contemporary Books: Chicago, 2003); Craig Coenen, *From Sandlots to the Super Bowl: The National Football League, 1920–1967* (Knoxville: The University of Tennessee Press, 2005); Michael MacCambridge, *America's Game: The Epic Story of How Pro Football Captured a Nation* (New York: Anchor Books Random House, 2005); Michael Oriard, *Brand NFL: Making and Selling America's Favorite Sport* (Chapel Hill: The University of North Carolina Press, 2007); Thomas Patrick Oates and Zack Furness (eds), *The NFL: Critical and Cultural Perspectives* (Philadelphia, PA: Temple University Press, 2014); Mark Dyreson and Jaime L. Schultz, *American National Pastimes – A History* (London: Routledge, 2015).
2. Clay Fowler, 'Super Bowl I: It All Kicked Off in the LA Coliseum,' Inland Valley Daily Bulletin, 6 February 2016, https://www.dailynews.com/events/20160206/super-bowl-i-it-all-kicked-off-in-the-la-coliseum (accessed 10 December 2016).
3. For more details on Super Bowl LI than anyone could ever digest see the official NFL of the game, https://www.nfl.com/super-bowl (accessed 7 February 2017).

4. For a fuller treatment of the argument that the Super Bowl has become the newest American holiday, see, Peter Hopsicker and Mark Dyreson, 'Super Bowl Sunday', in Len Travers (ed.), *The Historical Dictionary of American Holidays*, vol I, (Westport, CT: Greenwood Press, 2006), 30–55.

5. Crepeau, *NFL Football*; Weiss with Day, *The Making of the Super Bowl*; Coenen, *From Sandlots to the Super Bowl*; MacCambridge, *America's Game*; Oriard, *Brand NFL*; Oates and Furness, *The NFL*.

6. Hopsicker and Dyreson, 'Super Bowl Sunday'.

7. Sapna Maheshwari, 'During Breaks in Super Bowl, Advertisers Enter Political Debate', *New York Times*, 6 February 2017. https://www.nytimes.com/2017/02/06/business/super-bowl-ads-politics.html?_r=0 (accessed 7 February 2017); Bethonie Butler and Maura Judkis, The Five Most Political Super Bowl Commercials, *Washington Post*, 6 February 2017, https://www.washingtonpost.com/news/arts-and-entertainment/wp/2017/02/06/the-five-most-political-super-bowl-commercials/?utm_term=.2a3410c2586c (accessed 7 February 2017).

8. Curiously, the CEO of 84 Lumber argued the advertisement was not political and expressed admiration for Trump and support for the wall. 84 Lumber marketing executives, however, insisted that the CEO's personal views were not considered by the company when it designed the ad. Marissa Payne, '84 Lumber CEO: Super Bowl Ad Showing Trump's Wall Wasn't Intended to Be Political', *Washington Post*, 8 February 2017, https://www.washingtonpost.com/news/early-lead/wp/2017/02/04/company-re-tools-rejected-super-bowl-ad-but-you-can-still-see-the-original/?utm_term=.bae4e4aa3884 (accessed 8 February 2017). 84 Lumber Super Bowl Commercial: 'The Entire Journey': https://www.washingtonpost.com/news/early-lead/wp/2017/02/04/company-re-tools-rejected-super-bowl-ad-but-you-can-still-see-the-original/?utm_term=.bae4e4aa3884 (accessed 6 February 2017).

9. Christopher R. Martin and Jimmie L. Reeves, 'The Whole World Isn't Watching (But We Thought They Were): The Super Bowl and United States Solipsism', *Culture, Sport, Society* 4.2 (June 2001), 213–236.

Disclosure Statement

No potential conflict of interest was reported by the authors.

The Super Bowl at 50 or L

Richard Crepeau

ABSTRACT

In the short span of a half-century the Super Bowl has grown from a modest championship game between two football leagues into an outsized mid-winter holiday co-produced by the National Football League and the combined efforts of the American advertising and television industries. It has grown from a one-day into a two-week festival featuring a vast range of events, parties, and a championship football game. Fifty years on, half of the population of the United States and a worldwide television audience participate in Super Bowl activities and festivities either live or virtually. Television, marketing, and a wide range of media platforms have aided and abetted the growth of this celebration of football and consumption. Although there are many ways to describe the Super Bowl it is the nineteenth century vocabulary of the economist Thorstein Veblen that best captures its essence. In Veblen's words it is a case of 'conspicuous consumption' now running on steroids.

For those of us who remember the first Super Bowl it seems a bit surprising that the National Football League championship game has reached age fifty. Even more surprising may be the fact that this championship football game has morphed into a mid-winter national celebration on a scale that dwarfs all other sporting events in this country and rivals the biggest events across the globe. There are several stories within this development. First there is the narrative of growth, which resembles a tidal wave across a wide swath that engulfs and subsumes all in its path. Second there is a question of how and why this happened and involves obsessions over football, marketing genius, and the power of television. Third is the meaning of the Super Bowl as a cultural phenomenon that has risen to the level of national holiday.[1] Where does the story begin?

In the 1960s the challenge presented to the National Football League from the newly formed American Football League led to a costly war between the two organizations. The war ended with a merger of the NFL and AFL, an act of economic necessity and survival. One of the first fruits of the merger was the 'AFL-NFL World Championship Game' between the Green Bay Packers of the NFL and the Kansas City Chiefs of the AFL. This official yet awkward name was quickly replaced in the press by the term 'Super Bowl' and in some cases 'Super bowl'. The *New York Times*, *Sports Illustrated*, and the *Chicago American*, used 'Super

Bowl'. On the Packers home turf, the Milwaukee papers, the *Journal* and the *Sentinel*, used 'Super bowl' with the latter referring to the victorious Green Bay Packers as 'Supermen'. If that was not enough, 'Super' someone erected a sign at the Green Bay airport identifying the city as 'Super Titletown U.S.A.'[2]

Where the name Super Bowl originated is obscured by differing although not necessarily mutually exclusive stories. One version attributes the name to Lamar Hunt, founder of the AFL who suggested the name at a meeting of league officials after seeing his children playing with the 'Super Ball', a ball that bounced higher than normal balls and was popular with children. No one in the league meeting, including Hunt, cared much for the name and NFL Commissioner Pete Rozelle hated it. Whether the press picked up the name from Hunt or some NFL official, or whether someone just started using it is difficult to say, but what is known is that the press picked it up quickly. The following year, Super Bowl II, the name appeared on the Official Logo for the game, although not yet on the tickets. The game programme for the third Super Bowl did use the term on its cover and the term appeared on game tickets for the first time at Super Bowl IV.[3]

As for the use of Roman Numerals that practice too had a chequered beginning. Roman Numerals first appeared on the Game Logo at Super Bowl II, appeared on the game programme for Super Bowl III, was used in the press for Super Bowl IV, but did not appear on the tickets until Super Bowl V. The term 'World Championship Game' remained on the tickets though Super Bowl IV.[4]

Why Roman Numerals? Clark Haponstall of the Sports Management Department of Rice University claims that Commissioner Rozelle's decision to use Roman Numerals was made to avoid any confusion over the year of the game because the NFL season crossed two calendar years. Rozelle also thought 'it kind of gave that gladiator feel and was something that made the game special'.[5]

Perhaps Haponstall was correct and it was as simple as an attempt to avoid confusion. Whatever it was it seems that, particularly in retrospect, it was a perfect choice. Commissioner Rozelle would develop a reputation as a boy genius, a marketing wizard, and, above all, an all-powerful ruling figure over the league, a kind of Caesar Augustus in the imperial age of the NFL and America. He was after all the builder of an Empire that became the envy of the world of sport. In practice the Roman numerals became a marketing signifier of distinction that has set this game off from all other sporting events.[6]

It would have been difficult at Super Bowl I to foresee what a huge event the Super Bowl would become. First, the venue itself was not the first choice of the NFL. Rozelle wanted the game played in the Rose Bowl but college football forces prevented it, insisting that the amateur purity of college sport could not be associated with the crassness of the professionals who played the game for cash over glory. Instead the game took place at the Los Angeles Coliseum where the 90,000-seat facility would only attract two-thirds of its capacity. Television ratings were an impressive 65 million viewers, but not in the same stratosphere as they would subsequently be. The blackout of a 75-mile radius around Los Angeles, one of the largest television markets in the country, no doubt decreased the size of the TV audience. Perhaps more important was the fact that both NBC and CBS televised the game, and they had little difficulty selling out their commercial time at a modest rate of $80,000 per minute.[7]

The party scene in Los Angeles got little mention, although the game did attract a number of Hollywood celebrities. Among those sighted were Bob Hope, Jack Lemmon, and Henry

Fonda who were seated adjacent to the Packer fans led by Marie Lombardi wearing a gold-striped dress.[8]

The sight of over 30,000 empty seats at this first World Championship Game did not please Commissioner Rozelle. On the flight back to NFL headquarters Rozelle told his top aides, 'Never again is there going to be a championship game that isn't a sellout'. With time for serious planning for the second championship game in Miami the NFL built the foundation on which the Super Bowl would stand and expand over the course of five decades. The basics were to define target audiences, develop group sales, and to market the game. The targets would be 'television advertisers and sponsors … along with media organizations, sporting goods manufacturers, and anyone else with business ties to pro football'. The game was promoted as a 'big mid-winter, "must attend" media event … and a gala celebration lasting for an entire weekend'.[9]

Alvin 'Pete' Rozelle was a master marketing man with many contacts in New York City. A week before Super Bowl II the game was declared a sell-out. All tickets were sold, none given away. The price structure was changed slightly with the middle level price lowered by $2, making the prices 12, 8 and 6 dollars. Not simply the game was marketed. 'Basically we were following the college bowl game pattern selling the warm weather, the beach, the golf, the restaurants, and the entertainment of the host city. It would be a gala weekend no matter who played'.[10]

Indeed, it was, as Super Bowl II had very high ratings and favourable media comment. There was pageantry with an Air Force fly over and a halftime show featuring the Grambling University band. Another Packer victory rounded off a near perfect day.[11]

Super Bowl II in Miami foreshadowed a number of the markers of 'Superness'. The first claims of economic impact for the host city were made at Super Bowl II. Tourism in Florida in January usually went through a post-New Year's lull that picked up at the end of the month. Not so for Super Bowl II on January 14. By Super Bowl III hotel rooms were becoming dear as hoteliers reported selling out their accommodations. Eastern Airlines flights to Miami were fully booked. Travel agents were selling Super Bowl package tours. Miami restaurants were full with waiting lists for those who had not booked far enough in advance. An estimated $50 million was poured into the Miami economy. As for the game a sell-out was expected and achieved. Something clearly was beginning to happen around this game and the mid-January weekend as the corporate world became a major participant in it.[12]

It was Super Bowl III that sealed the appeal of this new American sports attraction. Again the game was in Miami and this time the new media star of pro football, Joe 'Willie' Namath, was the major attraction. On Thursday of Super Bowl Week at the Miami Touchdown Club, Namath was being honoured as the Player of the Year. He thanked the single girls of New York as other players had thanked their wives. Then from the back of the room someone shouted to Namath, 'we're going to kick your ass'. Namath's response turned out to be prophetic and therefore memorable: 'Hey, I got news for you. We're gonna win the game. I guarantee it'.[13] The Super Bowl now had its first major piece of folklore and it is quoted multiple times in every week prior to each Super Bowl since.[14]

The game was now big enough to capture the attention and elicit a comment from Marshall McLuhan, the internationally acclaimed media analyst and academic. He described the Super Bowl as 'a world theater … The world is a happening. In the speed-up of the electronic age, we want things to happen. This offers us a mosaic that the fans love – everything is in action at once'. He added that the games of every culture hold up a mirror to that culture while instant replay offered every fan another chance at participation.[15]

In the game itself the New York Jets dominated the Baltimore Colts and Joe Namath emerged as the toast of the town. Many observers of the NFL considered this game a key to solidifying the place of the Super Bowl in American sport as for the first time an AFL team had defeated the NFL team. Others argue that this did not happen until the Super Bowl IV when Kansas City dominated the Minnesota Vikings demonstrating that Super Bowl III had not been a fluke.[16]

For Super Bowl IV there was a change of venue. The league decided to move the game from city to city as long as the host site featured warm weather. As the party atmosphere during the week was growing, what better place for the big game than the city known for its decadence? New Orleans was a natural. Sportswriter George Vecsey saw this as a great matchup of 'Old New Orleans and nouveau riche football' with the French-Spanish city 'a perfect backdrop for the gaudy spectacle the barkers are trying to create'.[17]

The levels of display and spectacle were growing. There were 3,000 pigeons and one turtle dove released during pre-game ceremonies; a tableaux of the Battle of New Orleans and a Mardi Gras parade; Pat O'Brien read the words to the national anthem, backed by a chorus and band from Southern University and the trumpet of Doc Severinsen. It was called the second largest bash in America, second only to Mardi Gras. Halftime pageantry included many acts from the Ed Sullivan show, and the opera singer Marguerite Piazza offered her rendition of 'Basin Street Blues'. Astronauts, baseball stars, and celebrities were there to be seen, brought in to validate the importance of the event.[18]

The only downside was the weather, rain and cold that turned the outdated Tulane Stadium into a bit of a quagmire. There were shortages of hotel rooms and transportation. The pre-game pageantry had issues when a hot air balloon Viking failed to go upward and instead drifted into the stands. Despite these setbacks the party atmosphere was sustained, for it was after all New Orleans.[19]

Looking back on the game over 40 years later New Orleans residents remember it somewhat differently. Some talked of the neighbourhood feel of Tulane Stadium, people parking cars in their yards, and the nuns parking cars to raise money for the Ursuline Academy. There was no media frenzy or corporate dominance of tickets as a large percentage of the fans were locals and ticket prices low. There was very little tailgating and no security at the gates. In the press box the writers fought wind, cold, and the leaks in roof.[20]

Don Weiss, one of the leading architects of the modern Super Bowl as the NFL's public relations and operations guru from the late 1960s through the early 1990s, pointed to another sign that the Super Bowl was increasing its status:

> As if we needed it, one more reliable indicator proved to us that we had a hit on our hands. The instant the Super Bowl's drawing power become clear, celestial personalities swarmed around the game like moths lured to a dazzling light: entertainers, media moguls, corporate moguls, scions from the advertising world, sports heroes, and 'groupies' of every persuasion. Every time we turned around, people were clamouring to be part of our great January celebration.

In addition, there were agents who were trying their best to get their clients or companies into the Super Bowl mix. Weiss hit the mark when he wrote: 'The Super Bowl was more than a sports event. It was more than a media event. It was one big party. And everyone wanted to be there, even if some of them didn't have game tickets'.[21]

This was how it all began and by the end of the 1970s the Super Bowl had reached its position as a burgeoning national holiday, and a 'must see' and 'must be seen at' festival. In every aspect of the week-long event, the Super Bowl had achieved 'Superness'. From the 1970s onward it continued to grow geometrically. All now was simply multiplication and elaboration. At the Monday post-mortem with the press following Super Bowl IV, Commissioner Rozelle underlined the reality, pointing out that 23 million households were tuned in to the game and that the audience share was 69 per cent of sets in use. 'More people watched yesterday's Super Bowl game than watched Neil Armstrong walk on the moon last July', Rozelle added.[22]

Each year the show got bigger if not better, and by the time the Super Bowl reached its 'L' edition the NFL had set out the formulas and requirements for the mid-winter celebration. The dimensions of the Super Bowl have never been laid out in such detail as they were in 'Super Bowl LII-Host City Bid Specifications & Requirements'. This 154-page document reveals, among other things, the scope of the event. No detail is too large or too small to be laid out for potential bidders, and the demands made on host cities are on such a scale as to indicate the magnitude of the Super Bowl.[23]

The governing rule is set out at the start in clear terms. The NFL Events Department is the 'lead entity' responsible for 'the planning, management and execution of the Super Bowl, working closely with many other NFL departments, including Communications, Broadcasting, Football Operations, Finance, Security, Legal, Marketing & Sales, and Consumer Products'. The NFL was in control of this event in all its multitudinous dimensions. All commercial operations are owned or controlled by the NFL including rights and licensing.[24]

All aspects of stadium operations are handled by the NFL including parking, concessions, ATM machines, merchandise, credit cards, programmes, ticketing, staffing, and a host of other details. The Super Bowl ATMs must take only the debit and credit cards that are approved by the NFL. The NFL takes 100% of ticket revenue and handles all ticket distribution and allocation. Tales of NFL Commissioners and team owners scalping tickets are not mentioned.[25]

The NFL requires a tax exemption from state, county, city, and any other local taxes. Any NFL transactions that are not tax exempt must be paid by the Host Committee. The host city must create a Clean Zone, essentially a Super Bowl DMZ around the stadium that includes the NFL Experience sites and the headquarters hotels used by the NFL. The police for this operation will be supplied by the host city – at the city's cost. And, of course, the police will be at the command of the NFL. Among their law enforcement duties will be to work on the anti-counterfeiting unit whose major concern is suppressing counterfeit official NFL merchandise.[26]

The NFL also requires three golf courses to be supplied for the NFL Foundation Golf Classic, and two bowling alleys to be provided for the NFL Celebrity Bowling Classic. If the game is held in a winter climate, the NFL reserves the right to use the golf courses at any other time of the year. If there is cost involved in any of this, the host will pay the bill. All the rooms in at least one hotel will be taken over by the NFL, and all meeting and conference space provided without cost. All hotels are required to offer room rebates to the league.[27]

In the 'Transportation' section of the document, as well as in many other sections, there is one recurring phrase: 'at no cost to the NFL' or some variation thereof. This seems to be the 'Super Bowl Mantra' of the NFL. Similarly, the phrase 'exclusive use' and variations on it are found across the length of the document. The needs for limos, shuttle buses, and school buses as well as secure and exclusive parking facilities are listed for these and other NFL vehicles.[28]

The official NFL regulations require that the Host City 'will be responsible for providing' practice facilities for the participating teams equivalent to what is normal for the NFL team located at the host site. There are detailed specifications for these facilities down to water, ice, laundry, and catering. This section rambles on for several pages covering all imaginable items, and some that exceed the limits of the imagination.[29]

The requirements and lists of needs spread over the 154 pages reveal an insatiable appetite for freebies for the National Football League. If this seems excessive it also is a tribute to the power of the Super Bowl and the ability of a $9 billion business to masquerade as a sport. It was not hyperbole when the NFL referred to the Super Bowl as an unofficial holiday.[30]

The halftime show became another measure of Superness and it took a leap forward when the Walt Disney Company took over the role of halftime director. In the summer of 1976 Bob Jani, Disney's director of entertainment called Don Weiss, set up a meeting, and made a presentation for the halftime show at the Rose Bowl for Super Bowl XI. His pitch was impressive and incredibly enthusiastic. Weiss and the NFL accepted the Disney pitch. Jani put together a card show for 103,000 people in the Rose Bowl that was part of 'It's a Small World' theme for the show. Disney cast members, some 1,500, would help energize the crowd. From this point on halftime was a blockbuster entertainment of its own.[31]

The change in halftime entertainment from marching band shows to choreographed mass spectacles really began the year before, at Super Bowl X in Miami. The theme was the kick-off of America's Bicentennial. The Bicentennial logo appeared all over the Orange Bowl and the Super Bowl logo also reflecting the patriotic theme. 'Up With People,' a singing and dancing troupe sponsored by the conservative group Moral Re-Armament to counter the 1960s and 1970s 'counter culture', put on the Bicentennial extravaganza – the first of four shows that the organization staged at the Super Bowl.[32]

The NFL reached out to fans of all ages. In 1975 during the Bicentennial observance, the NFL tied itself to the patriotic celebration by sponsoring an essay competition for high school students. All those from the ages of 14 to 18 were eligible to enter the competition on the subject, 'The Role of the NFL in American History'. First prize was a $10,000 scholarship and an all-expenses paid trip for themselves and their parents to Super Bowl X. Second prize was a $5,000 scholarship. Ten runners up received a $1,000 scholarship.[33]

The next big show came at Super Bowl XXII in San Diego when Bob Jani, now at Radio City Music Hall, brought the iconic Rockettes to halftime. They danced onto a stage that was designed to look like a grand piano, with 88 white grand pianos ringing the field. The 1960s pop star Chubby Checker was featured at the keyboards. Logistics were difficult, but at the Super Bowl that was never an obstacle, only a challenge. At Super Bowl XXVII there was a change of style with a big headliner replacing the choreographed groups. Pop music superstar Michael Jackson provided the half-time show along with 3,500 youngsters from Southern California. A card section at the Rose Bowl did an encore.[34]

Pre-game festivities also evolved over the years. The National Anthem was joined in 1969 by the Pledge of Allegiance, an oath led by the astronauts from Apollo 8, the first manned-flight to orbit the moon. Military flyovers also became standard and soon served as a climax for the national anthem.[35]

The National Anthem was from the beginning a means for the NFL to tie itself to patriotism and performing the anthem at the Super Bowl was an honour coveted by many. As time went by and the Super Bowl approached the status of a national holiday, football-field sized flags were spread across the gridiron for the anthem. What is generally considered the greatest of these performances came in 1991 at Super Bowl XXV in Tampa on the eve of Operation Desert Storm, the US-led invasion to retake Kuwait from Iraq during the Gulf War. The NFL took the occasion to turn this Super Bowl into a patriotic storm of their own. The featured singer was Whitney Houston who delivered a national anthem that electrified the stadium and the television audience. It has such power that Houston's record company issued it as a single and it moved immediately to the top of the charts. After the September 11 attacks ten years later, Houston's recording returned to the charts.[36]

Television played a major role in the growth of the Super Bowl and at the same time reflected that growth. There are any number of ways to measure this. In terms of the deployment of the technical hardware in production the networks quickly escalated their coverage. At Super Bowl II, CBS used twelve cameras including one in the Goodyear Blimp, along with four video machines for isolated replays and highlights including stop-action and slow motion in colour. At Super Bowl XXIII, NBC deployed 23 cameras and 12 replay machines while for Super Bowl XXV in Tampa, ABC had 22 cameras operating around the stadium. On and on it went. Ten years later, CBS used 34 cameras while introducing freeze-frame technology.[37] The coming of flat screens and HD television added yet another dimension to the technology, and the Super Bowl has stimulated sales of these TVs. Consumer Electronics Association surveys have found that almost a quarter of television purchase are made specifically for the Super Bowl.[38]

Television, of course, remained the true gauge of the NFL's popularity. With the Super Bowl wrapped into contracts, the league drove the price of the contracts and of commercial time ever upward. The cost of thirty seconds of commercial time for the first Super Bowl telecast was $40,000. By 2010 the price jumped to the $3 million level. At each and every turn television was both growth engine and the measure of growth.[39]

Television generated money and interest and more money. 1981 was a record year for television ratings and it coincidentally was the year for contract renegotiation between the league and the networks. It was a year in which CBS made $25 million from its NFL operations. In 1982, CBS, NBC, and ABC signed a record five-year $2 billion contract with the NFL. In 1985, the Commissioner decided to bring ABC into the Super Bowl rotation. In the end ABC agreed to pay the NFL $650 million for the rights to Monday Night Football which included special prime time games on Thursday or Sunday, and $17 million for Super Bowl XIX. NBC followed agreeing to a deal at $590 million. CBS, after some hesitation, signed for $730 million.[40] The rapidly escalating prices were driven because the networks wanted the plum prize of the package, the Super Bowl.

Across five decades, television ratings followed an upward trajectory with only a few exceptions. In 2016, the game drew 111.9 million viewers and that was down for the second consecutive year. On the other hand, this was the third largest audience in history, with record audiences for six of the previous seven years. Four million others streamed the game, making up the difference. The largest TV audience for a Super Bowl was in 2015 with 114.4 million viewers. The second largest was in 2014. Network and NFL officials point out that Super Bowl audiences get undercounted because they do not calculate the number of people watching the game in large groups at parties and at sports bars. Nearly

17 million tweets were sent during the game by nearly 4 million different authors during Super Bowl 50(L). Over 72% of television sets in use were tuned to the game. To round out the story, *Sports Illustrated* reported that the top seven rated television shows in US history were Super Bowls.[41]

Television commercials provide another window on the growth of the Super Bowl – first reflected in the price of commercial time as it skyrocketed, then in production costs and quality, and finally in the fascination that television viewers developed for the commercials. In some ways, the commercials became the centerpiece of the Super Bowl as they were much anticipated by the viewing public. This led to various informal voting on the 'best' commercials and the posting of them online when that technology emerged, first post-game and more recently several days and, in some cases, weeks before the game. Sneak previews were also developed for the commercials. Some believe that these short films are the finest quality of film making extant, and advertising agencies used them to exhibit their creative and marketing skills.

The commercial that is now considered the most powerful as well as of the highest artistic quality was the 1984 Ridley Scott production that introduced the Apple Macintosh to the nation. *Forbes* offers this description:

> The commercial showed the future in a monochromatic hyperindustrial gray. Uniformly expressionless humans are assembled before a giant screen as big brother delivers a monotone about 'the great body of the state' and 'the unification of thought'. In the midst of all the dread, a young blonde woman (a model and former discus thrower Anya Major) wearing red shorts and a white Apple Macintosh t-shirt sprints through the assembled storm troopers and human drones to fling a sledgehammer at the screen. Over the sudden blast of glare, an announcer intones, 'On January 24th, Apple Computer will introduce Macintosh. And you'll see why 1984 won't be like "1984"'.[42]

All subsequent Super Bowl advertising has been measured against this path-breaking commercial. The product was in the stores on Tuesday and sales reached $3.5 million in short order. Over the next three months, $155 million worth of Macintosh computers were sold.[43]

Less profound but quite influential have been a series of Budweiser commercials produced for the Super Bowl. On set features the Budweiser Clydesdales and over the years they have appeared in many different settings. These are much anticipated each year and warmly and fondly received. Another set featured the 'Bud Bowl'. This was a faux football game between bottles of 'Bud' and 'Bud Light' that first appeared during Super Bowl XXIII. These proved so popular that they went on over several years and the Las Vegas odds makers put a line on the game. Overall there were eight Bud Bowls and some of them used Roman Numerals.[44]

The Super Bowl became an important vehicle not just for advertisers but for the networks themselves. Each network used it to promote its own programming. In the case of FOX, it used the NFL and the Super Bowl to raise its status to the level of 'major network' and in the process overpaid for the TV rights driving up the prices the networks must pay even further.

The coming of cable television in the 1980s offered expanding revenues to the NFL and, of perhaps greater importance, expanding coverage. This expansion added to the size and scope of the NFL's reach, and in turn enhanced the importance of the Super Bowl. Indeed, everything Super Bowl was swept up into this ascending trajectory of popularity and growth. Bigger is always better and every aspect of the Super Bowl came to reflect that reality.

One of the innovative start-ups that appeared with the advent of cable, Entertainment and Sports Programming Network (ESPN), used the NFL to capture an enormous audience and turn this experiment in twenty-four hour sports telecasting into a success. ESPN's contribution to Super Bowl madness beyond the 24/7 promotion of the NFL was its decision to saturate the network with Super Bowl programing during Super Bowl Week. This culminated with the practice of showing non-stop highlights of all the previous Super Bowls leading up to the start of the major network pre-game coverage some three or four hours before kick-off.[45]

Competing television networks have tried counter programming to attract an audience by offering block-buster movies and other programming to attract non-football fans – to no avail. Other networks created programming to ride the wave of Super Bowl popularity. The most successful and enduring of these is 'The Puppy Bowl' shown on the Animal Planet Network. The first airing was in February 2005, and it has become a standard part of Super Bowl Sunday viewing for dog and cat lovers.[46]

Another of the staples of Super Bowl week is the Commissioner's Party, first held at Super Bowl I. Not exactly a smashing hit, the first rendition saw the executives from the AFL line up on one side of the room, and those from the NFL on the other side. After this awkward start, it did not take long for the event to become the centrepiece of activities on the Friday night before the game. Like everything else associated with the Super Bowl it grew quickly and soon expanded beyond the capacity of a hotel to host it. The last hotel venue was in New Orleans at the Roosevelt Hotel for Super Bowl VI. The following year the Commissioner's Party was held on board the Queen Mary in Long Beach. At Super Bowl VIII in Houston, the party occupied the expanse of the Astrodome. A giant barbecue, with pigs roasting on spits, dotted the floor of the facility. Commissioner's parties in Miami were held at Hialeah Racetrack and at Miami Airport's International Terminal just prior to its opening.[47]

The cost of the Super Bowl XII party in New Orleans was $75,000, a figure that drew some critical comment. Responding to critics who found this excessive Commissioner Rozelle countered by saying that money in fact is the whole point with the Super Bowl implying that was a large part of its attraction. He added that 'you think about money all the time with the Super Bowl, more than any other sports event. That's because it's a one-shot event'. An Oakland Raider executive was closer to the mark: 'the measurement of what it means is this: It's the victory. It's the cult of Number Oneism'.[48]

The guest lists kept growing and gate-crashers became a problem. Among the 2,000 invited guests for the Super Bowl IX party were the media, the Commissioner's immediate family including the League office staff, league management and executives from each team, television executives, and sponsors. Players were not invited. Wives of the elite were. In addition, competing teams brought an entourage of staff and friends.[49]

The Commissioner's Party initiated more parties which grew in number and kind over the decades. Sponsors and television networks held their invitation-only events. CBS appeared to be the industry leader until the advent of ESPN whose party became the 'must be seen at' event. Various corporate sponsors staged parties during Super Bowl Week. Some used these to entertain clients while others offered them as incentive rewards for employees. The first to move in this direction were the major television sponsors such as Ford, General Motors, and Coca Cola. Eastern and National Airlines put together packages for early Super Bowls in Miami and the NFL was, according to Don Weiss, delighted to supply all the tickets they needed.[50] At Super Bowl VII in Los Angeles, 267 Chrysler dealers were rewarded with a trip to the game. Ford flew in 650 of its best people from their national convention being held in Las Vegas. By the time of Super Bowl XIX in Palo Alto, California, twenty-six corporations were active in the party scene. At Super Bowl XXX in Miami, 200 corporations took part in the party scene, and the large corporation spent up to $5 million to bring over 100 employees to the Super Bowl.[51]

As the Super Bowl has become basically a corporate event, the corporate tent became a common sight. At the scene of Super Bowl XXXV in Tampa in 2001 there were 17 huge tents, compared to nine in the same city in 1991. The first tents appeared in Tampa in 1984. Executives and their guests used the tents for pre-game and post-game bashes. The largest in 2001 was 100 × 360 feet and accommodated more than 1,500 people. The carpeted, climate-controlled structure contained everything from big-screen TVs to a giant ship's mast. In addition, the 800,000-square-foot corporate hospitality area was being transformed into a pseudo-beach populated by 10-foot-tall macaw statues, twenty-five-foot-tall lifeguard chairs, and a sandcastle.[52]

A tent complete with food and entertainment cost a company as much as $750,000, while added features could run the price to $1.5 million. Coca-Cola, Ford, and Prudential are noted for the opulence of their tents. The NFL keeps details under wraps because big corporate sponsors, unlike individuals, often do not want shareholders or customers to know how much they are spending. And no wonder. At one tent in Tampa, a staff of 500 served such entrees as Lower Keys Conch Chowder, prime rib and salmon along with upscale brands of liquor and such treats as Maryland crab cakes or leg of lamb. Several tents featured high-priced performers such as the Spinners and the Classic Rock All-Stars, a band that included Bernie Leadon and Randy Meisner, former members of the Eagles.[53]

For the largest companies, a four-day Super Bowl trip could cost as much as $10,000 per person, so if a company brings 150 guests, the cost would be about $1.5 million. It was one of the priciest events in the sports world and, of course, worth every tax-deductible dollar of it.[54]

Not to be overshadowed in the excess sweepstakes, for Super Bowl XXXV the City of Tampa dropped $350,000 into flowers and other landscape enhancements for public properties; while the county paid Team Sandtastic of Sarasota $628,000 to build a Super Bowl Sand Montage in Sand Key Park. Two thirty-foot tall NFL helmets with logos of the Ravens and Giants on either side of the Lombardi Trophy were surrounded by 29 other helmets 6-feet in height. All sculpted of sand, of course.[55]

Beyond the corporate jets, the skies were filled around the Tampa Bay Area producing an air traffic controller's nightmare. A B-2 Bomber provided the fly over while Ray Charles sang 'America the Beautiful' and the Air Force Thunderbirds graced the skies during the national anthem. A bevy of banner-towing planes, a brace of blimps, and fourteen helicopters provided shuttle service for the Fortune 500 fans, jammed the air corridors around Tampa at Super Bowl XXXV.[56]

If private planes and helicopters were too plebeian, 'Silent Wings II,' the modest 104-foot yacht featuring a staff of four including a gourmet chef was available for hire. The luxury accommodation featured a Jacuzzi along with 'his' and 'her' bathrooms in the largest of the suites. This package featured six luxury suites for the big game and a chauffeured Rolls-Royce – all of this for a modest $100,000. Indeed, the yacht may have been the best means of assuring a ticket to the game, if that really mattered to anyone. Most game tickets go to NFL officials, corporate sponsors, and politicians and are freebies.[57]

At Super Bowl XXXV, the corporate party took on another dimension with the emergence of The Playboy Party, The Maxim Party, and The Penthouse Party in the Battle of the

Soft-Porn Magazines. In recent years, the Maxim Party seems to have become the choice of the discerning in these matters. Through the first years of the twenty-first century, Rolling Stone, DirecTV, various celebrity hosted parties, the Leather and Lace Party, Ditka and Jaws Cigars with the Stars, the Player's Super Bowl Tailgate, and many, many more have joined the list. The one certainty is that this list will continue to grow.[58]

This party atmosphere of high rollers inevitably attracted practitioners of the world's oldest profession. A former prostitute reported that 'Pimps see the Super Bowl as a moneymaking opportunity sent by God'. From the services provided in the private suites to the half-time quickie, the laws of supply and demand were never better illustrated.[59]

It is at the grass roots level that the full sweep of the party scene can be observed. Neighbourhood and office groups offer a good measure of the ubiquity of the Super Bowl. In 1996 at Super Bowl XXIX, five friends from Chicago held their twelfth annual Super Bowl Party in Las Vegas. They use the same hotel and the same room, dress in the same pink warmup suits, and carry the same travel bags each year. No wives make the trip and no other men have ever been invited although some have asked. The 'Five Guys' do the usual Vegas things; drink, gamble, and of course watch the Super Bowl in their room, which is filled with all the party essentials one needs.[60]

Another variation was created by Bob 'Moose' Morrison of Fairfield, Ohio. This party is by invitation only for 100 guests, and you cannot buy your way in. Preparations go on year round. 'Moose' begins freezing ice cubes in the form of footballs at Thanksgiving storing them in a large freezer in his garage. Two seven-foot tall plywood helmets are bolted to the front of the house and painted in that year's team colours. The doorknobs are in the shape of footballs. Each room has a television and the carpet in the house is taped to look like yard lines.[61]

Many people share the viewing experience with the same group of friends or colleagues each year. Some people set up bleachers in their home to enhance the authenticity of the experience. For those not in the United States for this major holiday there are gatherings in many of the major cities of the world. London pubs offer the late night Super Bowl for the large American community there. Moscow kick-off is at 2 a.m. and in 1993, 600 people gathered in a Moscow hotel ballroom for a watch party. American servicemen around the world gather for the game, and in recent years some have been featured on the telecast of the game.[62]

For Super Bowl XLIII friends from Florida gathered with their children, grandchildren, and a crowd of 200 others at the Bourbon Street Inn. This was not in New Orleans but rather on a dusty side street in Bangkok 9,000 miles from Tampa. The party began at 5:30am, necessitating a 4:30 wake-up call. The establishment run by a Louisiana native was decked out in the colours of the Pittsburgh Steelers and Arizona Cardinals, and the patrons were dressed in the colours of their favourite team. The Black and Gold of the Steelers dominated as it did in the game itself. Richard Turkiewicz described it this way:

> There we had a choice of New Orleans style breakfast price fixe or an alternative breakfast price fixe which included all the beer or 'Bloody Mary's' you wished to accompany your breakfast. All the meats for the breakfast are flown in from New Orleans and you think you are actually in New Orleans. The restaurant has that much flavor. The main difference is that all the waiters and servers are Thai and there is no lack of either.[63]

The NFL did its best to encourage the parties and the emergence of the tents near the stadium. Another aspect of the party atmosphere was the inauguration of the NFL

Experience in 1992 prior to Super Bowl XXVI in Minneapolis. This is essentially an NFL theme park with football fun and games set up in a central location in the week prior to the game. There are inactive experiences, the opportunity to meet the great players of the past and present, exhibits of the Super Bowl rings and the Lombardi Trophy. Perhaps most important is the Super Fan Shop where the NFL helps fans dispose of their excess income on the largest offering of official NFL limited-edition merchandise and the latest in authentic NFL products. The NFL Experience generally has a sponsor and for Super Bowl 50 Hyundai was the chosen one.[64]

In recent years the Super Bowl experience has broadened via the internet and social media. The NFL has expanded its activities for the day and the week with a strong PR effort to instil a social conscience into the festivities. The Super Bowl website was created to promote the game, the activities of the week, and provide yet another outlet for sponsors and advertisers. The Super Bowl website quickly became a centre for sponsors. In 2000, the lead Site Sponsor was Miller Lite. Joining the list of major sponsors was Web MD, VISA (where you could acquire an official NFL credit card), RCA's Direct Satellite System, U.P.S., E*Trade (which offered web visitors their Knowledge Center), Hotjobs.com, and Mel Gibson's latest movie.[65]

At Superbowl.com, nearly the entire Super Bowl experience was available. There were highlights of past games; live shots of host city hot spots and other important landmarks; and a RealSlideshow of all the championship games. There were diaries by players and the wives of players each offering a variety of insights on the weekend. However, the highlights of Superbowl.com are Tips for Throwing a Super Bowl Party, animated Super Bowl greeting cards, an Electric Football Game, NFL for Her, and the Miller Lite Beer Pager. If you needed more ESPN.com sent Dan Patrick out on patrol for Celebrity Sightings in Atlanta. In point of fact there was no end to the variety of things that eventually turned up at Superbowl. com. One year, Dan Marino was featured at the Kraft Foods sponsor link where he served up the Kraft Party Playbook with fourteen appetizers, seven main dishes, and eight desserts, including the Super Bowl Cake. Marino was happy to send you all the recipes via email.[66]

To mute the garish character of the mid-winter celebration the NFL began placing a heightened emphasis on social action and social conscience. Taste of the NFL had its start in 1992 in Minneapolis and it grew rapidly under the slogan 'A Party with a Purpose'. NFL stars Kurt Warner and Donovan McNabb took part in the distribution of a donation of 10,000 cans of soup to the Second Harvesters Food Bank of Greater New Orleans in 2002. The NFL starting in 2000 partnered with Campbell Soup in the 'Tackling Hunger Program' as part of a 500,000 can Super Bowl donation and the six million cans donated that year as part of the 'Tackling Hunger Program'. NFL fans were invited to participate in the programme all year long by going to www.chunky and clicking on the helmet of their favourite team. Each click produced a one-can donation.[67]

One of the most interesting web sites was www.gospelcom.net. At this location you could order your Super Bowl outreach kit so that you could have a Christian Super Bowl party in your own home. The Kit came with a twelve-minute video (ideal for the halftime show) hosted by CNN's Fred Hickman and featuring All-Pros Brent Jones and Steve Wallace of the Super Bowl Champion San Francisco Forty-Niners. Jones and Wallace discuss their close friendship and mutual faith in Jesus Christ. Other players offer testimonies on such subjects as Racial Harmony and Salvation.[68]

All of this was available at The Reggie White Christian Super Bowl Web page and came with pre-game, half-time, and post-game prayer service suggestions. A Reggie White Video was credited with 30 young people being saved in Melbourne, while a reported 4,200 Reggie White Super Bowl parties led to 2,500 decisions for Christ.[69]

The Super Bowl has come to permeate all corners of American life. Sermons are given in churches on Super Bowl themes. Super markets push Super Bowl themed food in the weeks heading into Super Sunday with special snack packs, cakes in the shape of a football, cupcakes covered with icing in the participating team colours. The beer merchants are not among the largest advertisers on the game telecast, but their displays in supermarkets establish a clear identity between their product and the Super Bowl.

It may be difficult to put all of this into any sort of perspective and perhaps only the vocabulary created by Thorstein Veblen, the insightful Progressive Era economist and sociologist, is capable of fully capturing the Super Bowl scene. Veblen's *The Theory of the Leisure Class* coined those wonderful phrases, 'conspicuous consumption', 'conspicuous leisure', and 'conspicuous waste' to describe the habits of the rich in late-nineteenth-century America. Along with 'predatory barbarism', 'pecuniary emulation', 'vicarious consumption' and 'conspicuous waste', Veblen's colourful vocabulary is ideally suited for describing this distinctive American midwinter holiday. The difference is that the habits of the rich in the late nineteenth century have trickled down the social order to those riding the wave of corporate wealth and consumption in the second half of the twentieth century. This includes those middle and working class fans and non-fans who emulate those who actually attend the Super Bowl.[70]

All this has been cultivated by the marketing geniuses of the NFL, the advertising agencies in service to the consumer economy, and aided and abetted by the media in all its shapes and forms. The media no longer covers just the Super Bowl. As Mike Tanner wrote in the *New York Times* in 2010 'it covers itself covering the Super Bowl, self-referentially glorifying in the excess while gorging on television hours and column inches'. So after all this growth of excess 'hype has become metahype; excessive analysis of excess itself'.[71]

'Enough' is a word seldom heard in America, and never heard in connection with the Super Bowl. Indeed, too much is never enough. The snowball rolling down the hill for fifty years has become larger than the Alps and shows no signs of abatement.

Notes

1. Craig Coenen, *From Sandlots to the Super Bowl: The National Football League, 1920–1967* (Knoxville: University of Tennessee Press, 2005); Michael MacCambridge, *America's Game: The Epic Story of How Pro Football Captured a Nation* (New York: Anchor Books Random House, 2005); Richard C. Crepeau, *NFL Football: A History of America's New National Pastime* (Urbana: University of Illinois Press, 2010); Michael Oriard, *Brand NFL: Making and Selling America's Favorite Sport* (Chapel Hill: University of North Carolina Press, 2007); and Mark Yost, *Tailgating, Sacks, and Salary Caps: How the NFL Became the Most Successful Sports League in History* (Chicago: Kaplan Publishing, 2006).
2. See the *Milwaukee Journal* and the *Milwaukee Sentinel* for 15 and 16 January 1967; *Sports Illustrated*, 23 January 1967; *New York Times*, 11 January 1967; and Bryan Moritz, 'Kickoff to the Hype: Newspaper Coverage of Super Bowl I' (paper presented to the History Division Association for Education in Journalism and Mass Communication Conference, St. Louis, Mo., 10 August 2011), https://www.scribd.com/document/98332751/Kicking-off-the-hype-Newspaper-coverage-of-Super-Bowl-I.

3. MacCambridge, *America's Game*, 236–7; and Crepeau, *NFL Football*, 60–70.

4. http://www.nfl.com/photos/09000d5d8267533c; http://www.sportslogos.net/logos/list_by_team/593/Super_Bowl/.

5. Tad Hathaway, 'Touchdown Houston: History of Roman Numerals and the Super Bowl', Updated 2 January 2004, www.news24houston.com; and www.visualeditions.com.

6. The imperial character of the NFL and Pete Rozelle is a tendency that has long been recognized and one that I have written about for the last twenty-five years. Others have referenced this tendency including Michael Oriard, and Michael MacCambridge. More recent observations have been made by: Thomas Patrick Oates and Zack Furness, eds, *The NFL: Critical and Cultural Perspectives* (Philadelphia: Temple University Press, 2014); Steve Almond, *Against Football: One Fan's Reluctant Manifesto* (Brooklyn, NY: Melville House, 2014); Mark Edmundson, *Why Football Matters: My Education in the Game* (New York: The Penguin Press, 2014); Jeff Davis, *Rozelle: Czar of the NFL* (New York: McGraw Hill, 2008); and John Fortunato, *Commissioner: The Legacy of Pete Rozelle* (Lanham, MD: Taylor Trade Publishing, 2006).

7. Bradley Johnson, 'Super Bowl Supersized', *Advertising Age*, 26 January 2016, http://adage.com/article/news/super-bowl-supersized-4-5-b-ad-spending-50-years/302180/.

8. *Milwaukee Journal Sentinel*, 15 and 16 January, 1997; Harvey Frommer, 'Ten More Things I Learned Creating "When It Was Just a Game"', http://www.theepochtimes.com/n3/1897951-ten-more-things-i-learned-creating-when-it-was-just-a-game/.

9. Don Weiss with Chuck Day, *The Making of the Super Bowl: The Inside Story of the World's Greatest Sporting Event* (Chicago: Contemporary Books, 2003), 133–6.

10. Ibid., 138–9.

11. Ibid., 147.

12. Frank Litsky, 'Super Bowl is a Bonanza for Miami's Economy Lull', *New York Times*, 14 January 1968. Times Select.

13. MacCambridge, *America's Game*, 254.

14. For instance, see the recollection of Namath's boast in Paul Zimmerman, 'Guaranteed Cool', *Sports Illustrated*, 28 January 1991, 72–6.

15. Gerald Eskanazi, 'Viewers Drink in Underdog's Victory', *New York Times*, 13 January 1969, 33. Viewed in the *New York Times* Time Machine.

16. Fortunato, *Commissioner*, 83–4; and MacCambridge, *America's Game*, 271.

17. Weiss, *The Making of the Super Bowl*, chap. 12; and George Vecsey, 'Fans Celebrate in Vieux Carre', *The New York Times*, 11 January 1970, http://www.nytimes.com/1970/01/11/archives/fans-celebrate-in-vieux-carre-30000-join-in-festivities-opera-and.html?_r=0.

18. Ibid.

19. Weiss, *The Making of the Super Bowl*, chap. 12.

20. Tammy Nunez, 'Super Bowls at Tulane Stadium Lacked Glitz, Glamour of Modern Game But Were Still Special', *The Times-Picayune*, 13 January 2013, http://connect.nola.com/user/tnunez/index.html.

21. Weiss, *The Making of the Super Bowl*, 201.

22. Ibid., 181.

23. National Football League, 'Super Bowl LII Bid Specifications & Requirements', November 2013; https://www.documentcloud.org/documents/1513830-nfl-super-bowl-lii-host-city-bid-specifications.html.

24. Ibid.

25. Ibid.

26. Ibid.

27. Ibid.

28. Ibid.

29. Ibid.

30. Ibid.

31. Weiss, *The Making of the Super Bowl*, 183–7.

32. Ibid., 190.

33. Red Smith, 'N.F.L. in American History', *New York Times*, 16 November 1975, sec. 5, 3.

34. Weiss, *The Making of the Super Bowl*, 191–7.
35. Ibid.
36. http://www.espn.com/espn/feature/story/_/id/14673003/the-story-whitney-houston-epic-national-anthem-performance-1991-super-bowl.
37. 'CBS Costs Soar for Super Bowl', *New York Times*, 14 January 1968, 'Times Select; Super Bowl Coverage', *USA Today*, 20–22 January 1989; 27 January 1995; 3–5 February 2006; and 'Advertising Supplement', *New York Times*, 26 January 2001.
38. Keith B. Grant, 'Why the Super Bowl Makes for Super TV Sales', 25 January 2014, CNBC, http://www.cnbc.com/2014/01/24/er-bowl-makes-for-super-tv-sales.html.
39. Crepeau, *NFL Football*, 192.
40. Fortunato, *Commissioner*, 116.
41. http://www.nielsen.com/us/en/insights/news/2016/super-bowl-50-draws-111-9-million-tv-viewers-and-16-9-million-tweets.html; See also Richard Sandomir, 'Super Bowl Was a Stunner, and That's Just the Size of the TV Audience', *New York Times*, 2 February 2015; and Associated Press, 'Super Bowl Gets 111.9 Viewers, Down From Last Year', 8 February 2016, http://www.si.com/nfl/2016/02/08/super-bowl-50-tv-ratings-media-circus.
42. http://www.forbes.com/sites/patrickhanlon/2014/01/30/apple-1984-spot-won-the-game-30-super-bowls-ago/#32094e2e27d0.
43. Richard C. Crepeau, 'Super Bowl Superness', Sport and Society for Arete, 4 February 2016, http://stars.library.ucf.edu/onsportandsociety/102/; and 'Sport and Society for Arete Columns are Available at the Website of the Sport Literature Association', http://www.uta.edu/english/sla/sportsoc.html. Pre-1996 articles, as well as later ones, are also available at the electronic website at the University of Central Florida library, http://stars.library.ucf.edu/onsportandsociety/).
44. http://www.si.com/nfl/2015/11/04/bud-bowl-super-bowl-commercial.
45. Oriard, *Brand NFL*, 169–74.
46. http://www.rollingstone.com/culture/news/americas-other-cuter-super-bowl-the-story-of-the-puppy-bowl-20140131.
47. Richard C. Crepeau, 'Super Bowl: Corporate Excess and Roman Numerals', Sport and Society for Arete, 30 January 1994, http://stars.library.ucf.edu/onsportandsociety/360; Weiss, *The Making of the Super Bowl*, 236–8; and Judy Battista, 'Super Bowl 50 Marks Landmark Occasion for NFL's Biggest Stage', 1 February 2015, http://www.nfl.com/news/story/0ap3000000465802/article/super-bowl-50-marks-landmark-occasion-for-nfls-biggest-stage.
48. Gerald Eskenazi, 'Money is the Root of All Super Bowl Matters', *New York Times*, 14 January 1978. Times Select.
49. 'New Orleans Game Plan Offers "Super Party" and All That Jazz', *New York Times*, 8 January 1975. Times Select.
50. Weiss, *The Making of the Super Bowl*, 136–8.
51. Tom Buckley, 'Business in the Front Seat for Today's Super Bowl', *New York Times*, 14 January 1973; Richard C. Crepeau, 'Super Bowl XXXV and Its Excesses', Sport and Society for Arete, 25 January 2001, http://stars.library.ucf.edu/onsportandsociety/618; Richard C. Crepeau, 'Super Bowl Excesses', Sport and Society for Arete, 24 January 1997, http://stars.library.ucf.edu/onsportandsociety/222; and Richard C. Crepeau, 'Super Bowl XXIX', Sport and Society for Arete, 25 January 1995, http://stars.library.ucf.edu/onsportandsociety/408.
52. Crepeau, 'Super Bowl XXXV and Its Excesses'.
53. Ibid.
54. Kyle Parks and Jeff Harrington, 'Corporate America Buys Star Execs Ultimate Party', *St. Petersburg Times*, 29 January 2001, http://www.sptimes.com/News/012901/SuperBowl2001/Corporate_America_buy.shtml.
55. Edie Gross, 'Super Bowl Sculpture Rises from Sand', *St. Petersburg Times*, 20 January 2001, http://www.sptimes.com/News/012001/SuperBowl2001/Super_Bowl_sculpture_.shtml.
56. 'Notable Flyovers at Sports Events', *Sports Illustrated*, http://www.si.com/more-sports/photos/2014/06/27/notable-flyovers-sports-events; and Jean Heller, 'Corporate Jets Blitz

Bay Area for Super Bowl', *St. Petersburg Times*, 22 January 2001, http://www.sptimes.com/News/012201/SuperBowl2001/Corporate_jets_blitz_.shtml.

57. Crepeau, 'Super Bowl XXXV and Its Excesses'.

58. http://www.espn.com/travel/news/story?id=3853138 lists parties in Tampa for Super Bowl in 2009.

59. Richard C. Crepeau, 'The Super Bowl: New Forms of Excess', Sport and Society for Arete, 24 January 2003, http://stars.library.ucf.edu/onsportandsociety/559; http://www.espn.com/page2/s/superbowl/sex.html.

60. Gary Mihoces, 'Bash Keeps Us Going Rest of the Year', *USA Today*, 27–29 January 1995, sec. A, 1–2.

61. Ibid.

62. Benita Hussain, '10 Places Around the World to Watch the Super Bowl', http://matadornetwork.com/sports/10-places-around-the-world-to-watch-the-super-bowl/.

63. E-mail note and personal conversation with Richard Turkiewicz, June, 2009; 'The Super Show', *Time*, 10 January 1977.

64. http://www.sfbaysuperbowl.com/nfl-experience#gDfv7Y5IkjY9ByKE.97; David Leon Moore, 'Pasadena Puts its New Look on Parade', *USA Today*, 29 January 1993, sec. E, 1.

65. The Super Bowl websites chronicle each individual Super Bowl year and are not archived. The original superbowl.com websites for past Super Bowls are no longer available. The current Super Bowl website can be found at https://www.nfl.com/super-bowl.

66. Ibid.

67. Russell Adams, 'Campbell Soups Sack's NFL Mothers', *Wall Street Journal*, 27 August 2008; 'NFL Moms Shine in Campbell's Chunky Soup TV Commercials', *PR Newswire*, 5 September 2002, http://www.wsj.com/articles/SB121979854864874981 http://www.prnewswire.com/news-releases/nfl-moms-shine-in-campbells-chunky-soup-tv-commercials-75639392.html.

68. The original website for www.gospel.com site is no longer available, but the activities have continued and a good overview is available at www.superbowlgospel.com.

69. This website is no longer available but there are many sources available that discuss Reggie White's strong commitment to and advocacy for Christianity. See for example: The Baptist Press website http://www.bpnews.net/19790/reggie-white-who-used-football-to-spread-gospel-dies-at-43 and a 1996 *Sports Illustrated* article on White http://www.si.com/vault/1996/09/02/217042/up-from-the-ashes-packer-reggie-white-preaches-that-god-can-raise-a-man-to-the-super-bowl-and-a-church-from-ruins; https://www.sportsspectrum.com/articles/2013/01/26/reggie-white-minister-of-defense/.

70. Peter Hopsicker and Mark S. Dyreson, 'Super Bowl Sunday: An American Holiday?' in Len Travers (ed.), *Encyclopedia of American Holidays and National Days*, (Westport, CT: Greenwood Press, 2006), 54–60; and Richard C. Crepeau, 'Thorstein Veblen Explains the Super Bowl', http://stars.library.ucf.edu/onsportandsociety/223/ is the first of several 'Sport and Society' pieces in which variations of this analysis can be found.

71. Mike Tanner, 'Excess Reigns at the Super Bowl', *New York Times*, 10 January 2010.

Disclosure Statement

No potential conflict of interest was reported by the author.

'Superbowling': Using the Super Bowl's Yearly Commentary to Explore the Evolution of a Sporting Spectacle in the American Consciousness

Peter M. Hopsicker

ABSTRACT

In the days following Super Bowl III, *New York Times* columnist Robert Lipsyte coined the phrase 'superbowling'. Consisting of the 'chatter' and diverse perspectives voiced throughout the nation in the days surrounding each Super Bowl, superbowling includes the off-the-wall psychiatric evaluations and epic gloating by football fans, political reactions and sociological analyses concerning the game's affect on the nation's institutions, as well as the hasty generalizations by alarmed moralists and university professors. This paper utilizes the 'superbowling' penned between Super Bowls I and XXXVI as evidence that provides insight into 'the variety of ways in which Americans understood and enacted their political culture at a specific time'. By investigating the varieties of superbowling topics highlighted within each yearly Super Bowl, one cannot only better understand the evolution of Super Bowl Sunday, but can also understand its relationship to the prominent historical happenings and personalities of the time. It is concluded that by the turn of the millennium, superbowling revealed at least three enduring qualities of Super Bowl Sunday: 'conspicuous consumption', 'shared experience', and 'national holiday'.

Many of today's American football fans would agree with the Reverend Dr. Norman Vincent Peale's often-used quotation, 'If Jesus were alive today, He would be at the Super Bowl'.[1] Yet this may not have always been the case. While the media dubbed the professional football championship game the 'Super Bowl' immediately upon the merger of the AFL and NFL in 1966[2], the NFL did not employ the phrase 'Super Bowl' on the official game programmes until its third edition in 1969 nor on the official game tickets until its fourth edition in 1970. Furthermore, the media surrounding the first two 'AFL-NFL World Championship Games' often questioned the legitimacy and premature nature of using the superlative 'super' to describe this fledgling event – in hindsight, perhaps rightly so. In 1986, in fact, writers in *Sport* magazine, commenting on the quality of the first twenty Super Bowls, suggested that at least during versions I and II, if Jesus had wanted to reach a mass audience, He would have likely been elsewhere.[3]

As one of the six key stipulations agreed upon as a result of the 1966 merger of the American Football League (AFL) into the National Football League (NFL), an annual professional football championship game pitting the winners of each league in a climactic clash has capped each season since 1967.[4] Described as a 'once-in-a-lifetime sports attraction' months before the 1967 inaugural coin toss, NFL Commissioner Pete Rozelle predicted the largest sports viewing audience in history, a sell-out crowd with a million dollar gate, and the highest fee paid by any television broadcasting network for any single sports event.[5] Yet in the days before kick-off, roughly 40,000 'first-come, first-served' tickets remained available in the cavernous Los Angeles Memorial Coliseum. Backlash from the NFL's decision to blackout the game in local viewing areas, the perception that the outcome was a foregone conclusion due to the belief that NFL teams were far superior to AFL teams, and the game being televised on both NBC and CBS provided excuse for the lagging ticket sales. Seventy-two hours before kick-off, Rozelle conceded, 'it would be hard to get a sell-out at this point'.[6]

Thirty thousand seats remained empty at the Coliseum as the NFL's Green Bay Packers predictably defeated the AFL's Kansas City Chiefs, 35–10. The NFL fell roughly $250,000 short of its projected million-dollar gate, and the game left no mark in the annals of historically high (or low) television ratings.[7] Sports columnists did not hesitate to level judgement on the unimpressive nature of this original 'super' game. William Wallace of the *New York Times* dryly noted how the Super Bowl had piqued the nation's curiosity for 'about 150 minutes', resolving questions of 'no great significance', displacing 'sports-minded Americans out of the routine of their lives for an afternoon', and, when the game was over, we all simply went 'back to what we were doing before'.[8] Columnist Jack Gould, also of the *New York Times*, compared the game to a mediocre Hollywood production. 'The advance build-up was more impressive than the show and the script fell apart in the second act', Gould complained adding, 'There is a million-dollar dud in everyone's closet'.[9] Super Bowl anthologist Danny Peary's more recent description of Super Bowl I encapsulates the day's tepid evaluation: the fleeting national attention and average television ratings 'pretty much reflected the indifference the American public felt toward the game'.[10]

The second instalment, while achieving higher television ratings and a sell-out crowd at Miami's Orange Bowl (perhaps due to lowered ticket prices) enjoyed similar morose accolades. 'Only the importance of the game saved it from bordering on dullness', grumbled Arthur Daley of the *New York Times*. Daley described the Green Bay Packers' 'manhandling' of the AFL's Oakland Raiders as a 'cold-blooded execution that almost seemed to lack inspirational fervour', further observing that 'if the gap between the two leagues is narrowing, it is not yet visible to the naked eye'.[11] The Super Bowl continued to suffer from a perceived lack of parity between the AFL and NFL teams, and the unimpressive nature of its showcase championship event only fuelled that perception. Football fans seemed more concerned with the drama surrounding Vince Lombardi's resignation shortly after the game than with his Packers winning Super Bowl II.[12]

Super Bowl III marked a turning point in public interest in the game. After New York Jets quarterback Joe Namath predicted and then delivered the first Super Bowl victory for an AFL team, sportswriters praised the brazen quarterback for making the event significant. William Wallace of the *New York Times* gave Namath credit for putting 'competition, anticipation and equality into an extravaganza that needed a justification for its continued existence'.[13] In the eyes of many pundits the Super Bowl had risen to an equal footing with the Kentucky Derby, the World Series, and the Masters. Commentators found significant ink-worthy value in 'superbowling' – a phrase coined by *New York Times* columnist Robert Lipsyte in the aftermath of Super Bowl III.[14] Lipsyte, known for his inventing of trenchant terms, such as 'SportsWorld', which refers to the sports-centric 'infrastructure' of American society that both exposes and influences patterns of behaviour,[15] employed superbowling as a method of revealing the championship game's profuse and pervasive effect on the nation's psyche. Consisting of the 'chatter' and diverse perspectives voiced throughout the nation in the days surrounding each Super Bowl, superbowling includes the off-the-wall psychiatric evaluations and epic gloating by football fans, political reactions, and sociological analyses concerning the game's impact on the nation's institutions, as well as the (sometimes) hasty generalizations by alarmed moralists and university professors.[16] Written as both criticism and praise, superbowling allows for the perpetual deliberation of the meaning of Super Sunday as a functioning part of SportsWorld – as part of the underlying cultural foundation that 'touches everyone and everything'.[17]

Reviewing the superbowling composed between 1967 and the turn of the millennium provides evidence of the all-out-blitzing nature this championship event had on the American psyche.[18] Occurring each winter for the past half century, superbowling provides ongoing opportunities to explore the nation's consciousness through the critical examination of an immensely popular American sporting event. The Super Bowl is ultimately revealed as a special place within SportsWorld where both critics and advocates make meaning of this recurring moment of shared American experience. It further reveals our affinity for 'conspicuous consumption' – to 'get stoned', as Lipsyte puts it, through 'absurd excesses (that) reassure us that we're okay'.[19] It also reveals the spectacle's relationship to the prominent historical happenings and important historical patterns that ultimately have cemented the game's national holiday status.

To be sure, several unflattering superbowling portrayals shrouded Super Bowls I and II. Not all the commentaries were negative – and some accurately prophesized that the game would eventually become a major cultural spectacle.[20] During Super Bowl I, for example, journalists described the New York and Kansas City metropolitan areas as 'gripped by a giddy fever', consumed by a 'vague madness', and a never before seen excitement characterized by a 'rapt, hypnotic stare' at television sets throughout the cities.[21] These cities, stirred by 'Football's Day of Decision', found its men in front of the television, its women waiting in the kitchen, its children cancelling birthday parties and trips to movie theatres, its bars packed with football fans who vacated their homes and apartments to watch the game, its businesses closing early, its church services rescheduled, and its political figures pausing from other national interests to partake in the spectacle.[22] In the days following Super Bowl II, superbowlers noted the 'complex cultural changes' that were taking place on football Sundays.[23] Shortly after the Jets victory in 1969, some superbowlers, perhaps forgetful of their indifference to Super Bowls I and II, reversed their previously pessimistic perspectives on the event and would concisely characterize the game's growing cultural relevance as it entered the 1970s. Annulling his initial cynical evaluations, for example, William Wallace, predicted that from Super Bowl III and beyond, 'Pro football will never quite be the same again'.[24]

Wallace's comment proved precedent. The Super Bowl quickly commanded influence in SportsWorld as a shared American experience of national holiday status born from conspicuous consumption. Indeed, within two decades of its existence, the game was such a part of the nation's calendar that superbowlers dubbed Super Sunday an American holiday. By the 1990s, it represented 'the winter version of the Fourth of July celebration'.[25] In the days following the turn of the twenty-first century, superbowling scholars Peter Hopsicker and Mark Dyreson used the iconoclastic sociologist Thorstein Velben's economic theory to characterize Super Bowl Sunday as a national holiday 'created by the modern entertainment industry to celebrate the national appetite for conspicuous consumption' and further described it as a 'blueprint for the way in which [future] holidays are constructed'.[26] From its first edition to the turn of the millennium, the Super Bowl emblazoned itself into the nation's consciousness as a shared American experience one specific winter Sunday at a time. Indeed, a review of the superbowling written in the 1970s through the early 2000s provides evidence for these accolades and reveals not only the growth of the event itself, but also its perpetual presence and influence on American culture.

Superbowling in the 1970s

Entering the 1970s, Super Bowl 'fever' began to infect not only the hometowns of the competing teams but the entire United States as well. Indeed, immediately after Super Bowl I, travel agencies began attracting vacationers to Super Bowl host cities by adding game tickets to vacation packages. By the 1970s, they used the game as a 'springboard for winter vacations' and a marketing tool to give a 'powerful shot in the arm' to the January tourism slump, which occurred after New Year's Day.[27]

The masses who did not book a winter sojourn to the sunbelt watched the game on their television sets. Television ratings and shares grew quickly after Namath and the Jets won the third Super Bowl. The fourth version attracted the largest television audience for a single sports event recorded up to that time, and television advertising rates followed suit increasing by more than 40%.[28] In fact, since Super Bowl II, the NFL has enjoyed television shares in the sixties and seventies, and since Super Bowl VI (with the exception of Super Bowl XXIV with a rating of 39), television ratings of over 40. These indicators provide early evidence of the game's enduring popularity and shared experience nature. On one winter Sunday per year since 1970, almost three-quarters of all operating televisions and almost half of all existing televisions in the United States have been tuned in to the Super Bowl.[29]

The 1970s also witnessed the increasing parity between the two former leagues as they merged into one NFL with two conferences – the American Football Conference that included all of old AFL franchises plus the NFL's Baltimore Colts, Pittsburgh Steelers, and Cleveland Browns; and the National Football Conference that included the remaining teams from the old NFL. In 1970, on the cusp of the merger, the AFL's Kansas City Chiefs' victory over the NFL's heavily favoured Minnesota Vikings in Super Bowl IV proved that the Jets' upset the previous year was no fluke and tied the Super Bowl series with two victories for each league as they moved towards their new amalgamation. The Chiefs' win alleviated questions of competitive parity and convinced the nation that the game was worth watching. Superbowlers did not miss the opportunity to note how the victory solidified the successful merger of both leagues under one shield. 'The American Football League commenced operations 10 years ago and it was a joke', wrote Arthur Daley in the *New York Times*. 'It ceased its existence as an entity in the Super Bowl yesterday', Daley observed, 'and [because of its convincing victory] made its exit laughing'.[30] By the middle of the decade, few could argue against the Super Bowl's growing presence on the American calendar as exemplified by one superbowler who noted how the Super Bowl brunch of scrambled eggs and Bloody

Marys constituted 'as much of an institution in American suburbs as eggnog parties at Christmas or picnics on the Fourth of July'.[31]

In the early part of the decade, however, superbowlers honed in on three new problems associated with the event's rapid growth to success.[32] First, the Baltimore Colts and the Dallas Cowboys combined for 16 major errors and 14 penalties in Super Bowl V, raising questions about the quality of the game. One pundit blamed two weeks of 'preparation, build-up, and clamour' for the errors, but concluded that the errors made the game 'zany and fun' rather than detracting from its entertainment value.[33] Second, while the NFL enjoyed sell-outs since Super Bowl II, by Super Bowl III the league office changed its ticket distribution policy from 'how many do you want?' to 'this is how many you can have' and this is who can have them.[34] The availability of 'no strings attached' tickets for the 'little guy' evaporated. 'Rarer than snowflakes in Miami', announced one newspaper report, revealing that only one thousand tickets were made available for those 'without a connection to some team or somebody' for Super Bowl V.[35] By Super Bowl IX, tickets for the average fan were almost non-existent.[36] Even those who knew 'somebody' were not guaranteed tickets causing some VIPs to experience, in the words of one superbowler, 'disappointment, embarrassment, and anger'.[37] Third, while the game enjoyed high television ratings, backlash continued from the NFL's television blackout policy 'exorcising' the local commoner from watching it on TV. While the other 64 million football fans who could not attend the game contributed to the Nielson ratings, the ongoing television blackouts in the cities that hosted the Super Bowl fuelled a growing number of 'caustic comments' about the rapacious commercialism surrounding the game.[38]

Growing pains aside, politicians found immediate value in positive connections to the Super Bowl, and by the mid-1970s, their connections became regular fodder for superbowling chatter. Reports that Senators Robert F. Kennedy and Jacob K. Javits 'hardly moved away from the television set' during Super Bowl I,[39] and stories of Vice President Elect Spiro Agnew (native Marylander and Governor of Maryland) being asked to leave the Baltimore Colts' bench before the kick off of Super Bowl III (his presence 'violated league policy')[40] indicated early political connections. However, President (and Miami Dolphins fan) Richard Nixon's inaugural congratulatory phone call to quarterback Len Dawson and the victorious Kansas City Chiefs after Super Bowl IV certainly set the precedent for the association of future presidents with the game.[41] While Nixon's initial phone call did not draw much ire from superbowlers, his suggestion of a 'down-and-in' play to Dolphins' coach Don Shula before Super Bowl VI did. A satirical superbowler wondered, 'If Presidents can suggest game plans to football coaches, can football coaches suggest new game plans for Presidents?'[42] After the play failed, a White House staff member defended Nixon's offensive strategy noting how 'No politician sensitive to economic issues would ever call a 'down-and-out''.[43] The next year, President Nixon's defection from the Dolphins to the 'home team' Washington Redskins for Super Bowl VII did not go unnoticed by superbowlers nor did the absence of a play-call from 'Coach Nixon'.[44] Perhaps the ongoing war in Vietnam and the growing Watergate scandal diverted Nixon's attention from drawing up offensive plays.

Conscious of the size and scope of the Super Bowl audience, politicians later in the decade often tried to remain neutral on favouring one team over another in order to cleverly avoid alienating any potential voters. Just before Super Bowl XIII, for example, President Jimmy Carter bet $5 on the Cowboys against his mother, Miss Lillian, who took the Steelers (a bet that she won). That same year, Vice President Walter Mondale and New York City Mayor

Ed Koch picked the Vikings and the Jets, respectively, mindful of their hometown states, but forgetful that neither team finished that season with a winning record or make the playoffs, let alone the Super Bowl.[45]

Layered on top of growing political associations to the Super Bowl, nationalism found a home at the game tinting every aspect with hues of red, white, and blue. However, the patriotic images of the pregame U.S. Air Force flyover during Super Bowls II and VI, the presence of the Air Force Academy Choir and the U.S. Marine Corps Marching Band at Super Bowl VI, and the leading of the Pledge of Allegiance by the Apollo 8, Apollo 11, and Apollo 17 astronauts before Super Bowls III, IV, and VII, respectively, nudged some superbowlers out of their patriotic comfort zones. A *New York Times* 'Letter to the Editor' observing that the 'pomp surrounding the Super Bowl activities might as well have taken place in a country governed by a military junta' provides an early example of questions surrounding the game's growing nationalistic connections. Lamenting the overbearing 'military intrusion' on 'even this aspect of American life', the letter-writer warns that such overtones would 'no doubt contribute unfavourably toward this country's image'.[46] Such questions, however, did not derail Super Bowl X being positioned as the official kick-off of the nation's bicentennial celebration in 1976, an honour that came on the heels of the release of Thomas Harris' novel, *Black Sunday*, in which Arab extremists attempted to blow up a stadium during the Super Bowl.[47]

During this formative period time sportswriter Hunter S. Thompson began superbowling in his well-known gonzo journalistic fashion.[48] Writing two articles in *Rolling Stone* magazine under the title 'Fear and Loathing at the Super Bowl' (Super Bowls VII and VIII), Thompson raged on the 'inseparable' and 'unholy' nature of his 'extremely twisted…relationship with God, Nixon and the National Football League'. At one point he attempted to convince the Super Bowl press corps into 'praising God and singing the national anthem'.[49] At times referring to the Super Bowl as 'predictable' with the outcome often 'painfully clear less than halfway through the first quarter', Thompson compares the purported excesses of Super Bowl week (including free meals and drinks for the sportswriters as well as the lavish Commissioner's Party) with the speed and dullness of the actual game – comparing the latter to a 'molasses farm'.[50] He argued that professional football's charge to success came about through its connections to television and the NFL's ability to create a 'personal relationship' between a 'huge coast-to-coast audience of armchair fans who 'grew up'…with the idea that pro football was something that happened every Sunday on the tube'.[51] Thompson also described how the NFL spectator-base had transformed from a rough yet 'hip' and 'private kind of vice' in the 1960s to 'a sort of half-rich mob of nervous doctors, lawyers and bank officers who would sit through the whole game without ever making a sound'.[52] Troubled by this change in the live Super Bowl audience demographic, Thompson noted how he would rather have 'stayed in [his] hotel room and watched the goddamn thing on TV; or maybe in some howling-drunk bar full of heavy bettors'.[53]

In hindsight, Thompson's 1970s rants epitomized superbowling. They covered a variety of topics that would reappear in superbowling threads for years to come – often with extreme prejudice such as his characterization of the NFL as 'the last bastion of fascism in America'.[54] Yet, he was not the only critic of the Super Bowl production who revealed themselves more prominently in the 1970s. Superbowlers less enamoured with the growth of the day's status, such as David Condon of the *Chicago Tribune*, were quick to characterize the event as 'Pete Rozelle's travelling crap game'. Lamenting the day's already recognized holiday status, Condon ranted, 'The way you guys are going ape on Super Bowl Sunday, you'd think it was the most important holiday of the season, [but] George Allen wasn't born in a manger [and] Don Shula isn't one of the Pilgrim fathers cooking up turkey and venison for a Thanksgiving spread'.[55] Others noted how the quality of the game continued to suffer for the sake of making money. 'Peter Roselle's VIII annual production of the Super Bowl was a yawner', one *Chicago Tribune* editorial ranted. 'The teams played with little enthusiasm – it was all business (which I suppose it was meant to be)'.[56] *Sports Illustrated* described the same game as having 'all the excitement and suspense of a master butcher quartering a steer'.[57] The following year, Red Smith, the nation's most renowned sports columnist, suggested that the 'promotional overkill by the [television] networks' caused the negative reviews of the games. 'It isn't that the title game is necessarily duller than many in midseason', Smith continued, 'it only seems so because expectations are built so high...It isn't talent that is lacking, but a sense of proportion'. The word 'super' in Super Bowl, Smith concluded in his superbowling exercise, simply promises more than any promoter can deliver.[58] Smith's comments echo Thompson's assessment of Super Bowl VII. 'The game itself was hopelessly dull', Thompson complained, 'like all the other Super Bowls'.[59]

Still, by the time Super Bowl X kicked-off the nation's bicentennial celebration,[60] one superbowler preached that to 'escape mention of the Super Bowl...one must almost resign from the human race'.[61] In 1977, *New York Times* sportswriter Jon Nordheimer designated the Super Bowl as a 'national social spectacle' in which the 'rhythm of midwinter America on a Sunday afternoon will change'.[62] Another columnist characterized Super Bowl Sunday as a 'slice of Americana' that 'taxed the limits of hyperbole'.[63] An additional columnist opined that collectively the first ten Super Bowls had 'produced a sense of [American] history'.[64] Still another writer added that the 'the church, the theatre, the family and the political process having let us down, we need to believe in the Super Bowl'.[65]

These homages to the unifying power of the Super Bowl in American society did not stop superbowlers from wrestling with the quality and place of the actual game within the day's activities. On the one hand, they identified Super Bowl Sunday as a 'national social spectacle' and a 'slice of Americana'. On the other hand, they lamented the 'sleep-inducing' and 'disappointing' nature of the first 10 'Stuper Bowls', and complained how the game itself no longer served as the focus of the day and had receded into being just 'part of the background'.[66] Some pundits even proclaimed that the conference playoff games had become ultimately more exciting than the 'big game'.[67] Shortly before Super Bowl XII, even Commissioner Rozelle admitted that the day was 'probably more of an event than simply a game'.[68]

The American masses largely overlooked these critical opinions. Regular superbowlers acclaimed the day's impact on American culture regardless of whether or not the Super Bowl itself generated an exciting spectacle. The *Washington Post's* Tony Kornheiser contended that 'Americans caress the Super Bowl as much they caress any event in contemporary culture'.[69] Celebrity superbowlers from other walks of life chimed in as well. The novelist Kurt Vonnegut observed that watching the Super Bowl was 'a perfectly normal American thing [to do]', while playwright Arthur Miller's wondered if Super Bowl Sunday had become a 'religious holiday'.[70] By the end of the 1970s, Super Bowl Sunday had become a defining part of the nation's culture. *New York Times* columnist John Leonard defined it as an event where Americans 'participate with ourselves as a nation'. Leonard confessed: 'Once a year,

I would like to be doing what everyone else is doing, and 95 million people is a lot of everybody elses'.[71]

Superbowling in the 1980s

Yearly increases in the cost of Super Bowl television commercial time, growth in Super Bowl television audiences, and the first international transmission of the game to London, England in 1981 (although superbowlers described the audience as 'almost entirely American') confirmed increasing interest in the Super Bowl throughout the 1980s.[72] Consumerism secured its place at the Super Bowl during this economically booming decade. American businesses began to treat the event as a kind of 'corporate convention', using the game to attract clients and sponsors from across the country for a week of networking.[73] With a nod towards conspicuously consumptive practices, the Super Bowl became, as one superbowler noted, 'synonymous with money' and one of the country's 'truly intriguing financial and sociological phenomenons'.[74]

The corporate takeover of the Super Bowl led to a ticket price increase from $30 to $100 over the course of the decade, with scalpers reportedly receiving five-times those amounts.[75] The addition of 'Ad Bowl' in the 1980s, the corporate television advertising showcase during the Super Bowl, spawned by the release of a $1 million dollar commercial for Apple Computer, doubled advertising rates to $700,000 for a 30-second spot in the second half of the decade.[76] While the Super Bowl continued to grow as a shared 'American experience' on the nation's calendar, these two data points vividly demonstrate the economic exclusivity now intrinsic to the event. By the middle of the 1980s, as a *Newsday* superbowler poignantly observed, the Super Bowl had become an event 'for the royalty to attend and for the peasants to watch on TV, a situation that does not cause the NFL any guilty feelings'.[77] This class division would continue to increase dramatically in the following decades, and by the end of the 1990s, both ticket prices and advertising rates would almost triple these amounts.[78]

Super Bowls in the 1980s also galvanized the promotional and economic value of hosting the game, and host cities netted increasing estimates of economic development. In 1977, host city Pasadena, California, reported the influx of 75,000 out-of-towners spending approximately $14 million dollars on round-trip airline tickets and roughly $11 million dollars a day in town.[79] The Miami Chamber of Commerce, nostalgic for the economic gains made by hosting earlier games, described the Super Bowl as 'the biggest single event a community can have economically', and estimated that the game brought a $40 to $50 million economic boost for the host city.[80] Four years later, an economic analysis showed considerable growth in the financial power of the game. Economists estimated that Super Bowl XIX generated more than $113 million for the San Francisco Bay area and predicted that Super Bowl XX would produce at least $90 million for the city of New Orleans.[81] Towards the end of the decade, host cities were vying for an estimated $150 million in revenue, motivating superbowler Tony Kornheiser to label the day as 'corporate America's annual holiday...built to honour conspicuous consumption'.[82]

During the 1980s, the White House also solidified its relationship with the Super Bowl. While Vice President George Bush created monster traffic problems with his motorcade when he attended Super Bowl XVI,[83] President Ronald Reagan endured the most superbowling ink during the cold war era. After Super Bowl XVIII, President Reagan's phone call to the victorious Los Angeles Raiders' locker room (televised live in split-screen format) included various cold war references to 'secret weapons', 'silos', and 'MX missiles'.[84] The phone call, which usually sought, in the words of one superbowling sport philosopher, to 'demonstrate that [the President's] office identifies with the values that brought the [winning] team to this level of success',[85] did not achieve this purpose. 'The President jerked us back to the reality that we had been trying to escape', an angry superbowler howled. 'He is the person whose arms build-up I am watching the game to forget', the writer complained further lamenting how 'sport is one of our last refuges from the man in the White House and his incessant baiting of the Kremlin'.[86] Other superbowlers implored the President to 'stay out of our locker room' because 'to most people nuclear arms are not funny'.[87] These sorts of commentaries led NBC to interview President Reagan before Super Bowl XX, hoping to supplant 'the frequently awkward' and 'ludicrous' postgame telephone call from the White House.[88]

As awkward as these phone calls could be for any president, George Vecsey of the *New York Times*, who admitted to loathing the Super Bowl,[89] continued to stoke this particular storyline through the next two years by referencing a 'character actor' who made 'bizarre' and 'weird' bomb and missile jokes.[90] President Reagan's flippant references to the tools of nuclear war during Super Bowl XVIII, however, failed to motivate the media to more rigorously cover the 1985 Geneva Summit held between President Reagan and Soviet leader Mikhail S. Gorbachev, nor did these comments quell their lust to cover the 20th instalment of the championship game. NFL officials issued 2,400 media credentials for Super Bowl XX – roughly 1,400 more than the number requested for the Summit.[91] This juxtaposition of media resource allotment suggests that even discussions of world peace could not compete with the attention routinely devoted to the Super Bowl.

By the middle of the decade, superbowlers began to point out that 'indifference' to the Super Bowl would clearly be 'damning information' for any political candidate.[92] The timeliness of Reagan's cold war references could not have been more noticeable as the country anxiously awaited his announcement to seek a second term.[93] Unfortunately for Reagan, one year later the newly re-elected president would unintentionally clash once again with the Super Bowl culture. As early as 1983, speculation swirled about the potential of Super Bowl Sunday and Inauguration Day landing on the same date, 20 January 1985.[94] When this potential became reality, the White House etiquette office moved the public inauguration ceremony to the Monday after the Super Bowl. Superbowlers paid no attention to the nuances of protocol, however, and leaped on this switch, believing that the championship game had supplanted the American ceremony. Seeking solutions, one *New York Times* superbowler, Richard Reeves, suggested a constitutional amendment to remedy the issue. 'Congress shall make no law respecting an establishment of events, institutions or encumbrances of any kind interfering with the playing of the Super Bowl', Reeves proposed in his constitutional draft. 'No business shall be conducted by any Federal official, specifically including the President of the United States on the day of America's game', Reeves admonished. By replacing 'a political event as the symbolic holiday of America's civic religion', Reeves concluded, 'we now know [the Super Bowl is] a higher holiday than the day when we crown our king'.[95]

Reeves and other superbowlers had failed to do their research on inaugural procedures. In fact, the six previous Inauguration Days that landed on a Sunday were also moved to the following Monday.[96] While James Monroe (1817), Zachary Taylor (1849), Rutherford B. Hayes (1877), Woodrow Wilson (1917), and Dwight D. Eisenhower (1953) followed this accepted practice for their Sunday inaugurations without the pressures of a national sporting event (or, with the exception of Eisenhower, the pressures of televised coverage of the inauguration), the American public seemed uninterested in this historical standard and instead elevated the power of the Super Bowl over one of the nation's most profound political ceremonies. The Capitol's expert on inaugurations adamantly denied that the power of the Super Bowl moved inauguration. 'It reads well and tells wells', he admitted, 'but it just ain't true'. The public swearing-in of the President had been postponed, not because of football, but because of the political tradition of avoiding Sunday public inaugurals.[97]

While Reagan had little control over this inauguration narrative, he did take steps to ensure his connection to the estimated 100 million Americans predicted to watch Super Bowl XIX – the largest television audience of that year.[98] Hours after the private inauguration ceremony held in Washington D.C., Reagan became the first president to perform the official Super Bowl coin toss – a task he achieved via a satellite link to Palo Alto, California, in order to stay in Washington for the Monday public inauguration ceremony. Superbowlers did not miss this opportunity to note that the inaugural ceremony would most likely get single-digit ratings, while the coin-toss would probably break television records – and that the difference between the two should 'tell us something about what's really important around here'.[99] One superbowler proposed defusing the tension caused by both events falling on the same day by actually fusing the two events together – hold the inauguration ceremony during the Super Bowl halftime, he suggested. 'The NFL should be happy because football will begin and end the day's events. The White House should be happy because the situation will offer the largest live and television audiences ever for a Presidential inauguration. And the networks should be happy because they will be spared the costs of covering major happenings on opposite coasts on the same day'.[100] The suggestion of fusing the Super Bowl and politics appealed to Reeves as well. 'The coin in the air – and on the air – could serve as the symbol of the partnership of sports and politics in our time', Reeves suggested. The Super Bowl had become, Reeves affirmed, 'such a national holiday now that the President has to be a part of the game to prove he really is the President'.[101] Such a statement would be indicative of future superbowling commentary highlighting the presidential and political associations to the Super Bowl each winter.

In addition to these political connections, nationalism continued to bleed through all aspects of the event highlighted in 1981 by the adornment of the New Orleans Superdome, the Philadelphia Eagles and Oakland Raiders players, and every fan in attendance of Super Bowl XV with a yellow ribbon in recognition of the Iran Hostages freed days earlier.[102] Likewise, the premier of the game in London became, as one superbowler noted, an 'expression of the patriotism often felt by citizens overseas, especially at times of national stress at home'.[103] The following year, columnist Russell Baker compared watching the game to Thanksgiving turkey and other uniquely American traditions. 'If eating turkey is what you have to do to qualify for fellowship in the American community, I'll force myself to do it', Baker proclaimed, 'just as I force myself to watch the Miss America Pageant, the Academy Awards and the Super Bowl on television. If the whole county is going to engage in these things, who am I to be snooty about them?'[104]

As the 1990s approached, Super Bowl Sunday clearly had firm roots in America's midwinter calendar, and its branches connecting it to the political, social, commercial, and economic tenets of the nation annually bore positive fruit for the NFL. Now permanently connected to the American psyche, superbowlers throughout the 1980s regularly conferred holiday status on the Super Bowl, declaring it the 'first [holiday] of the year',[105] a 'favourite holiday',[106] and a 'national party'[107] in which participation qualifies one for 'fellowship in the American community'.[108] The superbowlers positioned it positively on America's list of 'national holidays'[109] as well as somewhat negatively as a 'patriotic substitute for [other] increasingly esoteric national holidays'.[110] Additionally, some superbowlers characterized it as a 'symbolic holiday of America's civic religion'[111] and a 'high holy day'.[112] Perhaps overstepping the boundaries of propriety, one *Houston Chronicle* superbowler even suggested that the Super Bowl had replaced Easter as America's primary religious holiday. 'What are 80 million American's doing on the day that the two conference champions play for the National Football League title on a Sunday in January?' the correspondent quipped. 'Attending Mass?'[113]

As during the 1970s, superbowlers continued to bash the NFL about the fading relevancy of the actual football game seemingly lost amidst the corporate, commercial and political spectacle.[114] Described by some as 'unbearably dull',[115] lacking 'high drama',[116] and a 'Siberia of the soul',[117] the quality of the game simply could not live up to the hype in the minds of some superbowlers, and each final score often verified their perspectives. Only two Super Bowls were determined by less than seven points in the 1980s, and by the end of the decade, the average margin of victory for all Super Bowls was over two touchdowns. Observers began to speculate that most of the audience had developed a powerful apathy towards the teams actually playing in the games. 'The teams involved do not matter much', wrote one pundit. 'What matters is who comes [to the game]'.[118] Some national polls demonstrated the growing indifference to which teams were actually vying for the Lombardi Trophy. The *New York Times*/CBS News polls for Super Bowls XVI and XXI indicated that 40% of the audience admitted to 'not caring who wins the Super Bowl [rather] than prefer either team'.[119] Even the players understood that fandom for a particular team did not drive the national passion for the Super Bowl. At Super Bowl XVI, a group of players described the game as a 'sideshow' and 'for kids'.[120] Other superbowlers, perhaps unknowingly channelling the shared experience qualities of the game, called the Super Bowl 'a national holiday' in one breath before adding, but 'I don't really care about the game'.[121] Commenting on this disinterest, and echoing one superbowler's complaint from the previous decade,[122] Vecsey observed, 'the real problem is the Super Bowl itself' adding it's 'an event that takes so long to deliver so little'.[123]

However 'little' football the day delivered, by the end of the 1980s Super Bowl Sunday had established deep roots in American culture and branches beyond the country's boundaries. The American Forces Television and Radio Network broadcast the spectacle to over 30 countries and 200 ships at sea, in order to 'let [the US Armed Forces] know that the American way of life is still worth living'.[124] By the mid-1990s, the Super Bowl aired in 174 countries to an estimated potential global audience of 750 million.[125] By the start of the 1990s, the Super Bowl traversed the geographic borders of the United States – at least according to the press releases from NFL marketing gurus. Super Bowl Sunday had become, as Vecsey pointed out, 'the world's problem now'.[126]

Superbowling in the 1990s

The Super Bowl would continue to experience rising costs during the 1990s both from a fan and a corporation perspective. Ticket prices grew from $125 to $325 during the course of the decade and television advertising rates for 30-second commercial slots more than doubled from $700,000 to $1.6 million. In response to the '$43,333 A Second'[127] advertising rate for Super Bowl XXXII, superbowlers reiterated how the event continued to serve as an advertiser's goldmine. 'There are few opportunities for marketers to appeal to an audience as broad as the Super Bowl's', one pundit proclaimed. 'Every year, the championship football game is by far the most-watched television show, gathering 130 million to 140 million viewers before the electronic hearth for what has become a midwinter orgy of commercial culture'.[128] Unable to dismiss the 'demographic desirability' of a diverse and national audience, companies continued to use the Super Bowl as a means to an ends, to sell their products and prove their companies' worth before the nation, and to win the annual 'Ad Bowl'.[129] By the turn of the millennium, corporate executives believed that no other media event eclipsed the marketing potential of the Super Bowl.[130]

The Super Bowl matured during the 1990s as a corporate capitalist spectacle, confirming commentator Tony Kornheiser's 1989 assessment of the day as 'corporate America's annual holiday…built to honour conspicuous consumption'.[131] Similarly, by the 1990s few would challenge the notion that the event functioned as 'appointment television',[132] a 'shared American experience',[133] and a 'common American moment'.[134] Still some superbowlers wondered if growing competition from cable and satellite television as well as the growing opportunities afforded by the Internet might in the near future erode the massive but captive Super Bowl audience.[135] Solid television ratings and shares during the 1990s through Super Bowl 50 would indicate otherwise. Furthermore, while Don Weiss, former Executive Director of the NFL, urged the league not to 'forget about the game', [136] the economic impact of the Super Bowl largely clouded the original purpose of the event behind a shower of dollar signs. Rather than the superlatives normally associated with sporting events – skill performance and kinaesthetic prowess of participating teams and athletes – the sale of billion dollar advertising deals, multi-million dollar television contracts, accolades marking the year's highest consumption of chips, popcorn, pretzels, and snack nuts, and ticket prices that put game attendance out of the reach of the middle class dominated Super Bowl narratives.[137] By 1995, even the president of NBC Sports, Dick Ebersol, confessed that the teams playing in the game did not 'really matter' in terms of how many people tuned in to watch.[138]

The Super Bowl's maturation into a Nielsen ratings powerhouse and conspicuous consumption showcase, however, did not alleviate the NFL from its regular and sometimes contentious juxtaposition of politics and nationalism in the spectacles. In the early 1990s, the NFL thrust itself into the political arena by relocating Super Bowl XXVII out of Arizona due to that state's unwillingness to recognize Martin Luther King Day.[139] NFL Commissioner Paul Tagliabue recommended the move in 1990 while ironically proclaiming that the NFL was not 'a political advocacy group'. 'The NFL's goal is to focus the Super Bowl on football, not election controversy', Tagliabue argued. 'The Super Bowl is a stage for great quarterbacks and linebackers…not a platform for political strategies and demonstrations'.[140]

In response to the Arizona controversy, and in some ways resuscitating Hunter S. Thompson's 1970s charge of NFL fascism, superbowler Ira Berkow of the New York Times criticized the league for its 'heavy-handed' decision, but conceded that such actions are 'not unusual for an NFL undertaking'.[141] Berkow and other superbowlers, savvy to the economic ramification of hosting the game, also pointed out the Super Bowl's $200 to $250 million value to the host state. Furthermore, they insinuated that both the NFL and Arizona feared 'boycotts by sponsors and civil rights groups', which would reduce both constituents' bottom line. Critics also observed the potential publicity damage to both the NFL and Arizona should 'the game become secondary to [these political statements]' – a development that might have undermined the Super Bowl's showcase appeal.[142] Tagliabue, however, danced around these pitfalls. The commissioner described the Super Bowl as 'one of sport's extraordinary spectacles…covered by 1,500 representatives of an international news corps…[and] watched by 100 million Americans and millions of additional fans in 60 other countries'. He made no mention of the positive or negative financial implications of playing the game in Arizona when justifying his decision. Instead, he argued for removing the Super Bowl from the political discussion and allowing 'Arizona to continue its long-time political debate over the King holiday'. Tagliabue concluded his public remarks on the issue with a pragmatic query: 'Why should politicians or pundits force the league to become stuck at the centre of prolonged political debate when it can be minimized?'[143]

In spite of Tagliabue's efforts, the NFL and the Super Bowl remained at the centre of this controversy. *The New York Times'* Berkow forgave the NFL for any improper intentions but remained critical of the NFL's actions. 'It is one thing…to enact laws and ordinances to insure equality in jobs, in housing, in education, in where to sit on a bus and in seating at luncheon counters', he opined. 'It is yet another to make an attempt…to twist the arm of an electorate to pay homage by dint of a symbol'.[144] While Tagliabue would be accused of 'muddling' the manner in which the league handled this decision, Arizona would ultimately approve the King holiday in 1992 and, according to one report, would be awarded Super Bowl XXX in 1996 as a 'consolation' to 'appease Arizonans and the Phoenix Cardinals' owner, Bill Bidwill'.[145]

While Commissioner Tagliabue attempted to keep the NFL out of the King holiday politics and avoid 'political football', another prominent example of Super Bowl politicking unavoidably arose even before the Arizona referendum was tallied. The outbreak of the Gulf War in August 1990 raised questions about playing or cancelling the twenty-fifth anniversary of the Super Bowl. Superbowlers approached this question on several fronts. 'I can't help thinking that there will be something obscene about going ahead with our annual orgy of football now that a war actually has started', wrote Lowell Cohn of the *San Francisco Chronicle*, taking a contrarian stance. 'It would be like Uncle Bob bringing a TV set to a funeral because he simply can't miss that all-important game. Somehow, all the Super Bowl parties, the happy-go-lucky halftime shows, and for heaven's sake, that awful Bud Bowl will seem so out of place in relation to the reality of the world trying to blow itself to bits in the Middle East'. By the end of his essay, Cohn recommended postponing the game at least a week. 'If after that, the world is still going crazy, you can cancel it altogether', he observed. Cohn further warned that if anyone [players, networks, sponsors, fans] thinks cancelling the game is a 'major inconvenience', perhaps they should 'consider what's going on in the Persian Gulf'.[146]

Other superbowlers supported playing the game citing justifications of historical precedent. 'Along with any other business', Dave Anderson of the *New York Times* asserted, 'sports in America should try to maintain itself during a war. As it has during other wars in America's history' (*sic*). Referencing how the assassination of President Kennedy, the bombing of Pearl Harbor, the Korean War, and the Vietnam War did not drastically curtail America's sports consumption, Anderson recommended playing the game, but subduing the partying.[147]

Tony Kornheiser, writing in the *Los Angeles Times*, also agreed that the Super Bowl should be played. 'It's a diversion', he opined, 'something to chase our minds away from the horror of war', because 'the living need some reassurance', and because 'the soldiers themselves are probably eager for the Armed Forces Network to broadcast the Super Bowl. They might see it as a hopeful symbol'. With greater passion than Anderson and Cohn, Kornheiser also recommended toning down the Super Bowl's 'excesses'. He advised the NFL to simply 'let it be a game'. 'Spare us the American Dream theme park, the jet flyovers, the orchestral anthems, and the omnipresent flags', he pleaded. 'Spare us the ostentatious parties with the egregious tons of gourmet foods and the wall-to-wall celebrations of greed and glitz', he continued. 'Spare us the false solemnity by the broadcasters', Kornheiser begged. 'Don't insult our intelligence or goose our passions with stentorian monologues about the meaning of it all'.[148]

Just two days before the scheduled playing of Super Bowl XXV, however, questions remained about postponing or cancelling the event. Commissioner Tagliabue, perhaps drawing on the years of nationalism associated with the event, cried that the Super Bowl had 'become the winter version of the Fourth of July celebration'. Worried that the events in the Middle East might pre-empt the game's television coverage, the commissioner insisted that the NFL wanted 'an audience to watch our game' – an audience estimated to be 750 million viewers worldwide – and if that was not possible, then the game should be postponed.[149]

While the game was ultimately played and televised on its scheduled date, 27 January 1991, the only obvious major reduction in the Super Bowl excess was the cancellation of the commissioner's annual party. Ignoring the superbowlers' recommendations, the NFL staged a 'patriotic spectacular'. President George Bush, commander in chief during the Persian Gulf War, ordered a 'breath-taking display of military might' allowing the 56th Tactical Training Wing Air Force jets to fly over Tampa Stadium after Whitney Houston's seismic performance of the national anthem.[150] The NFL could not have picked a better uniform colour scheme to fit Super Bowl XXV's patriotic theme – both the New York Giants and the Buffalo Bills donned their usual red, white and blue.

Superbowling in the 2000s

The NFL's use of the elevated patriotic timbre in the United States during Super Bowl XXV set off alarms for some superbowlers. As the twenty-first century dawned, those warnings grew more intense for some chroniclers of the Super Bowl and American culture. While *Miami Herald* sports columnist Edwin Pope noted that 'right from the start, [the NFL] wanted the Super Bowl to be intensely American...and there was never any question they would use patriotism as their motif',[151] superbowlers often debated the appropriateness of linking militarism and nationalism to the Super Bowl as early as the 1970s. The Gulf War had heightened questions of this association's propriety. Those questions would be reignited with the horrors of the 9/11 terrorist attacks in 2001. In contrast to Tagliabue and Ebersole, who labelled the Super Bowl 'a winter version of the Fourth of July'[152] and 'a national party that rivals the Fourth of July',[153] respectively, superbowler Robert Klein scolded the American public for treating Super Bowl Sunday as a 'patriotic substitute for increasingly esoteric national holidays'. Referring to the Super Bowl as both a 'quintessential American creation' as well as a 'simple game', Klein caustically observed: 'To many, the Fourth of July has come to mean a celebration of the invention of the firecracker and injury statistics.

Veterans Day means no alternate-side-of-the-street parking. We continually trivialize the national heritage we purport to honour. George Washington was a great leader. What other nation celebrates the birthday of its father every year with a mattress sale?'[154] Superbowling regular Kornheiser took a similar stance. 'You cheapen patriotism by selling it like laundry detergent', he ranted. 'Can't anyone have a sense of decorum about the flag decals on the helmets, and the flag patches on the jerseys?' he implored.[155]

Super Bowl XXXVI, held five months after the 9/11 terrorist attacks and themed by the NFL and Fox Sports as 'Heroes, Hope & Homeland', included even more patriotic pageantry in its 'flag-centric' celebration, so much so that Hunter S. Thompson wondered if the 'NFL had been drafted into the 'war effort'.[156] While few adamantly disagreed with the NFL's tribute honouring not only those killed in the attacks but also those serving in Operation Enduring Freedom, superbowlers still identified some nationalistic inconsistencies. For example, reacting to overt displays of American patriotism during this 'Patriot Bowl', superbowler Michael Davis of the *Washington Post* declared: 'With the helium steadily leaking out of Memorial Day, a holiday few Americans observe by actually attending events that honour the sacrifices of war, and Labor Day devolving into little more than cookouts and mattress sales, the Super Bowl is filling the void'.[157]

Superbowling scholars also provided insight and cautionary counsel. Treating the Super Bowl as any other commodity, sociologist Jay Coakley argued that 'Patriotism now seems to be an acceptable hook for [this] kind of packaging'. Coakely added that 'Just as manufactures use red, white, and blue to legitimize their products at other points during the year, the Super Bowl and its sponsors have done the same thing'.[158] Counselling some restraint in these judgements, football historian Michael Oriard asserted that 'the desire to honour the policeman, firefighters and others who died on September 11 is a genuine impulse'. Oriard admitted that 'unfortunately, when it gets entangled with the Super Bowl, it is also a calculated marketing strategy, and it risks cheapening the very thing that they are celebrating'.[159] Ironically, a 2015 report would reveal that the military actually used taxpayer dollars to fund patriotic displays at NFL events between 2012 and 2015. Arguably, both the military and the NFL benefited from this marketing agreement, yet after a slew of negative publicity, the NFL returned the funding earmarked for this 'paid patriotism'.[160]

To be certain, significant events, such as war and terrorism, often motivate scribes to seek deeper meaning in things than what might normally be the primary focus of attention – to emphasize, borrowing from a mid-1980s superbowler, 'what's really important around here'.[161] While the Gulf War, the 9/11 attacks, and the wars in Afghanistan and Iraq undoubtedly provoked such attention primarily to the nationalism associated with the event, overwhelming evidence suggests that the NFL has continuously engaged since the earliest staging of the game in connecting 'Americanness' to the Super Bowl.[162] While this connection may not have been the most ink-worthy aspect of the Super Bowl in the past, the United States' increasing presence during the first decade of the 2000s in conflicts around the world, vividly expressed since at least 2000 by regularly televised shots of United States armed service men and women stationed overseas and watching the Super Bowl, has certainly garnered greater visibility in recent years. If anything, as previous scholars have pointed out, these wartime Super Bowls confirm that, similar to the 'conspicuous consumption' and 'shared experience' aspects of the game, the event's connection to the traditional patriotic values of the United States would also be propagated in perpetuity.[163]

Superbowling as Shared Language

In the weeks before the 9/11 Super Bowl (XXXVI), Hunter S. Thompson described football as a 'universal language that cuts across many cultures and personality types'.[164] Thirty-three years earlier, on the heels of the Jets' Super Bowl III victory in 1969, Robert Lipsyte's enthusiasm for superbowling unwittingly provided a tool useful for speaking and interpreting that language. Over the years, superbowling has provided a forum for debating the value and meaning of this de facto national holiday within SportsWorld – an on-going discussion that would ultimately engage the globe. An analysis of superbowling content each winter since 1967 reveals that the Super Bowl not only exemplifies an important day of shared experience on the American calendar, but also contributes and interacts with the cultural happenings of the United States and other global communities. Superbowling provides a place for superbowlers, like Thompson, to declare in one breath that 'the NFL sucks',[165] and in the next breath that football fans 'are legion, and football is often the only thing we have in common'.[166] In essence, superbowling provides space for both critics and supporters to wrestle with issues that concern diverse populations and often reveal contrasting perspectives of 'what's really important around here'.[167]

In the 1960s and 1970s, superbowling illuminated not only the struggles of establishing a new event on America's sports calendar, but also the challenges of navigating its immediate growth and success. Superbowlers questioned the competitive parity and quality of the game amidst its blossoming commercialization and over-promotion. Its overall value as a legitimate sporting spectacle in contrast to it value as an entertainment and profitmaking phenomenon garnered significant debate. Within its first decade of existence, however, the commodification and over-promotion of the championship game did not derail it from its path to becoming a yearly shared experience on America's calendar. Superbowlers, including politicians and celebrities from diverse perspectives, recognized the day-altering nature of the event and wagered on its future appeal.

By the beginning of the 1980s, after managing its initial growing pains and establishing itself as a shared experience and commercial powerhouse, the Super Bowl became more visibly attached to politics and capitalism. President Reagan's coin toss certainly propelled the Super Bowl-White House relationship to new levels of consideration. As the viewership of the game both live and on television continued to expand nationally (and globally), 'being part of the game' became exponentially more important. Taking part in Super Sunday events became an important feature of what it meant to be a United States citizen – as something that qualifies one for 'fellowship in the American community'.[168] While the actual playing of the game fought against marginalization amidst the Super Bowl's 'conspicuous consumption' practices, the event's growing power as a shared experience generated arguments that the event deserved national holiday status. Furthermore, throughout the 1980s, the scope of the Super Bowl's influence widened considerably to include international interest. By the end of the decade, few could argue against the Super Bowl's significance as a classic component of Americana.

By the 1990s, the NFL and the Super Bowl clearly enjoyed political clout within the American psyche. While the NFL publically expressed a neutral position during the Martin Luther King holiday discussions in Arizona, the league clearly influenced the outcome by retracting a bid to host a Super Bowl. At the same time, Operation Desert Storm raised questions about the importance of a football championship game within the context of wartime America. The Super Bowl production that emerged from these debates highlighted the NFL's use of nationalistic strategies to promote its signature event. The terrorist attacks of 2001 would compound this attention a decade later. Setting aside the past superbowling topics often associated with commercialism and overbearing promotion, superbowlers during this decade when the United States was enmeshed in foreign wars focused more on the Super Bowl as a shared American experience. It became a place where Americans could collectively share, at least for one Sunday, a highly anticipated and regularly repeated element of American life. The Super Bowl served as a place where Americans could share their common language of football while wrestling with the potential horrors of international military conflict. It solidified its significance, like other national holidays, as a place to gather for common purpose.

While superbowling certainly continued from the turn of the millennium to present day, the first 35 years of superbowling highlight at least three enduring characteristics of the event: 'conspicuous consumption', 'shared experience', and 'national holiday'. To be sure, television ratings, commercial advertising costs, and ticket prices will most likely continue to rise into the future and will continue to fuel the former two tenets. Diversification in television outlets and the expansion of online markets will certainly intensify those as well. As for achieving 'official' national holiday status, one can only speculate. Certainly, the Super Bowl's presence in the American consciousness shows no signs of diminishing nor does there seem to be any indication that discussions supporting formal holiday status will wane. Regardless of the progress to this end, one thing is for sure: one can no longer question the use of 'super' in Super Bowl.

Notes

1. Attributed to Super Bowl X in Richard C. Crepeau, *NFL Football: A History of America's New National Pastime* (Urbana: University of Illinois Press, 2014), 204.
2. Don Weiss with Chuck Day, *The Making of the Super Bowl: The Inside Story of the World's Greatest Sporting Event* (New York: Contemporary Books, 2003), 158–159; 'National Football League Set to Open Season That Will End in Super Bowl', *New York Times*, 4 September 1966, 153; 'TV Executives Get the Picture of Super Bowl: Color It Gold', *New York Times*, 22 October 1966, 34; Dave Anderson, 'Merged Leagues to Meet Today To Chart Super Bowl and Draft', *New York Times*, 9 November 1966, 69.
3. Paul Fichtenbaum, and John Rolfe, 'Super Bowl I vs. Super Bowl XX: That was Then, This is Now', *Sport* 77, no. 2 (February 1986), 31.
4. Weiss, *The Making of the Super Bowl*, 45.
5. 'TV Executives Get the Picture of Super Bowl', 34; Dave Anderson, 'Super Bowl Hopes for $1-Million Gate', *New York Times*, 8 December 1966, 70; 'Empty Super Bowl Seats? Probably Not', *Chicago Tribune*, 5 January 1967, E2.
6. 'Judge Ok's TV Blackout, Super Bowl Sales Boom', *Chicago Daily Defender*, 10 January 1967, 24; George Strickler, 'Super Bowl Tickets Sales Still Lagging', *Chicago Tribune*, 12 January 1967, 11; James M. Gavin 'Super-Sunday Sounds Super', *Chicago Tribune*, 13 January 1967, C10.
7. Anderson, 'Super Bowl Hopes for $1-Million Gate', 70; 'Financial Facts, Figures On Super Bowl Game', *New York Times*, 17 January 1967, 64.
8. William N. Wallace, '60 Million to Watch Packers and Chiefs Play Today on TV', *New York Times*, 15 January 1967, S1.
9. Jack Gould, 'A Typical Coast Show: Super Bowl Is Unable to Measure Up to Advance Billing as TV Attraction', *New York Times*, 16 January 1967, 33.
10. Ibid.
11. Arthur Daley, 'Clear-Cut Superiority', *New York Times*, 16 January 1968, 32.

12. William N. Wallace, 'Lombardi Quits as Packers' Coach, but Stays with Club', *New York Times*, 2 February 1968, 41.
13. William N. Wallace, 'Super Bowl's Status: Game Rated in Class with World Series After American League's Major Upset', *New York Times*, 14 January 1969, 48.
14. Robert Lipsyte, 'Sports of the Times: Superbowling', *New York Times*, 18 January 1969, 36. A review of the *New York Times*, and specifically the writings of Lipsyte until he left the *New York Times* in 1971, reveals that he did not use this term in any ongoing fashion.
15. Robert Lipsyte, 'Absurd Excesses Abound in Sports: Sports World: An American Dreamland', *Chicago Tribune*, 25 April 1976, B1, B14; Robert Lipsyte, *Sportsworld: An American Dreamland* (New York: Quadrangle/New York Times Book Co., 1975).
16. Lipsyte, 'Sports of the Times: Superbowling', 36.
17. Robert Lipsyte, 'Absurd Excesses', B1.
18. While superbowling certainly occurs through present day, the scope of this paper is limited to 1967 through the early 2000s.
19. Robert Lipsyte, 'Absurd Excesses', B1.
20. Fichtenbaum and Rolfe, 'Super Bowl I vs. Super Bowl XX', 31–35; Paul Zimmerman, 'Day One: The Aspirations of the AFL Met the Arrogance of the NFL in Super Bowl I', *Sports Illustrated*, 83, no. 15 (Fall 1995), 74–81; Danny Peary (ed.), *Super Bowl: The Game of Their Lives*, (New York: MacMillan, 1997); Weiss, *The Making of the Super Bowl*.
21. Bernard Weinraub, 'Husbands Stare -- and Wives Glare: City's Males Spend Day at TV Sets at Home, in Bars', *New York Times*, 16 January 1967, 33.
22. 'The Super Bowl: Football's Day of Decision Stirs Nation', *New York Times*, 15 January 1967, S1; Weinraub, 'Husbands Stare -- and Wives Glare', 33.
23. Gerald Eskenazi, 'It's Fourth Down with Nowhere to Go', *New York Times*, 22 January 1968, 38.
24. Wallace, 'Super Bowl's Status', 48.
25. Gerald Eskenazi, 'Tagliabue Calls Game 'Winter 4th of July'', *New York Times*, 26 January 1991, 45.
26. Peter Hopsicker and Mark S. Dyreson, 'Super Bowl Sunday: An American Holiday?' in Len Travers (ed.) *American Holidays and National Days* (Westport: Greenwood Press, 2006), 30–54. Richard Crepeau also cites Veblen's 'conspicuous consumption' here: Richard C. Crepeau, 'Thorstein Veblen Explains the Super Bowl', *On Sport and Society*, (1992), paper 223 (http://stars.library.ucf.edu/onsportandsociety/223).
27. Display Ad #632, *New York Times*, 1 December 1968, sec. XX, 4; 'News and Notes from the Field of Travel', *New York Times*, 8 December 1968, 646; Jay Clarke, 'Why Florida's Season 'Suddenly Caught On'', *New York Times*, 7 March 1971, sec. XX, 8; Dena Kleiman, 'Some Super Bowl Tours Snagged', *New York Times*, 14 January 1978, 13, 14.
28. 'More Eyes on Football: Super Bowl Game in January Drew Largest TV Audience for Sports Event', *New York Times*, 15 February 1970, 171.
29. Weiss, *The Making of the Super Bowl*, vii-x.
30. Arthur Daley, 'Sports of the Times: Exit-Laughing', *New York Times*, 13 January 1970, 50.
31. Jon Nordheimer, 'Super Bowl Spectacle Today to Rivet Interest of Millions', *New York Times*, 9 January 1977, 1, 29.
32. William N. Wallace, 'Super Bowl 'Overcome' by Success', *New York Times*, 19 January 1971, 43.
33. Ibid.
34. Weiss, *The Making of the Super Bowl*, 158.
35. 'Tickets for Super Bowl Are Rarer Than Snowflakes in Miami', *New York Times*, 10 January 1971, S1.
36. 'Crimp in Economy Not Cramping 80,997 Styles'. *New York Times*, 12 January 1975, 194.
37. 'Tickets for Super Bowl Are Rarer Than Snowflakes in Miami'.
38. Philip H. Dougherty, 'Super Bowl Means Super-Sell Time is Here Again' *New York Times*, 17 January 1971, F13.
39. Weinraub, 'Husbands Stare – and Wives Glare', 33.
40. Weiss, *The Making of the Super Bowl*, 162.
41. Ibid., 180.

42. James Reston, 'Coach Nixon's Game Plan', *New York Times*, 5 January 1972, 37.

43. Red Smith, 'What Do They Do Now, Mr. President?' *New York Times*, 17 January 1972, 39.

44. Dave Anderson, 'Nixon Pledges Allegiance to Redskins', *New York Times*, 2 January 1973, 47.

45. 'Super Bowl: 48 Views and Nonviews', *New York Times*, 21 January 1979, S2.

46. Joseph Muntz, 'Military Intrusion', *New York Times*, 23 January 1972, E32.

47. Weiss, *The Making of the Super Bowl*, 208–210; Christopher Lehmann-Haupt, 'Books of the Times: Steelers, Vikings and Arabs', *New York Times*, 9 January 1975, 33.

48. Kevin T McEneaney, *Hunter S. Thompson: Fear, Loathing, and the Birth of Gonzo* (Lanham, MD: Rowman & Littlefield, 2016).

49. Thompson's *Rolling Stone* superbowling essays published in the 1970s were reprinted as a chapter in Hunter S. Thompson, 'Fear and Loathing at the Super Bowl' in *The Great Shark Hunt: Strange Tales from a Strange Time* (New York: Warner Books, 1979), 50, 56.

50. Thompson, 'Fear and Loathing', 85.

51. Ibid, 77.

52. Ibid, 84.

53. Ibid, 78.

54. Ibid, 59. Thompson's career took many twists and turns until his death in 2005. After penning his 'Fear and Loathing at the Superbowl' essays in *Rolling Stone* magazine, his writing on the NFL and the Super Bowl became virtually none existent until he contributed a series of essays on ESPN.com's 'Page 2' under the title 'Hey Rube'.

55. David Condon, 'The Super what? Bah! Humbug! Pete', *Chicago Tribune*, 14 January 1973, B3.

56. 'Super? Some Doubts About It', *Chicago Tribune*, 18 January 1974, C3.

57. Quoted in Michael R. Real, 'Super Bowl: Mythic Spectacle', *Journal of Communication* 25, no. 1 (1975), 31–43.

58. Red Smith, 'Super Sunday' *New York Times*, 12 January 1975, 240.

59. Hunter S. Thompson, 'Fear and Loathing at the Superbowl: No Rest for the Wretched', *Rolling Stone* (online), 15 February 1973, http://www.rollingstone.com/sports/features/fear-and-loathing-at-the-superbowl-no-rest-for-the-wretched-strobe-notes-and-strange-memories-on-a-dreary-weekend-in-los-angeles-19730215 (accessed 3 November 2016).

60. Weiss, *The Making of the Super Bowl*, 208.

61. William N. Wallace, 'Super Bowl Grows into Oversized Revel', *New York Times*, 11 January 1976, S3.

62. Nordheimer, 'Super Bowl Spectacle Today to Rivet Interest of Millions', 1, 29.

63. Gerald Eskenazi, 'Big Game Provides Slice of Americana, A Spectacle for Millions on Television', *New York Times*, 10 January 1977, 38.

64. Dave Anderson, 'X Marks the 10th' *New York Times*, 18 January 1976, 164.

65. John Leonard, 'Critic's Notebook: Being and Knottiness on the Air', *New York Times*, 24 January 1976, 29.

66. Stephen Banker, 'The Stupor Bowl', *New York Times*, 9 January 1977, 195; Eskenazi, 'Big Game Provides Slice of Americana', 38. Nordheimer, 'Super Bowl Spectacle Today to Rivet Interest of Millions', 1, 29.

67. Dave Anderson, 'The Super Bowl Needs a New Formula', *New York Times*, 11 January 1977, 51; 'Sports Editor's Mailbox: The Super Bowl', *New York Times*, 22 January 1978, S2.

68. Tony Kornheiser, 'Super Bowl a Cultural Phenomenon in Prime Time', *New York Times*, 9 January 1978, C12.

69. Ibid.

70. 'Super Bowl: 48 Views and Nonviews', S2.

71. John Leonard, 'Yahwek, Monty Hall, Gilchrist, Or Why I Will Be Watching', *New York Times*, 21 January 1979, S4.

72. William Borders, 'Super Premiere Plays for London Fans', *New York Times*, 27 January 1981, B15-B16.

73. Pamela G. Hollie, 'Super Bowl a 'Corporate Bash'', *New York Times*, 19 January 1980, 29.

74. Murray Chass, 'Super Bowl Brings Millions in Business', *New York Times*, 18 January 1981, S1.

75. William N. Wallace, 'Day of Superlatives at the Super Bowl', *New York Times*, 26 January 1981, C6.

76. Bernice Kanner, *The Super Bowl of Advertising: How the Commercials Won the Game* (Princeton: Bloomberg Press, 2004). Also see Matthew McAllister and Elysia Galindo-Ramirez, 'Fifty Years of Super Bowl Commercials, Thirty-Two Years of Spectacular Consumption', *International Journal of the History of Sport* (2017), (this issue).

77. Benjamin Rader, *In Its Own Image: How Television Has Transformed Sports* (New York: The Free Press, 1984), 98.

78. Weiss, 'Appendix A: Super Bowl Data' in *The Making of the Super Bowl*, 352–388.

79. Nordheimer, 'Super Bowl Spectacle Today to Rivet Interest of Millions', 1, 29.

80. Chass, 'Super Bowl Brings Millions in Business', S1; Bruce Horovitz, 'Orange County to Reap a Bonanza from Super Bowl', *Los Angeles Times*, 21 August 1986, B4.

81. Michael Janofsky, 'When Action Starts, A Nation Stops', *New York Times*, 20 January 1986, sec. C, 9, 20.

82. Tony Kornheiser, 'The NFL Shows Its Money, But No Heart', *Washington Post*, 21 January 1989, sec. D, 1.

83. Weiss, *The Making of the Super Bowl*, 204–208.

84. William Zinsser, 'The President is Spoiling My Party', *New York Times*, 29 January 1984, 1; Bob Bach, 'Reagan's Uncured Lines About Nuclear Arms', *New York Times*, 2 February 1984, A18.

85. Phil Hersh, 'The Super Bowl: 'Weird' is the Word That Says It Best', *Chicago Tribune*, 26 January 1986, O4.

86. Zinsser, 'The President is Spoiling My Party', 1.

87. Ibid.; Bach, 'Reagan's Uncured Lines About Nuclear Arms', A18.

88. Robert McG Thomas, Jr., 'Sports World Specials: Pre-game Packaging', *New York Times*, 13 January 1986, A1; George Vecsey, 'Super Bowl Fever', *New York Times*, 17 January 1986, A21.

89. Vecsey, 'Super Bowl Fever', A21.

90. George Vecsey, 'The Longest Day', *New York Times*, 20 January 1985, S13; George Vecsey, "Fans" Moment of Truth', *New York Times*, 20 January 1986, C15.

91. Richard Reeves, 'Heads of Tails? Government of Football?' *New York Times*, 20 January 1985, sec. 5, 1, 2; Janofsky, 'When Action Starts, A Nation Stops', 9, 20.

92. Mark Russell, 'It's Bigger Than Reagan! Even Cosby!' *New York Times*, 26 January 1986, S2.

93. Phil Gailey, 'The Method Behind the Super Bowl Madness', *New York Times*, 13 January 1984, A16.

94. Carl Stein, 'Come Jan. 20, 1985', *New York Times*, 12 August 1983, sec. A, 22; Henry H. Heins, 'Inauguration and the Super Bowl, Too', *New York Times*, 21 August 1983, sec. E, 16.

95. Reeves, 'Heads of Tails?', 1, 2.

96. Barack Obama's 2013 public inauguration ceremony was also moved to Monday.

97. James F. Clarity and Warren Weaver, Jr., 'Washington Talk: Briefing', *New York Times*, 18 September 1984, sec. A, 24; 'The Upscale Inauguration: Capital Uncorks the Champagne', *San Francisco Chronicle*, 18 January 1985, 1; Seth S. King, 'For Visitors, Fun, Politics, and Protests', *New York Times*, 20 January 1985, 18.

98. Peter W. Kaplan, 'Reagan May Join Super Bowl Ceremonies After Taking Oath', *New York Times*, 4 January 1985, A10; 'President Set for Coin Toss', *New York Times*, 16 January 1985, B9.

99. Reeves, 'Heads of Tails?', 1, 2.

100. Stein, 'Come Jan. 20, 1985', 22.

101. Reeves, 'Heads of Tails?', 1, 2.

102. Weiss, *The Making of the Super Bowl*, 223; Henry L. Griggs, Jr., 'Fumbles at the Mike Fill the Super Bowl', *New York Times*, 1 February 1981, 1.

103. Borders, 'Super Premiere Plays for London Fans', B15-B16.

104. Russell Baker, 'Sunday Observer: Bird of a Different Feather', *New York Times*, 19 December 1982, SM28.

105. Michael Katz, 'Super Bowl Week: The Hoopla Begins', *New York Times*, 17 January 1982, sec. S, 1.

106. William E. Geist, 'On Super Sunday, Super Party XVII', *New York Times*, 31 January 1983, sec. B, 4.
107. William E. Geist, 'When TV Sets Become TD Sets', *New York Times*, 25 January 1982, B2; Geist, 'On Super Sunday, Super Party XVII', B4.
108. Baker, 'Sunday Observer', 28.
109. Chass, 'Super Bowl Brings Millions in Business', 6, 8.
110. Robert Klein, 'Views of Sport: America's Pastime: Selling the Big Game', *New York Times*, 28 January 1990, sec. S, 12.
111. Reeves, 'Heads of Tails?', 1, 2.
112. Leonard J. Grimaldi, 'Frivolity for the Super Bowl', *New York Times*, 30 January 1983.
113. Jack Smith, 'Dissecting the First Art of Football in American Culture', *Houston Chronicle*, 8 October 1986, 2.
114. Geist, 'When TV Sets Become TD Sets', B2; Geist, 'On Super Sunday, Super Party XVII', B4.
115. Russell Baker, 'Right After This Shark', *New York Times*, 29 January 1986, A23.
116. Janofsky, 'When Action Starts, A Nation Stops', 9, 20.
117. George Vecsey, 'Gracious Wasteland', *New York Times*, 24 January 1982, S1.
118. Pamela G. Hollie, 'Super Bowl a 'Corporate Bash'', *New York Times*, 19 January 1980, 29.
119. Adam Clymer, ''38% Like the 49ers; 40% Don't Care', *New York Times*, 22 January 1982, A25; 'Poll Finds Preference for Giants', *New York Times*, 25 January 1987, S6.
120. Katz, 'Super Bowl Week', S1.
121. Geist, 'When TV Sets Become TD Sets', B2; Geist, 'On Super Sunday, Super Party XVII', B4.
122. Red Smith, 'Super Sunday', *New York Times*, 12 January 1975, 240.
123. Vecsey, 'Gracious Wasteland', S1.
124. Vecsey, 'The Longest Day', S13.
125. Leonard Shapiro, 'Super Sunday: 'A Shared American Experience'', *Washington Post*, 29 January 1995, A1; Interestingly, these estimates do not calculate actual ratings but only 'potential' viewers who would be able to tune in. See Christopher R. Martin & Jimmie L. Reeves, 'The Whole World Isn't Watching (But We Thought They Were): The Super Bowl and United States Solipsism', *Culture, Sport, Society* 4. 2, (2001), 213–236.
126. Vecsey, 'The Longest Day', S13. Also see Ian Adams, 'A Century of British Readings of America through American Football: From the *Fin de Siècle* to the Super Bowl', *International Journal of the History of Sport* (2017), (this issue); Mark Dyreson, 'The Super Bowl as a Television Spectacle: Global Designs, Glocal Niches, and Parochial Patterns', *International Journal of the History of Sport* (2017), (this issue); Lars Dzikus, 'Amerika: The Super Bowl and German Imagination', *International Journal of the History of Sport* (2017), (this issue); Craig Greenham, ''Super Bore'': The Canadian Media and the Grey Cup-Super Bowl Comparison', *International Journal of the History of Sport* (2017), (this issue); Kohei Kawashima, ''We Will Try Again, Again, Again to Make it Bigger'': Japan, American Football, and the Super Bowl: Past, Present, and Future', *International Journal of the History of Sport* (2017), (this issue).
127. Stuart Elliott, 'Ad Bowl Serves Up Chips, Both Snack and Computer', *New York Times*, 23 January 1998, sec. D, 1.
128. Ibid.
129. Stuart Elliot, 'Advertising', *New York Times*, 26 January 1996, sec. D, 4.
130. Elliott, 'Ad Bowl Serves Up Chips, Both Snack and Computer', 1.
131. Kornheiser, 'The NFL Shows Its Money, But No Heart', 1.
132. Shapiro, 'Super Sunday', A1.
133. Ibid.
134. Richard Rodriguez, 'Super Bowl: The Demise of America's Moment', *Los Angeles Times*, 25 January 1998.
135. Shapiro, 'Super Sunday', A1; Rodriguez, 'Super Bowl'.
136. Weiss, *The Making of the Super Bowl*, 245.
137. Elliot, 'Advertising', 4.; Elliott, 'Ad Bowl Serves Up Chips, Both Snack and Computer', 1; Jayne Clark, 'Super Bowl Hits and Myths', *USA Today*, 26 January 2001, sec. D, 1; Wayne Friedman, 'Super Bowl Ads Sell Super Early', *Advertising Age*, 73 23 (10 June 2002), 3, 66;

Weiss, *The Making of the Super Bowl*; Bernice Kanner, *The Super Bowl of Advertising: How the Commercials Won the Game* (Princeton: Bloomberg Press, 2004).

138. Shapiro, 'Super Sunday', A1.
139. 'Arizona Holiday for Dr. King May Face Ballot Test in 1990', *New York Times*, 26 September 1989, sec. A, 28; Ira Berkow, 'Sport of the Times: Dr. King and the Super Bowl', *New York Times*, 10 November 1990, 43; Thomas George, 'NFL Is Nearly Unanimous in Stand on Phoenix Super Bowl Issue', *New York Times*, 21 March 1991, sec. B, 16.
140. Paul Tagliabue, 'The Super Bowl: Not a Political Football', *New York Times*, 23 December 1990, S10.
141. Berkow, 'Sport of the Times', 43.
142. George, 'NFL Is Nearly Unanimous in Stand on Phoenix Super Bowl Issue', 16.
143. Tagliabue, 'The Super Bowl', S10.
144. Berkow, 'Sport of the Times', 43.
145. George, 'NFL Is Nearly Unanimous in Stand on Phoenix Super Bowl Issue', 16.
146. Lowell Cohn, 'At Least Delay the Super Bowl', *San Francisco Chronicle*, 17 January 1991, sec. D, 1.
147. Dave Anderson, 'Sports of the Times: In a War, Sports Here Continue', *New York Times*, 17 January 1991, sec. B, 11.
148. Tony Kornheiser, 'Commentary: When Winds of War Shift, Games Will Matter', *Los Angeles Times*, 20 January 1991, 9.
149. Eskenazi, 'Tagliabue Calls Game 'Winter 4th of July'', 45.
150. Hopsicker and Dyreson, 'Super Bowl Sunday', 45, 47. .
151. Quoted in Michael Davis, 'The Patriots Bowl: United We Sit, Watching a Football Game That's Become An American Ritual', *Washington Post*, 3 February 2002, sec. F, 1.
152. Eskenazi, 'Tagliabue Calls Game 'Winter 4th of July'', 45.
153. Shapiro, 'Super Sunday', A1.
154. Klein, 'Views of Sport', 12.
155. Kornheiser, 'Commentary', 9.
156. Hunter S. Thompson, 'Domestic Terrorism at the Super Bowl', *ESPN.com: Page 2*, [magazine on-line] 11 February 2002, http://sports.espn.go.com/espn/print?id=1,328,312&type=page2Story (accessed 13 October 2004).
157. Davis, 'The Patriots Bowl', 1.
158. Ibid.
159. Ibid.
160. Darren Rovell, 'NFL Returning $723 K for Sponsoring Military Tributes', *ESPN.com* (on-line) 19 May 2016, http://espn.go.com/nfl/story/_/id/15,611,052/nfl-returning-723000-taxpayers-paid-military-tributes (accessed 28 July 2016).
161. Reeves, 'Heads of Tails?', 1, 2.
162. Davis, 'The Patriots Bowl', 1.
163. Hopsicker and Dyreson, 'Super Bowl Sunday'.
164. Hunter S. Thompson, 'Braced for the Last Football Game', *ESPN.com* (on-line) 29 January 2002, http://www.espn.com/page2/s/thompson/020129.html (accessed 4 November 2016).
165. Hunter S. Thompson, 'Fear & Loathing on Super Sunday', *ESPN.com* (on-line) 15 January 2001, http://proxy.espn.com/espn/page2/story?id=1,016,761 (accessed 4 November 2016).
166. Hunter S. Thompson, 'Braced for the Last Football Game', *ESPN.com* (on-line) 29 January 2002, http://www.espn.com/page2/s/thompson/020129.html (accessed 4 November 2016).
167. Reeves, 'Heads of Tails?', 1, 2.
168. Baker, 'Sunday Observer', 28.

Acknowledgement

The author expresses special thanks to Ms. Allessia Zanin-Yost, Reference and Instruction Librarian at Penn State Altoona, for her tremendous help in researching this paper.

Disclosure Statement

No potential conflict of interest was reported by the author.

Fifty Years of Super Bowl Commercials, Thirty-Two Years of Spectacular Consumption

Matthew P. McAllister and Elysia Galindo-Ramirez

ABSTRACT

This article will explore the role and visibility of advertising during the Super Bowl over the years as a model for strategies of modern advertising and the resulting commercialization of US society. It uses the concepts of 'spectacular consumption' derived from Guy Debord and the 'commodity audience' from Dallas Smythe to frame the commercials' cultural transformation and influence. The spectacular nature of Super Bowl commercials and the special commodity worth of its audience were not present in the early days of the event, but gained momentum with Super Bowl XVII and its airing of Apple's '1984' commercial that became mythologized in the advertising industry. After 1984, both the rising inflation-adjusted CPM ('cost-per-thousand') and the increased media coverage indicate an increased spectacularization. This also manifested in such phenomena as the influential, decades-long Doritos user-generated content contests and the *Greatest Super Bowl Commercials* TV specials, and was a forerunner of such post-millennial advertising strategies as branded entertainment and content marketing, all designed to integrate advertising as a legitimate form of entertainment culture and prevent the avoidance of advertising by audiences.

On 15 January 1967, the day of the first AFL-NFL World Championship – what the press called even then the Super Bowl – an article in the *New York Times* announced, 'A Super 60 Seconds Costs $85,000', an alarming-enough figure to justify a headline.[1] Many advertisers at the time thought this was an outrageous amount. The year before, a vice president (VP) for advertising agency Foote, Cone & Belding (FCB) called pro football TV ad prices 'ridiculous' and argued that, '[at] some point in time, advertisers just won't be able to go along with the higher prices that result from competitive network bidding without commensurate increases in audience values'.[2] This feeling was shared by the automaker Ford: before the first Super Bowl, the automaker held out until the last minute, trying to negotiate a lower price from Columbia Broadcasting System (CBS), one of the two television networks that broadcast the first Super Bowl.[3]

So was the VP at FCB correct? Did advertisers balk at high football ad prices? When adjusted for 2016 inflation, the $85,000 figure would be over $600,000. Although this increase would certainly be shocking to those in 1967, imagine their disbelief if told that $600,000 would buy less than 4 seconds of Super Bowl commercial time 50 years later – even when adjusted for inflation – given its $5 million per 30-s price tag (see Table 1). The longevity of the Super Bowl and its advertising obviously show that advertisers did not abandon the event, despite prices rising much more than would have been predicted in 1967.

However, from another perspective perhaps the VP *was* right: maybe advertisers have gone along with this unimaginable (in 1967 minds) increase because, somehow, the 'audience values' have become more attractive to advertisers. From an advertiser perspective, the value of the Super Bowl has indeed increased for advertisers over the years. Yet, this value did not significantly increase until a specific historical moment that not only transformed advertising, but also came at a social and cultural cost that has continued throughout the modern Super Bowl era.

The Super Bowl is clearly a key event for the advertising industry, being by far the most expensive US televised event each year in which to place advertising and is a much discussed venue within the advertising industry. Super Bowl commercials, though, are more than this: they are themselves a highly visible, anticipated, and influential cultural event, one that explicitly celebrates and promotes commercialism. The Super Bowl is not just a football game; it is a beloved 'Ad Bowl', a commercial status that according to historians Peter Hopsicker and Mark Dyreson in an analysis of this mega-event represented 'an unprecedented development in American consumer culture'.[4] In many ways, the Super Bowl has permanently raised the bar for intrusive commercialism. This article will explore the role and visibility of advertising during the Super Bowl over the years as a model for strategies of modern advertising and the resulting commercialization of US society. It uses the concepts of 'spectacular consumption' derived from Marxist theorist Guy Debord and the 'commodity audience' from political economist Dallas Smythe to frame the commercials'

Table 1. Super Bowl commercial prices, 30-s spot, select years.

Year	Then-current cost	Adjusted for 2016 inflation	Viewers (mil)	CPM (adjusted)
1967	$40,000	$289,000	24.4	$11.8
1970	$78,200	$482,000	44.2	$10.9
1975	$107,000	$476,000	56.1	$8.5
1980	$222,000	$649,000	76.2	$8.5
1984	$368,200	$848,000	77.6	$10.9
1985	$525,000	$1.17 mil	85.5	$13.7
1995	$1.15 mil	$1.81 mil	83.4	$21.6
1999	$1.6 mil	$2.30 mil	83.7	$27.5
2000	$2.1 mil	$2.92 mil	88.5	$33.0
2005	$2.4 mil	$2.94 mil	86.1	$34.1
2015	$4.5 mil	$4.54 mil	114.4	$39.7
2016	$5.0 mil	$5.00 mil	111.9	$44.7

Sources: For all cost and ratings from 1970 to 2009, and ratings from 1967 to 2009: http://tvbythenumbers.zap2it.com/2009/01/18/historical-super-bowl-tv-ratings/ Costs for 1967 are an average of NBC and CBS; see 'Sponsors Sign for Super bowl TV', *Broadcasting*, 32.

Costs for 2015–2016: Nick Schwartz, 'Stunning Infographic Charts the Skyrocketing Cost of a Super Bowl Ad', *USA Today*, 6 February 2016, http://ftw.usatoday.com/2016/02/how-much-does-super-bowl-ad-cost (accessed 19 July 2016).

Ratings for 2015: Scott Collins, 'Super Bowl 2015: Sunday's Game a Ratings Winner for NBC', *Los Angeles Times*, 3 February 2015, http://www.latimes.com/entertainment/tv/la-et-st-super-bowl-2015-ratings-20150203-story.html (accessed 19 July 2015).

Ratings for 2016: F. Pallotta and B. Stelter, 'Super Bowl 50 Audience is Third Largest in TV History', *CNN.com*, 8 February 2016, http://money.cnn.com/2016/02/08/media/super-bowl-50-ratings/ (accessed 23 May 2016).

To adjust for inflation, the CPI calculator at the US Bureau of Labor Statistics was used: http://www.bls.gov/data/inflation_calculator.htm. Calculations for CPM were done through the ClickZ CPM Calculator at https://www.clickz.com/static/cpm-calculator.

cultural transformation and influence.[5] However, the spectacular nature of Super Bowl commercials and the special commodity worth of its audience were not present in the early days of the event, but gained momentum, as many have argued, with Super Bowl XVII and its airing of Apple's '1984' commercial that became mythologized in both the advertising industry and recollections of Super Bowl advertising. The subsequent spectacular nature of the Super Bowl commercial and its surrounding cultural discourse manifested in such phenomena as the influential, decades-long Doritos user-generated content (UGC) contests and the *Greatest Super Bowl Commercials* TV specials has served as a crucial forerunner of such post-millennial advertising strategies as branded entertainment and content marketing, all designed to integrate advertising as a legitimate form of entertainment culture and prevent the avoidance of advertising by audiences.

Spectacular Consumption and the Audience Commodity

The idea of modern spectacle originates from the work of Guy Debord, an activist and scholar associated with the 1960s' French Situationalist movement.[6] For Debord, modern capitalist society is exemplified by spectacle: large-scale manufactured and visually dominant events, driven by commodity logic. The concept therefore combines elements of McLuhan-esque medium theory with Marxism and the Frankfurt School.[7] For Debord, spectacle was inherently ideological, depoliticizing citizens and falsely separating spectacle from the commodity relations that gave rise to it. Later, Debord argued that the collapse of the cold war introduced a combination of US- and Soviet-style 'integrated spectacle', a concept that often is applied to large-scale coordinated media events/franchises that may involve multiple outlets and tie-ins.[8] As early as the mid-1970s, sports media scholar Michael R. Real saw the connection between the Debordian 'mythic spectacle' and sporting events like the Super Bowl.[9]

Spectacle that is especially tied to saturation advertising or promotion is a form of 'spectacular consumption' where a marketing campaign or pervasive brand takes on a broad cultural resonance, and has been applied to Hollywood films, music, and children's entertainment.[10] Spectacular consumption often involves the use of multi-modal and integrated marketing forms, including advertising, public relations, merchandising, sales promotion, media coverage, and web outlets such as social media. Scholars have also used the concept to critique large-scale sports-related marketing, including the athlete-oriented Niketown promotions of the late 1990s and 2000s, and the Budweiser 'Whassup' campaign that originated as a 2000 Super Bowl XXXIV commercial.[11] The racial politics of the 'Whassup' commercial – seeing black friendship as both universal, authentic, but still racially stereotyped – is embedded in the sizeable scope of the campaign, its (transient) creation of celebrity for the campaign's actors, and its many promotional manifestations.

Modern Super Bowl commercials certainly seem to qualify as spectacular consumption.[12] Super Bowl commercials transcend their 30-s commercial space as other media forms, including news and television specials discuss, celebrate or are influenced by the commercials, as well as the growing percentage of viewers who report watching the broadcast exclusively for the ads.

The spectacularization of Super Bowl commercials is tied to the political economy of sports broadcasting. Specifically, a key element in understanding how a Super Bowl commercial went from being simply the ad in a highly watched event like the Oscars or the World Series to becoming its own highlighted and anticipated cultural event is tied to television's revenue model and its economic relationship with advertising. Dallas Smythe's concept of the 'audience commodity' is particularly useful for understanding the spectacularization of Super Bowl ads.[13] Influenced by Marxist theory, Smythe theorized the role of the audience in advertising-supported media content, arguing that the audience serves as the key commodity being sold by the media to advertisers. But not all audiences, Smythe contends, are equally valuable. The most valued audience commodity is that which is plentiful (so a mass viewership, in the case of television), 'pure' in terms of desirable demographics that advertisers wish to reach (such as 18–49-year-old males; those with disposable income and the willingness to spend), and 'pliant' consumer audiences (or those especially receptive to the advertisers' persuasive messages).[14] This form of commodification skews the programming that broadcasting and other ad-supported media offer, both privileging content that attracts some audience commodities over others and offering content that flows well with the consumption-oriented messages of advertising (thus encouraging an 'advertising-pliant' mindset). Smythe also argued that audiences may be seen as a form of labour in advertising systems, given that advertising exposure is not normally the goal of media users (with viewing ads being then a form of labour), and the promotional functions that audiences may fulfil by disseminating advertising messages through their thinking of advertising messages, talking about them with others, and their own consumption behaviours. In the era of data-mining digital advertising, where digital media systems are designed to collect user information with the goal of creating targeted advertising, Smythe's audience labour metaphor has seen a resurgence in critical political economy of the media.[15]

Spectacular consumption and the audience commodity intersect especially in the case of the modern Super Bowl, where motivated viewing of advertising is seen as a key part of the event, and this drives the value of the audience commodity before and during the event. However, such a dynamic was not always the case. As the next section describes, before the mid-1980s, the Super Bowl was a valuable way to reach audiences as was any high-profile sporting event, with large audiences and desirable demographics. But audiences did not become the pliant super-commodity until several years after the Super Bowl began.

Pre-Spectacular Super Bowl Advertising

Information about commercials during either the NFL or AFL championship games before the first 'Super Bowl' in 1967 is sparse. Much of the footage of early championships is lost, especially the commercials. Articles in the popular press were rare, and, when they wrote about it at all, the business press discussed the nature of the audience commodity: how much it cost to advertise during the championship, and how much the networks paid for football broadcasting rights to be able to offer this commodity.[16] One exception is a notable advertising campaign that aired during the 1959 NFL Championship between the Baltimore Colts and the New York Giants – the latter making their second consecutive trip to the championship game. According to a report in *Advertising Age*, five Giants players including future Hall-of-Famer Sam Huff appeared in commercials for Philip Morris-owned cigarette brands (or 'cigaret' as was spelled in the article), all comically interacting with TV personality Max Shulman. As an early version of integrated marketing, these TV commercials were teased by complementary radio spots airing before the game, and by the Giants players who toured the country touting brands such as Marlboro and Philip Morris. Alpine and Parliament cigarette commercials also aired during that game.[17]

In the 1964 NFL Championship, major sponsors included Ford and Philip Morris, each of which, according to the trade journal *Broadcasting*, had advertising time for one quarter of the championship.[18] Other signed sponsors included Union Carbide, and Socony Mobile (later ExxonMobil), and beer brands Ballantine, Falstaff, Hamm's, Schmidt, Wiedmann, and National Brew. The latter, a sponsor of the Baltimore Colts, may have advertised Colt 45, named after running back Jerry Hill,[19] who played in that game. Although no specific sponsors were listed for the AFL Championship game, season sponsors – which may have included the championship broadcast – included Champion Spark Plugs, Goodyear, Pearl Brewing, and R.J. Reynolds.[20]

Beginning with the first Super Bowl in 1967, advertisements began to garner a bit more press attention. However, through Super Bowl XVIII in 1984, the limited coverage mainly focused on the list of advertisers or the nature of the cost of Super Bowl ads.[21] Simulcast on two networks (the only Super Bowl to do so),[22] deals with advertisers for the inaugural Super Bowl included Chrysler, R.J. Reynolds, and American Airlines for NBC, and Philip Morris, Falstaff, and Ford – eventually, after last-minute negotiations – for CBS. McDonald's was among the sponsors signed to advertise on both broadcasts.[23] In one way, though, Super Bowl I was prescient about how much advertising could eventually influence the broadcast of the game. The second half had to be kicked off twice, likely because the officials did not wait long enough for NBC to return from its commercial break (for Winston cigarettes), although apparently audience members were not informed that the irregularity stemmed from the television networks' advertising schedules.[24]

It is telling about the early Super Bowls that the most noteworthy commercials *as* Super Bowl commercials featured football stars, signalling that the sports element was still perceived as much more dominant than the advertising per se. From 1972, three years after his upset victory in Super Bowl III, Joe Namath was slathered in Noxzema shaving cream by a then-unknown Farrah Fawcett, and helped establish male-fantasy, double-entendre humour as a trope in the game ('I'm so excited, I'm about to get creamed'); this commercial became celebrated as the Super Bowl's 'first high-profile spot',[25] but at the time it received little press.[26] The other especially recognizable ad is the Coca-Cola commercial featuring Pittsburgh Steeler 'Mean' Joe Greene tossing his jersey to a young fan as he exits a tough game. That spot was ranked by *USA Today* in its 50th anniversary coverage as the greatest Super Bowl commercial of all time.[27] However, the Coca-Cola commercial actually debuted during the regular NFL season, three months before its broadcast during Super Bowl XIV in 1980.[28] While the ad also spawned two sequels and a parody, they all were produced well into the spectacular consumption era of the Super Bowl, more than 20 years after the original aired.[29] Nevertheless, these commercials and their celebrated status solidified links between advertising and professional athletes in the television age.

Triggering Spectacularization: '1984', Audience Commodity Values and Media Coverage

Through the early 1980s, advertisers saw the Super Bowl as a valuable, but not especially celebrated, vehicle for marketing campaigns. In the estimation of most industry-insiders, the Academy Awards broadcast represented a more prestigious venue.[30] As many have noted,

1984 marked a key year in the ascendance of Super Bowl commercials. One particular advertisement from 1984 has received much of the credit for this transformation, a spot for the Macintosh computer. Called by various writers 'The Big Bang',[31] 'the most storied Super Bowl spot of all time',[32] 'the best TV commercial ever',[33] the commercial 'that changed advertising',[34] and 'the first "event" ad',[35] this commercial illustrated the power of the Super Bowl to draw attention from viewers and the media as an advertising-centred venue. Directed by Ridley Scott, a then-rising star in Hollywood for his science fiction epics *Alien* (1979) and *Blade Runner* (1982), the minute-long '1984' ad aired during the Super Bowl's second half. Scott's vision cost between $400,000 and $600,000 to produce, and $1 million to broadcast.[36] The complex cinematic semiotics of the commercial – most clearly referencing George Orwell's Big Brother but also *The Wizard of Oz* – has been analysed by rhetoricians and advertising critics.[37] Significant press attention followed throughout that year given its cinematic nature and cost, and its introduction of the easily dramatized PC/Mac market battle. As a result of it being covered in the news and the commercial's replay during television news segments, Apple may have received as much as $150 million in free publicity.[38] In the computer industry, the brand image that the commercial established – Apple as rebellious and youthful, IBM/PCs as establishment and old – was profoundly successful and continued for decades afterward.[39] The next year, Apple followed '1984' with 'Lemmings', a notoriously ill-received commercial that nevertheless generated significant attention.[40]

The '1984' Macintosh commercial moved Super Bowl commercials into spectacularizing status in two significant ways. The advertisement created enhanced audience commodity values and it also generated increased attention to Super Bowl ads by the media – trends that began to take off the following year. Table 1 illustrates trends in the advertising rates, ratings, and audience commodity value during the 50-year history of the Super Bowl. Several factors influenced the ad rates and the cost to reach a thousand viewers (CPM) in particular years and to various degrees. These include the 1969 upset victory by the AFL's New York Jets in Super Bowl III, a victory that sparked additional publicity and made the games more compellingly competitive,[41] the removal of cigarette advertising from all television broadcasting in 1971,[42] the placement of the game into primetime beginning with Super Bowl XII in 1978,[43] and the ebb and flow of the digital economy, including the 'Dot-Com Super Bowl' that featured 17 different Internet companies buying commercials in 2000 but just three the next year.[44]

Despite these often short-term influences, the Super Bowl historically generated steady growth for the categories of then-current advertising prices for a 30-s spot and size of audience. The cost of a 30-s ad, for example, crossed the $1 million mark in 1995, an event that received coverage in newspapers across the country.[45] However, when one adjusts the CPM for inflation – adjusting the price for 2016 equivalents – then a different pattern emerges. Specifically, adjusted CPM is mostly flat during the first 18 years of the Super Bowl, basically between 8.5 and 11 (factoring in the additional cost CBS charged during the Super Bowl I compared to NBC). This figure began to climb steadily starting in 1985, the year after the Macintosh commercial. This shift clearly shows that the audience commodity became more valuable after this year. Since 1985, advertisers have been willing to pay more each year, even when accounting for inflation.

What accounts for the increase in adjusted CPM beginning in 1985? Recall the earlier discussion that the value of the audience commodity involves the size, demographics, and consumption receptiveness of that product. In this case, the increase in CPM starting in 1985 is likely not because the audience grew – if anything, this should make the cost per person less expensive as efficiencies of scale apply. Nor is it necessarily only about the demographic makeup of the audience, given that the Super Bowl audience is less likely to be male-dominated than a typical football broadcast. Females made up 46% of the audience for the 2011 Super Bowl, compared to 43% nine years earlier; the 18–34 age demographic remained constant at 23%.[46]

What seems to be the most logical explanation for the increase is the creation of a revered commercial cocoon during Super Bowl broadcasts, an environment cultivated especially starting in 1984. After this year, the advertising and broadcast television industries realized that the commercials were a unique element of the broadcast and for television generally – offering commercials to be watched along with, or maybe even instead of, the game, rather than as a necessary evil for audiences to receive the game.

The historical timing of this transformation also reveals some of the unique factors about the Super Bowl as unique commodity. The Super Bowl became an advertising-centred event that mitigated long-term trends in the television and advertising industries. Broadcast television faced competition from cable and satellite systems, both offering basic channels such as MTV but also advertising-free premium channels, including HBO. These premium channels featured original programming and drained especially desirable demographics that could afford such options.[47] A fourth broadcast network, Fox, would debut just a few years later, and afterwards smaller networks like The CW appeared. In addition, the remote control and VCRs (and eventually DVRs and streaming options) allowed audiences to avoid exposure to advertising by easily changing the channel or fast-forwarding through previous-recorded programmes.[48] For advertisers, cable networks and later the Internet allowed more effective demographic targeting. However, they also complicated media buying, especially for brands seeking a large audience and impact.[49]

Essentially what the Super Bowl does is freeze the network television system in the age where the TV commercial – and its audience commodity logic – was the pinnacle of mediated selling. In the 1960s, there were only three commercial networks sharing the entire audiences, ratings were high, and very few people had remote controls for easily avoiding the commercials. There were no video game systems or Internet access to distract viewers. During the Super Bowl, no one uses the remote control to avoid ads. The Super Bowl is often watched in group settings at Super Bowl parties, perhaps a throwback to the early days of television family viewing. A huge percentage of people watch the game, so diverting alternatives are put on hold; the Internet is used as a 'second screen' to complement viewing, including advertising viewing, rather than detract from ad exposure.[50] The Super Bowl, then, remains as broadcast network television's 'last hurrah'.[51]

As a result, audiences in this commercially protected environment are more expensive than those out in the wild. While watching the modern Super Bowl, viewers become advertising attentive, not only tolerating advertising but actively watching it, seeking it out in advance and after the game, and discussing it with others. In this way, the Super Bowl audience is the most desirable kind of ad-centred audiences in the current media environment that has been labelled 'the marketplace of attention'.[52] The '1984' ad and its philosophy of epic marketing also plugged into the Super Bowl as an unofficial holiday that manifests in group viewing, often-elaborate parties, network promotions of programmes, and conspicuous consumption of food, beer, and football fandom that flows with the commercial images between plays.[53] This translates into increased revenue for the networks: the spectacular consumption of the Super Bowl, triggered by the '1984' ad, enhances the political economy of the basic system.

Predictably, then, the rise in the price (and value) of the audience commodity is linked to a second trend that can measure the impact of '1984': the increased media coverage of Super Bowl commercials. Table 2 surveys 50 years of Super Bowl coverage in three major American newspapers – the *New York Times*, *Chicago Tribune*, and *Los Angeles Times*. These three newspapers were chosen both for their prominence and for their geographic distribution – East Coast (*New York Times*), Midwest (*Chicago Tribune*), and West Coast (*Los Angeles Times*). Articles represented in this table included mention of Super Bowl advertising in the headline, abstract, or lead paragraph.[54]

The findings indicate a post-1984 cultural shift in the importance of Super Bowl advertising. As seen in Table 2, pre-1984 coverage was both minimal and inconsistent. In particular, *Los Angeles Times* gave Super Bowl advertising no dedicated coverage until the mid-1970s and then only devoting an average of one article per year pre-1984.

Post-1984, the amount of coverage devoted to Super Bowl advertising begins to slowly rise. This rise continues through the 1990s and into the 2000s. It should be noted that while this growth has seemingly plateaued in recent years, this table does not include new, non-print forms of coverage. While currently not indexed within most research databases, newspaper-produced blogs such as *Company Town*, the *Los Angeles Times* entertainment industry-focused blog, and *Media Decoder*, the now-defunct *New York Times* advertising and entertainment blog, have produced Super Bowl advertising coverage not included in the physical editions of their parent newspapers.[55]

This pattern of coverage seems consistent with the trade press. Taking coverage of Super Bowl advertising in the most visible journal of the advertising industry, *Advertising Age*, from 1967 to 1984 (17 years), this outlet produced four stories about the Super Bowl, but none appeared on the prestigious front page. During the next five years – 1985–1990 – it offered 10 stories, 5 of them on the front page. Television news coverage, too, is now a significant part of Super Bowl commercial discourse: the cable and network morning news programmes cover the commercials with multiple and extensive segments before and

Table 2. Number of articles primarily about Super Bowl advertising in *New York Times, Chicago Tribune,* and *Los Angeles Times* in five-year intervals, 1967–2015.

Period	NY Times	Chi Trib	LA Times	Totals
1967–1970	3	2	0	5
1971–1975	6	2	1	9
1976–1980	1	2	4	7
1981–1985	5	5	8	18
1986–1990	12	17	12	41
1991–1995	32	25	12	69
1996–2000	31	35	34	100
2001–2005	40	33	26	99
2006–2010	44	40	30	114
2011–2015	50	41	24	115
Totals	224	202	151	577

Notes: Search terms used were the phrases 'Super Bowl and advertising' and 'Super Bowl and ads'. Newspapers were accessed through multiple databases. *Chicago Tribune* and *Los Angeles Times* through ProQuest using publication-specific search. *New York Times* through ProQuest (for articles through 2013) and NYT.com (for articles published 2014 and later). In the light of the Super Bowl's shifting dates and the possibility of post-event advertising coverage, a year was defined as running from March 1 to March 1.

after the game.[56] After the Super Bowl broadcast in 2004, the NFL Network repeated the commercials in consecutive order, *removing* the game itself from the commercial spectacle.[57]

The nature of the coverage also has changed. Early articles tended to focus on the price of Super Bowl ads, how the ratings indicated the cost efficiency of advertising during the Super Bowl, and a list of the advertisers.[58] But with the post-1984 era of spectacular consumption, specific campaigns, advertisements, and strategies are previewed before the Super Bowl and reviewed after the event.[59]

Symbolic of the attention that newspapers began paying to the commercials beginning in the 1980s is *USA Today*'s Ad Meter feature. Beginning in 1989,[60] the newspaper rated and ranked the commercials based on evaluations from focus groups. In 2012, the national daily added input from Internet users by employing social media via a partnership with Facebook where commercials were posted, rated, and shared by users.[61] Using a device that measures viewer reactions, commercials are given a numerical score that signifies scientific measurement. The first 'winner' of Ad Meter ranking was an American Express commercial featuring comedic actors Dana Carvey and Jon Lovitz with a score of '7.52'.[62] As with many such ad ratings, their criteria centred not on what commercials were effective at persuasion but rather on what ads were most entertaining. Humorous or poignant ads scored especially high in this metric.

Ad Meter itself has become part of the spectacle. As indicated by the use of the LexisNexis database, over 270 stories or features appeared in *USA Today* that mention the Ad Meter from January 1989 to February 2016, an average of 10 per year. The Ad Meter feature is also significantly covered in other news outlets.[63] A low Ad Meter rating has been known to cause advertisers to change agencies.[64] A high score could deliver an ad executive bonus.[65] High scores could even affect the value of stock for corporations that advertised their brands at the Super Bowl.[66]

This increase in news coverage is sparked by both advertisers' realization that high-profile ads can be supplemented by other marketing techniques including media placement, and the receptiveness of the media to offer exposure to such promotional efforts. The movement towards advertising treating Super Bowl placement as the lynchpin of a larger coordinated campaign involving public relations, sales promotion, and eventually teaser spots and webpage and social media support arguably began with or was greatly influenced by '1984'. In its 10-year retrospective of the Apple commercial, *Advertising Age* noted that the news coverage the commercial received 'would change the advertising game' (as is supported by Table 2). An advertising industry leader noted '1984' marked 'the beginning of the new era of integrated marketing communications'.[67] Just after the commercial aired, Apple placed 20-page inserts in the magazines *Newsweek*, *Time*, and *Fortune*, thus complementing the buzz and free media coverage the commercial received.[68] The next year, in 1985, the *Wall Street Journal* asked: 'When is a TV ad not an ad? When it's hyped as an event'.[69]

In addition to clever marketing tactics, a receptive media system is essential for such hype to work. In the mid-1980s, before the Internet and social media created additional competition for ad dollars, traditional media such as broadcast television and newspapers were concerned about their shrinking piece of the advertising pie. As mentioned earlier, cable television and the Fox broadcast network increased the outlets that could carry advertising and offered targeted demographics.[70] Ownership concentration of newspapers and television outlets – many diversified into cross-media ownership that included entertainment subsidiaries – both increased corporate debt because of acquisitions and created an environment friendly to large-scale advertising buys.[71] A Reagan-era deregulatory environment of media industries also emboldened commercial trends.[72] As media became incentivized to cater to advertisers to maintain revenue, the 1980s saw the growth of hybrid advertising and promotional forms such as infomercials, college football bowl sponsorship, advertorials, toy-based children's programming, and home shopping channels.[73] In this environment, the willingness of the news media to cover Super Bowl advertising was financially encouraged. For advertisers, media coverage of Super Bowl commercials offered a double benefit: the 'value-added' bonus of additional exposure for Super Bowl advertisers to justify the expensive costs of the event and an enhanced consumption-friendly environment for advertisers who place their ads around such news coverage.

These two factors – the increase in the audience-commodity and the increase in news coverage – illustrate the idea that well before their 50th anniversary, Super Bowl commercials were not seen as ads per se, but as celebrated forms of culture in-and-of-themselves, on par with blockbuster movies for generating audiences coveted by the media/adverting industries. From the standpoint of Super Bowl 50, the commercials have become spectacularized forms of media. They feature Hollywood talent who normally avoid routine advertising. In 1984, Ridley Scott pioneered the new format. Since then, Clint Eastwood and other A-listers have joined the Super Bowl ad-making lineup.[74] These spots are teased by pre-event commercials (ads for ads) as part of integrated campaigns using traditional and digital media.[75] They are viewed outside of the Super Bowl context. In 2015, consumers spent more than 800 million min watching Super Bowl commercials on YouTube, with over one-third of these views coming before the game. The Star Wars-themed VW commercial (with a Darth Vader-costumed kid seemingly starting his dad's car with the Dark Side) was a key advertisement for revealing online exposure. Internet users viewed it online 17 million times before the game, generating a huge buzz well before kickoff.[76] Recent ads are shared by users throughout social media. In 2015, the top-10 most viral Super Bowl commercials were shared 4.5 million times.[77] They are previewed and reviewed in the media, through Ad Meter and other metrics. They influence and inspire other forms of culture, including the films *Little Giants* (1994) and *Space Jam* (1996).[78] They benefit the media's marketing efforts. The Super Bowl provides an important platform for the broadcasting networks to promote their own programming during the event,[79] and for Hollywood to launch the hype for forthcoming summer blockbuster films.[80] Given these trends, it should not come as a surprise that the advertisements encourage an increasing number of viewers to watch the Super Bowl *exclusively* for the commercials. According to surveys, the percentage of the audience that tunes into the Super Bowl solely for the commercials has risen from 2% in 1996 to 10% in 2005 to 22% in 2010.[81]

Doritos' 'Crash the Super Bowl' and the *Super Bowl's Greatest Commercials*

Two particular case study histories illustrate the depth of how Super Bowl advertising perpetuates spectacular consumption trends. One is the decades-long 'Crash the Super Bowl' campaign for Doritos (ending with Super Bowl 50), and the second the *Super Bowl's Greatest Commercials* CBS television specials that aired nearly every year beginning in 2001 and continuing at least through 2016. As with many trends initiated or refined by Super Bowl commercials, these two continuing artefacts have normalized trends in the commercialization of everyday life and US culture.

The Doritos' 'Crash the Super Bowl' (CTSB) campaign is one of the most notable and unique examples of Super Bowl advertising in the 2000s. Organized around a contest for the best consumer-created Doritos ad, CTSB was an early and particularly successful UGC campaign. Running from 2006 to 2016,[82] the contest received over 36,000 entries, most from inside the United States as international submissions were not allowed until 2013.[83] Many of these entries were made available on both YouTube and the Doritos website. In 2016, for example, the top 50 entries as pre-screened by Doritos were posted for user viewing, voting, and sharing at their specially designated CTSB site, and supported by social media such as a Facebook page.[84] In this way, the campaign extends, de facto, the number of commercials seen by viewers from the ones airing on the Super Bowl to literally hundreds over the life of the campaign. The contest is designed to be viral, and the CTSB winner for Super Bowl 50 was the most shared commercial of that year.[85] The contest was also known for revealing the winner live during the Super Bowl itself and for airing the ads of the top two or three finishers (rather than just the winner). Additionally, the campaign managed to produce multiple ads that took first place in *USA Today*'s Ad Meter survey, an achievement for which Frito Lay monetarily rewarded participants. Joe and Dave Herbert, producers of the first CTSB spot to top the Ad Meter survey, were rewarded with $1 million dollars and a day-long celebration in their hometown.[86]

A rare example of an ongoing Super Bowl campaign, CTSB received a considerable amount of media coverage over the years. Within this coverage, there is a notable emphasis on the amateur nature of the contestants and on the contest's ability to provide crucial Hollywood connections for finalists. However, like many UGC contests both before and after CTSB, finalists tended to come from backgrounds in advertising or film. In the 2007 contest, four out of five finalists were either film-makers, employed by advertising agencies, or had previously produced commercials.[87] This was a pattern that not only continued but was seemingly embraced by Doritos as later editions of the contest included opportunities to work with film-makers such as Michael Bay and Zack Snyder as part of the grand prize.

Although the campaign was discontinued after Super Bowl 50, Frito Lay and Doritos did not entirely abandon the idea of UGC. Rather, they launched a new, year-round campaign, 'Legion of the Bold', which 'involves asking the general public for creative ideas throughout the year on everything from Vine videos to banner ads' and winning entrants are 'paid based on the complexity of the brief'.[88] Further, in an interview in *Advertising Age*, Frito Lay North America Chief Marketing Officer Ram Krishnan pointed to the generational shift that has occurred since the inception of CTSB, with Gen Z consumers 'earning success by putting out their own YouTube channel and creating content for that' – a trend that Krishnan sees as altering the ways in which the brand can offer value to the consumer.[89]

As *Advertising Age* declared, Doritos' 'Crash The Super Bowl' contest 'is widely seen as a groundbreaking program that put crowdsourced ads on the map',[90] thus serving as a role model for the advertising industry of how to involve consumers not just in the reviewing and sharing of commercials, but also as creators of commercials, further encouraging a consumerist (or, for the contest submitters, advertiserist) mindset. It also illustrates the ways in which digital media have shaped the nature of commercial content presented within the Super Bowl.

Super Bowl's Greatest Commercials (*SBGC*) is a series of television specials that traditionally air on CBS the week before the Super Bowl, starting in 2001 and appearing every year since – except 2003.[91] Typically, the 60-min, primetime specials collect and report user votes about past commercials (available on a tie-in website) to determine which is the 'greatest'. They also feature other entertaining commercials organized by themes ('Animals', 'At The Office'), entice viewers with previews ('sneak peeks') of commercials to be aired on that particular year's Super Bowl, include interviews with the stars of the commercials, and offer 'behind-scenes' or 'making-of' features of the upcoming commercials. The specials air on CBS whether the network carries the Super Bowl that particular year or not. They have also been rerun on The NFL Network.[92] Although the content of the specials themselves are all about the celebration of advertising, the specials sell ad time to other advertisers (that may or may not be advertisers for that year's Super Bowl) and, as with all broadcast network programmes, are interrupted by these commercials throughout the special. In fact, these specials are ads within ads, a perfect advertising-friendly environment. The existence and rhetoric of the specials clearly situate commercial culture as a legitimate form of popular culture.[93]

The *SBGC* specials were not the first television specials devoted to advertising, but the Super Bowl influenced perhaps the earliest series of specials, *The Best Commercials You've Never Seen (And Some You Have)*, which debuted on ABC in May 1998, with new or rerun episodes airing until 2002. The host for the first instalment was Ali Landry, a former Miss USA who was made a national celebrity by her appearance in Super Bowl Doritos commercials.[94] Later versions were hosted by two actors made famous by the Super Bowl Budweiser 'Whassup' ads.[95] In one of its last versions, ABC aired the special immediately after the *SPGC* on CBS in 2002, in a kind of inter-network lead-out programming strategy.[96] Other manifestations such as *World's Funniest Commercials* on the cable network TBS, airing in 2006 through 2010, and *Greatest Animal Commercials Countdown* on The CW network in 2016, typically include commercials from the Super Bowl. These ad-related specials are produced by the same company, Robert Dalrymple Productions.[97]

From the first airings in 2001, *SPGC* has been promotional not just for old and new Super Bowl commercials, but also for the networks. Co-hosts often include a star of a CBS programme, such as Mike O'Malley and Anthony Clark from the then-hit sitcom *Yes, Dear* in 2002 to Katharine McPhee of the crime procedural *Scorpion* in 2016.[98] The specials are also supported by tie-in news stories on morning news programmes, thus serving as a double promotion for the specials and the upcoming commercials. The public relations efforts of the brands recognized in the specials provide additional layers of support.[99] Obviously, the programmes themselves are a celebratory environment for the commercials, arguably more so than the Super Bowl itself, and explicitly frame the ads as a form of entertainment. The hosts and 'behind-the-scenes' features talk admiringly about the commercials, and certain categories of commercials which with modern eyes appear unseemly, such as cigarette commercials, are not included in the programmes.[100]

Ratings have generally increased for these specials. The audience for the first 2001 special was 6.5 million viewers.[101] In 2015, the *SBGC* special attracted 10.8 million, at a time when broadcast audiences were generally smaller than 15 years earlier.[102] Although many of the specials since 2001 were broadcast during the ratings-challenged nights of Friday and Saturday before the game, in 2016, for Super Bowl 50, CBS aired two specials: one on Tuesday, 12 February, at 8:00 pm as a 2-h special, and then a follow-up 1-h special – a new version, not a rerun – on Saturday night.[103] At one point, a promo was aired for the second special during the first Tuesday night *Super Bowl's Greatest Commercial* telecast, creating an intricate onion-layering of commercialism in which a promotional spot for a programme about commercials, featuring images of ads, aired along with ads during the commercial break of another programme about commercials featuring images of ads.

Just as the Doritos' 'Crash the Super Bowl' became a leader in the integration of UGC in advertising, so might the *SBGC* help normalize the idea of advertising-based content as a form of entertainment. This trend is often referred to by such names as 'brand entertainment', 'product integration', and 'content marketing', where a brand becomes the centre of a film, web feature, television episode, or even a whole programme.[104] In the case of CBGC, it is not one brand that comprises the programming, but several. Nor is it the brand that is the hero, but the advertisement ('advertising entertainment'?). Regardless, since 2001, the commercial-based specials have shown how economically and promotionally successful such hybrid forms can be.

The 'Ad Bowl' and the Transformation of Commercials from Sales Pitches to Entertainment

The main characteristic of the post-1984 era was to offer an event that spectacularized consumption – reinforced by the rising economic value of the commodity audience – and as a result celebrates brands, advertising, and consumerism by constructing the ads as simultaneously more than ads and therefore denying their own 'ad-ness'. Through elaborate production values including the involvement of movie stars; media coverage of campaigns; fan involvement through sharing, rating, and in some cases creation of ads; teaser ads and larger promotional support; online access to the ads; and decades of television specials specifically celebrating the commercials, the Super Bowl has elevated the commercial. The Super Bowl, then, has been a vehicle, and perhaps a justification, to raise this persuasive form on the hierarchy of 'taste cultures'[105] from a crassly promotional nuisance designed to persuade consumers to the equivalent of film and television programming designed to please audiences. A 2016 survey found that 77% of respondents felt that Super Bowl commercials were 'entertainment', and only 5% reported that ads bothered them during the game.[106] Although ads are no doubt still disliked by many media users, the Super Bowl has nevertheless been a long-term public relations campaign for the industry and its artefacts.

Just as the Super Bowl ad has gradually become a form of entertainment, so has the event and its ads extended the commercialization of everyday life and culture. Integrated marketing, viral marketing, user-generated campaigns, and content marketing all have some roots in Super Bowl commercial innovations. In these ways, a form of commercial selling is taken out of its selling context where it becomes more difficult to recognize, categorize, and thus evaluate commercial persuasion. Of course, Super Bowl commercials are forms of persuasion that are intricately tied to the political economy of televised sports, as is other sports-connected advertising. Other forms of mediated sports, such as sponsored college football bowl games, arguably represent similar 'groundbreaking' forms of commercialism, or even 'hypercommercialism'.[107] But given the Super Bowl's 50-plus-year legacy in promoting advertising, it has perhaps been the single biggest force in moving contemporary American culture into a digital world in which the categories of advertising, promotion, and media content are increasingly blurred, and where this blurring is more anticipated and accepted.

Notes

1. 'A Super 60 Seconds Costs $85,000', *New York Times*, 15 January 1967, S2.
2. 'Professional Football Games Are Too Expensive, Says FC&B's Stern', *Advertising Age*, 7 February 1966, 50.
3. 'Ford Wants Better Super Bowl Price', *Broadcasting*, 2 January 1967, 103–4.
4. Peter Hopsicker and Mark S. Dyreson, 'Super Bowl Sunday: An American Holiday?', in Len Travers (ed.), *Encyclopedia of American Holidays and National Days*, vol. 1 (Westport, CN: Greenwood Press, 2006), 31–54.
5. Guy Debord, *The Society of the Spectacle* (New York: Zone Books, 1995); Guy Debord, *Comments on the Society of the Spectacle* (New York: Verso, 1990); Dallas W. Smythe, 'Communications: Blindspot of Western Marxism', *Canadian Journal Of Political and Social Theory* 1, no. 3 (1977), 1–27; and Dallas W. Smythe, 'On the Audience Commodity and Its Work', in *Dependency Road: Communication, Capitalism, Consciousness & Canada* (New Jersey: Ablex Publishing, 1981), 22–51.
6. Debord, *The Society of the Spectacle*; for a review and application to modern media phenomena, see Douglas Kellner, *Media Spectacle* (New York: Routledge, 2003).
7. Marshall McLuhan, *Understanding Media: The Extensions of Man* (New York: McGraw Hill, 1964); Max Horkheimer and Theodor W. Adorno, *Dialectic of Enlightenment* (New York: Herder and Herder, 1972).
8. Debord, *Comments on the Society of the Spectacle*; and James R. Compton, *The Integrated News Spectacle: A Political Economy of Cultural Performance* (New York: Peter Lang, 2004).
9. Michael R. Real, 'Super Bowl: Mythic Spectacle', *Journal of Communication* 25, no. 1 (Winter 1975), 31–43.
10. Kathy Hamilton and Beverly Wagner, 'An Exploration of Spectacular Consumption at the Movies', *Journal of Customer Behaviour* 10, no. 4 (Winter 2011), 375–90; Eric King Watts, 'An Exploration of Spectacular Consumption: Gangsta Rap as Cultural Commodity', *Communication Studies* 48, no. 1 (1997), 42–58; and Matthew P. McAllister, '"Girls with a Passion for Fashion": The Bratz Brand as Integrated Spectacular Consumption', *Journal of Children and Media* 1, no. 3 (2007), 244–58.
11. Lisa Penaloza, 'Just Doing It: A Visual Ethnographic Study of Spectacular Consumption Behavior at Nike Town', *Consumption, Markets, & Culture* 2, no. 4 (1998), 337–400; Eric King Watts and Mark P. Orbe, 'The Spectacular Consumption of "True" African American Culture: "Whassup" with the Budweiser Guys?', *Critical Studies in Media Communication* 19, no. 1 (March 2002), 1–20.
12. Much of the scholarship on Super Bowl advertising focuses on their effectiveness as marketing – see for example Jason Y.C. Ho, Tirtha Dhar, and Charles B. Weinberg, 'Playoff Payoff: Super Bowl Advertising for Movies', *International Journal of Research in Marketing* 26, no. 3 (September 2009), 168–79 – or on issues of gender and/or racial representation in the ads. Examples of this latter body of research include Michael A. Messner and Jeffrey Montez de Oca, 'The Male Consumer as Loser: Beer and Liquor Ads in Mega Sports Events', *Signs: Journal of Women in Culture and Society* 30, no. 3 (2005), 1879–909. Work that focuses on the cultural impact of the large-scale scope of the consumption and commercials includes Matthew P. McAllister, 'Super Bowl Advertising as Commercial Celebration', *The Communication Review*, 3 no. 4, 403–28; Lawrence A. Wenner, 'Super-Cooled Sports Dirt: Moral Contagion and Super Bowl Commercials in the Shadows of Janet Jackson', *Television and New Media* 9, no. 2 (2008), 131–54. General overviews of the history and social issues of Super Bowl commercials include William M. O'Barr, 'Super Bowl Commercials: America's Annual Festival of Advertising', *Advertising & Society Review* 13, no. 1 (2012), https://muse.jhu.edu/article/477906 (accessed 22 May 2016); and Bernice Kanner, *The Super Bowl of Advertising: How Commercials Won the Game* (Princeton, NJ: Bloomberg Press, 2004).
13. Smythe, 'Communications'; and Smythe, 'On the Audience Commodity'.
14. Matthew P. McAllister, *The Commercialization of American Culture: New Advertising, Control, and Democracy* (Thousand Oaks, CA: Sage, 1996). In refining Smythe's concepts, scholars have

also argued that how the audience is measured – the audience ratings system – could also be viewed as a commodity of broadcasting, especially given that such measurement systems lean towards likely consumers rather than a pure audience measurement per se. See Eileen R. Meehan, *Why TV Is Not Our Fault: Television Programming, Viewers, and Who's Really in Charge* (Lanham, MD: Rowman & Littlefield, 2005).

15. Lee McGuigan and Vincent Manzerolle (eds), *The Audience Commodity in a Digital Age: Revisiting a Critical Theory of Commercial Media* (New York: Peter Lang, 2014).
16. In terms of pre-Super Bowl NFL championship coverage, see 'CBS' Buy of National football League Championship Game Startles Other Nets', *Advertising Age*, 27 April 1964; and Val Adams, 'Football TV Ads Will Cost More', *New York Times*, 6 January 1966, 34.
17. 'Shulman, Grid Stars Sell on TV for Philip Morris', *Advertising Age*, 4 January 1960.
18. '$29 Million for 1964 Football', *Broadcasting*, 10 August 1964, 27–31.
19. David G. Moyer, *American Breweries of the Past* (Bloomington, IN: AuthorHouse, 2009), 61.
20. '$29 Million for 1964 Football', *Broadcasting*.
21. The web archive adland.tv does not begin its inventory of Super Bowl commercials until Super Bowl III in 1969. See http://adland.tv/SuperBowlCommercials. As Kanner notes, the audio of the NBC broadcast, including the commercials, is available at what originally was the Museum of Television and Radio (now known as The Paley Center for Media) in New York; Kanner, *The Super Bowl of Advertising*, 13.
22. CBS and NBC each claimed to have better advertising efficiencies – CPMs – given what was seen as a very high cost to advertise. See 'Who Took the Super Bowl CPM title? It Depends on Which Network's Version You Accept', *Broadcasting*, 13 February 1967, 46.
23. 'Sponsors Sign for Super Bowl TV', *Broadcasting*, 26 December 1966, 32–3.
24. 'TV Ad Timing Was Off in Super Bowl, CBS McPhail Says', *Advertising Age*, 23 January 1967, 2, 68; and Robert Raissman, 'The Super Bowl: Two Decades in the Spotlight', *Advertising Age*, 20 January 1986.
25. 'Close-up: The History of Advertising in Quite a Few Objects – No 69: Joe Namath's Super Bowl Commercial', *Campaign*, 5 July 2013, 16.
26. A search through *The New York Times*, *Advertising Age*, or the *Chicago Tribune* did not uncover discussions of Joe Namath commercial the year it aired, although it appears on lists of the greatest Super Bowl commercials. See for example Mackenzie Carpenter, 'Highlights and Fumbles from Super Bowl Commercials', *Pittsburgh Post-Gazette*, 6 February 2005, E8.
27. '50 Best Super Bowl Ads Ever – USA Today Ad Meter', *Dayton Daily News*, 7 February 2016, Z5.
28. Robert Philpot, '"Mean" Joe Greene Reunites with "Kid" from Super Bowl Ad', *Fort Worth Star-Telegram*, 29 January 2016.
29. The 2009 sequel featured then-Steeler Troy Polamalu reprising Joe Greene's role: Ed Bouchette and Jerry Micco, 'Step Aside, Mean Joe; Polamalu Will Star in Ad Reprise', *Pittsburgh Post-Gazette*, 21 November 2008, D3. The parody did have Joe Greene in it, coupled with comic actress Amy Sedaris, for Downy fabric softener, in 2012: Bruce Dowbiggin, 'NBC Dresses in its Sunday Best: Super Bowl Marketing Machine Clicks into High Gear', *Globe and Mail*, 4 February 2012, S3. CBS's promotion of the commercials during Super Bowl 50 featured a reunion spot with the Greene and the now-adult actor of the original commercial: Philpot, '"Mean" Joe Green Reunites with "Kid"'.
30. Stephen Battaglio, 'The "Shut Up and Watch" Standard: Super Bowl Advertisers Are Judged as much as the Players', *Los Angeles Times,* 4 February 2016, http://www.latimes.com/entertainment/envelope/cotown/la-et-ct-super-bowl-ads-20160204-story.html (accessed 20 July 2016).
31. Kanner, *The Super Bowl of Advertising*, 25.
32. Chuck Barney, 'Super Bowl 50: The 10 Best Super Bowl Ads Ever', *San Jose Mercury News*, 1 February 2016.
33. Steve Hayden, '"1984": As Good as It Gets', *Adweek*, 30 January 2011, http://www.adweek.com/news/advertising-branding/1984-good-it-gets-125608 (accessed 18 July 2016).
34. Bradley Johnson, 'Ten Years After Apple's "1984": The Commercial and Product that Changed Advertising', *Advertising Age*, 10 January 1994.

35. Charlie McCollum, 'The Ad Lineup', *San Jose Mercury News*, 30 January 2004, F1.
36. Alice Z. Cuneo and Richard Linnett, 'Apple Concocts Homage to "1984"', *Advertising Age*, 8 December 2003, 1, 37.
37. Sarah R. Stein, 'The "1984" Macintosh Ad: Cinematic Icons and Constitutive Rhetoric in the Launch of a New Machine', *Quarterly Journal of Speech* 88, no. 2 (2002), 169–92.
38. Karis Hustad, 'Why Apple's "1984" Commercial Is Still Talked about Today', *Christian Science Monitor*, 22 January 2014.
39. Daniela Hernandez, 'Tech Time Warp of the Week: 30 Years of Apple Ads, 1984 to the Present', *Wired*, 29 November 2013, http://www.wired.com/2013/11/tech-time-warp-of-the-week-apples-commercials/ (accessed 18 July 2016).
40. Douglas M. Bailey, 'Those "Epic" Computer Ads', *New England Business*, 17 June 1985, 70.
41. 'Jets Super Bowl Victory May Lead to Price Boost of AFL TV Minutes', *Advertising Age*, 20 January 1969, 20; and Raissman, 'The Super Bowl'.
42. 'Rozelle says N.F.L. Will Add Six Clubs for a Total of 32 in Coming Decade', *New York Times*, 3 January 1971, S2.
43. Kanner, *The Super Bowl of Advertising*, 23.
44. Stuart Elliot, 'In Super Commercial Bowl XXXV, The Not-Coms Are Beating the Dot-Coms', *New York Times*, 8 January 2001, C15.
45. For example, 'Super Bowl Ad Prices Topping $1 Million Level', *Cincinnati Post*, 11 January 1995, 4B; and 'Super Bowl XXIX Ad To Top $1 Million Mark', *Daily News of Los Angeles*, 1 November 1994, L18.
46. 'Gap Between Number of Male, Female Super Bowl Viewers Is Shrinking', *Sports Media Business Daily*, 1 February 2012, http://www.sportsbusinessdaily.com/Daily/Issues/2012/02/01/Research-and-Ratings/SB-demos.aspx (accessed 17 July 2016). Those who had a household income of over $100,000 increased during this time, but given that older viewers also increased, it is unclear if these demographic trends would increase the cost of advertising.
47. McAllister, *The Commercialization of American Culture*.
48. Robert V. Bellamy Jr. and James R. Walker, *Television and the Remote Control: Grazing on a Vast Wasteland* (New York: Guilford, 1996).
49. Joseph Turow, *Breaking Up America: Advertisers and the New Media World* (Chicago: University of Chicago Press, 1997).
50. Stephen Battaglio, 'Super Bowl Ads Whetted the Appetites of Viewers, Who Watched Them Again on Smartphones', *Los Angeles Times*, 10 February 2016, http://www.latimes.com/entertainment/envelope/cotown/la-et-ct-superbowl-youtube-ads-20160211-story.html (accessed 20 July 2016).
51. 'Close-up: The History of Advertising in Quite a Few Objects – No 69: Joe Namath's Super Bowl Commercial', *Campaign*.
52. James G. Webster, *The Marketplace of Attention: How Audiences Take Shape in a Digital Age*. (Cambridge, MA: The MIT Press, 2014).
53. Hopsicker and Dyreson, 'Super Bowl Sunday'.
54. In-brief style articles were an exception to this. While Super Bowl advertising was discussed in each piece included in this table, this was not always mentioned in the title or abstract or at least not as both are presented on the databases used.
55. 'Company Town', *Los Angeles Times*, http://www.latimes.com/business/hollywood/; and 'Media Decoder', *New York Times*, http://mediadecoder.blogs.nytimes.com/author/the-new-york-times/
56. McAllister, 'Super Bowl Advertising as Commercial Celebration'.
57. Bill Doyle, 'For Some, It's All About the Commercials', *Worcester Telegram & Gazette*, 30 January 2004, 22.
58. One early example is 'A Super 60 Seconds Costs $85,000', *New York Times*.
59. See, for instance, Super Bowl soft drink coverage in Stephen Chapman, 'The Cold War's History, but the Cola Wars Drag On', *Chicago Tribune*, 6 February 1992, D23; Denise Gellene, 'In Super Bowl of Commercialism, Pepsi Ads Score Best with Viewers', *Los Angeles Times*, 31 January 1995, 1; and 'Coca-Cola Flexes Muscles for a Blitz', *New York Times*, 21 January 1998, D9.

60. The first *USA Today* Ad Meter articles that report results were 'Ad Meter Ratings', *USA Today*, 23 January 1989, 4B. Other articles supporting Ad Meter appeared on the same page, such as Stuart Elliott, 'Funny, Furry Ads Win Hearts of TV Viewers', *USA Today*, 23 January 1989, 4B.
61. Stuart Elliott, 'Super Bowl Commercials Rated by Social Media', *New York Times*, 8 February 2012, B3.
62. 'Ad Meter Ratings', *USA Today*, 23 January 1989.
63. Elliott, 'Super Bowl Commercials Rated by Social Media', among hundreds of others by various media outlets.
64. Elliott, 'Super Bowl Commercials Rated by Social Media'.
65. Battaglio, 'The "Shut Up and Watch" Standard'.
66. Jin-Woo Kim, Luther Trey Denton, and Tien Wang, 'Assessing Stock Market Response to the Release of Ad Meter Rankings of Super Bowl TV Commercials', *International Journal of Integrated Marketing Communications* (2015), http://www.ijimc.com/ (accessed 20 July 2016).
67. Johnson, 'Ten Years After Apple's "1984"'.
68. Richard L. Cohen, 'Making News Is Good News for an Advertising Campaign', *San Francisco Business Journal*, 25 February 1985, 9.
69. Ronald Alsop, 'When is a TV Ad Not an Ad? When it's Hyped as an Event', *Wall Street Journal*, 21 March 1985.
70. McAllister, 'The Commercialization of American Culture'.
71. Robert G. Picard, 'Commercialism and Newspaper Quality', *Newspaper Research Journal* 25, no. 1 (2004), 54–65.
72. Tom Engelhardt, 'The Shortcake Strategy', in Todd Gitlin (ed.), *Watching Television* (New York: Pantheon, 1986), 68–110.
73. McAllister, *The Commercialization of American Culture*; Robin Andersen, *Consumer Culture and TV Programming*. (Boulder, CO: Westview, 1995); Matthew P. McAllister, 'College Bowl Sponsorship and the Increased Commercialization of Amateur Sports', *Critical Studies in Mass Communication* 15, no. 4 (1998), 357–81; Engelhardt, 'The Shortcake Strategy'; and Judi Puritz Cook, 'Consumer Culture and Television Home Shopping Programming: An Examination of the Sales Discourse', *Mass Communication & Society* 3, no. 4 (2000), 373–91.
74. Dan Farber, 'Clint Eastwood's Super Bowl "Halftime in America"', *CBS News*, 6 February 2012, http://www.cbsnews.com/news/clint-eastwoods-super-bowl-halftime-in-america/ (accessed 20 July 2016).
75. See, for example, *USA Today*'s collection of short teaser spots that touted commercials in advance of Super Bowl 50 at http://admeter.usatoday.com/2016/01/28/watch-5-super-bowl-50-ad-teasers/ (accessed 20 July 2016).
76. Battaglio, 'The "Shut Up and Watch" Standard'. For a discussion of viral advertising, see *Michael Serazio, Your Ad Here: The Cool Sell of Guerrilla Marketing* (New York: New York University Press, 2013).
77. Tim Nudd, 'The 10 Most Viral Ads of Super Bowl 50', *Adweek*, 8 February 2016, http://www.adweek.com/news-gallery/advertising-branding/10-most-viral-ads-super-bowl-50-169532 (accessed 20 July 2016).
78. McAllister, 'Super Bowl Advertising as Commercial Celebration'.
79. CBS devoted nearly 9 min of commercial time to promote its own programming; Nick Niedzwiadek, 'Super Bowls Broadcast by CBS Feature the Most Network Promos', *Wall Street Journal*, 11 February 2016, http://www.wsj.com/articles/super-bowls-broadcast-by-cbs-feature-the-most-network-promos-1455222395 (accessed 20 July 2016).
80. Ho, Dhar, and Weinberg, 'Playoff Payoff'.
81. These figures are from two different polling/survey firms (Eisner and Harris). For the 2% figure, see Eric Fisher, 'Ad Buyers Bet on Winners', *Washington Times*, 21 January 1998, B7. For the 10%, see Nathan Slaughter, 'Souping Up for the Super Bowl', *The Motley Fool*, 2 February 2005, http://www.fool.com/investing/high-growth/2005/02/02/souping-up-for-the-super-bowl.aspx (accessed 20 July 2016). For the 22%, see Wayne Friedman, 'Super Bowl Fans Relish Ads as much as the Big Game', *Media Daily News*, 27 January 2010, http://www.mediapost.com/publications/article/121428/super-bowl-fans-relish-ads-as-much-as-big-

game.html (accessed 23 May 2016). The fact that this statistic is measured at all is indicative of the importance of Super Bowl ads (thanks to Joseph Turow for this insight).

82. The 2007–2008 campaign focused on aspiring musicians, rather than traditional advertising, and offered a grand prize of having the winner's music video aired during the Super Bowl and receiving a recording contract.

83. Karen Robinson-Jacobs, 'As Doritos' "Crash the Super Bowl" Ends, North Texas Companies Look Back at Iconic Ads', *Biz Beat Blog*, 5 February 2016, http://bizbeatblog.dallasnews.com/2016/02/as-doritos-crash-the-super-bowl-ends-north-texas-companies-look-back-at-iconic-ads.html/ (accessed 20 July 2016).

84. 'Doritos Crash the Super Bowl Final Edition; Finalists', https://crashthesuperbowl.doritos.com/finalists (accessed 31 January 2016). 'Doritos Facebook Page', https://www.facebook.com/DoritosUSA/?fref=ts (accessed 31 January 2016).

85. Nudd, 'The 10 Most Viral Ads of Super Bowl 50'.

86. Stuart Elliott, 'Will the Key to the City Come in Nacho Cheese, Cool Ranch or Spicy Sweet Chili?' *Media Decoder Blog*, 10 February 2009, http://mediadecoder.blogs.nytimes.com/2009/02/10/will-the-key-to-the-city-come-in-nacho-cheese-cool-ranch-or-spicy-sweet-chili/ (accessed 20 July 2016).

87. Alana Semuels, 'Going Up Against Some Real Pros; Amateur Entrants in Contests to Create TV Ads for the Big Game Find Themselves Bowled Over', *Los Angeles Times*, 4 February 2007.

88. E.J. Schultz, 'How "Crash the Super Bowl" Changed Advertising', *Advertising Age*, 4 January 2016, http://adage.com/article/special-report-super-bowl/crash-super-bowl-changed-advertising/301966/ (accessed 20 July 2016).

89. Schultz, 'How "Crash the Super Bowl" Changed Advertising'.

90. Ibid.

91. The year and number of TV specials is confirmed by both Internet Movie Database (imdb.com) as well as a search of reviews or previews of the specials in newspapers as found in the database Newsbank.

92. *SBGC 2013: Super Bowl's Greatest Commercials*. Directed by Mark Ritchie. NFL Network, 31 January 2013, 8–9 pm EST.

93. Matthew P. McAllister, 'Is Commercial Culture Popular Culture?: A Question for Popular Communication Scholars', *Popular Communication* 1, no. 1 (2003), 41–9.

94. Greg Paeth, 'TV Highlights for the Upcoming Week', *Scripps Howard News Service*, 2 May 1998.

95. David Bianculli, 'Isn't that Special? Not by a Long Shot', *New York Daily News*, 4 December 2001, 79.

96. R.D. Heldenfels, 'Think We Have Enough Super Bowl-related Shows?' *Akron Beacon Journal*, 1 February 2002, B1.

97. 'TBS Spans the Globe to Find the WORLD'S FUNNIEST COMMERCIALS for One-Hour Special Hosted by Kevin Nealon and Susan Yeagley', *PR Newswire*, 26 July 2006, http://ezaccess.libraries.psu.edu/login?url=http://search.proquest.com.ezaccess.libraries.psu.edu/docview/448468212?accountid=13158 (accessed 20 June 2016).

98. Ted Cox, 'Championship of Advertising; Commercialism Runs Amok in CBS' Super Bowl Special', *Daily Herald*, 26 January 2001, 27; and Chuck Barney, 'Super Bowl 50 Specials Spotlight Commercials, Halftime Shows and Star Players', *Mercury News*, 27 January 2016, http://www.mercurynews.com/sports/ci_29439730/super-bowl-50-specials-spotlight-commercials-halftime-shows (accessed 20 July 2016).

99. 'Famed Tide to Go(R) Ad Named One of Top Ten Super Bowl Commercials of all Time', *PR Newswire*, 23 January 2009, http://ezaccess.libraries.psu.edu/login?url=http://search.proquest.com.ezaccess.libraries.psu.edu/docview/453640893?accountid=13158 (accessed 20 July 2016). As found in the Newsbank database, a local television story about the specials aired on *News 10 This Morning*, KWTX in Waco Texas, in 2 February 2007; and nationally *CBS This Morning* aired a segment on 30 January 2013.

100. Walt Belcher, 'This Show's For You', *Tampa Tribune*, 26 January 2001, BAYLIFE1.

101. 'Last Week's Top TV Shows', *Long Beach Press-Telegram*, 31 January 2001, A12.

102. Toni Fitzgerald, '"Super Bowl's Greatest Commercials" Surges', *Medialife*, 27 January 2015, http://www.medialifemagazine.com/surge-greatest-super-bowl-commercials/ (accessed 5 July 2016).

103. *Super Bowl's Greatest Commercials 2016*. Directed by Mark Ritchie, CBS, 2 February 2016, 8–10 pm EST; and *Super Bowl's Greatest Commercials All-Star Countdown*, CBS, 6 February 2016, 8–9 pm EST.

104. Jean-Marc Lehu, *Branded Entertainment: Product Placement and Brand Strategy in the Entertainment Business* (London: Kogan Page, 2007); and Mara Einstein, *Black Ops Advertising: Native Ads, Content Marketing, and the Covert World of the Digital Sell* (New York: OR Books, 2016). The Super Bowl commercial-influenced film *Space Jam* could also easily be considered brand entertainment, given the emphasis on Nike and Warner Brothers licenses like Bugs Bunny.

105. Pierre Bourdieu, *Distinction: A Social Critique of the Judgment of Taste* (Cambridge, MA: Harvard University Press, 1984).

106. Wayne Friedman, 'Super Bowl Viewers See Ads as Entertainment First, Marketing Second', *MediaPost*, 2 February 2016, http://www.mediapost.com/publications/article/268084/super-bowl-viewers-see-ads-as-entertainment-first.html (accessed 20 July 2106).

107. Matthew P. McAllister, 'Hypercommercialism, Televisuality, and the Changing Nature of College Sports Sponsorship', *American Behavioral Scientist* 53, no. 10 (2010), 1476–91.

Acknowledgements

The authors wish to thank Jeff Knapp of Penn State University Libraries, Mary Beth Oliver, Joe Turow, and Ross Wolin for their help with the ideas in this manuscript.

Disclosure Statement

No potential conflict of interest was reported by the authors.

'Super Bore': The Canadian Media and the Grey Cup-Super Bowl Comparison

Craig G. Greenham

ABSTRACT

A closer look at football illuminates some important truths in the Can-Am experience. Central to this discovery is the notion of the Grey Cup as Canada's anti-Super Bowl. Complete with folksy traditions and understated pageantry, the Grey Cup is emblematically Canadian and has historically served as a sharp rebuke to American cultural imperialism and excess, represented so perfectly by the Super Bowl. Like many aspects of Can-Am relations, however, the Super Bowl experience is not a simple narrative. Many Canadians have not only integrated the Super Bowl into their sporting calendars but prefer it to the domestic product. The growing cultural influence of the Super Bowl north of the border made national headlines in 2015 when ratings revealed that more Canadians, per capita, watched the Super Bowl than Americans. Traditionally the attitudes reflected in Canadian media demonstrate a clear bias that favoured the Grey Cup over the Super Bowl. The Super Bowl's prominence in Canada was written by Canadian sports scribes as regrettable and undeserved while the virtuous Grey Cup, they asserted, went under-appreciated, not just globally but increasingly domestically. This chauvinistic rhetoric supports and adds to the existing research that focuses on Canadian reaction to American mass culture.

The United States and Canada have enjoyed a largely harmonious relationship and, while meaningful differences exist, common traits prevail and bond the neighbouring nations. Shared experience of these peoples extends to the realm of professional team sport and three (National Hockey League, National Basketball Association and Major League Baseball) of the 'Big Four' leagues have club representation on both sides of the border. What much of the rest of the world calls the 'gridiron' version of football to distinguish it from association football and rugby football, remains the last holdout, segregated with a domestic league in each country – the National Football League (NFL) and the Canadian Football League (CFL). The CFL briefly had American franchises from 1993 to 1995 but historically this expansion effort was considered misguided. At different times, Vancouver, Montreal and Toronto were rumoured destinations for NFL franchises but nothing materialized past the speculation stage.[1] On some level, this separation appears curious. Football, at least

65

in the North American context of the word, does not enjoy the global presence of hockey, basketball and baseball. Instead, football remains mainly the preserve of Americans and Canadians. If ever two nations were joined together by a sport, football in the Canadian-American (Can-Am) context appears a likely candidate, particularly when the origins of Canadian and American football share an embryonic experience in 1874 before evolving along different paths.[2]

Aside from the geographical settings, differences persist between the Canadian and American brands of football. The Canadian field of play is larger, for example, and a handful of rule variations serve as a point of distinction – most notably the Canadian version employs a three-down system compared to the four-down method in the United States and fields 12-man teams instead of the American version of 11-man squads. In order to preserve Canadian content, the CFL limits roster spots for foreign players.[3] Of course, the financial fortunes of the two leagues differ drastically. The NFL is the picture of economic might while the CFL has struggled where money is concerned. [4]

A closer look at football illuminates some important truths in the Can-Am experience. Central to this discovery is the notion of the Grey Cup as Canada's anti-Super Bowl. Complete with folksy traditions and understated pageantry, the Grey Cup is emblematically Canadian and its place within the national psyche has historically served as a sharp rebuke to American cultural imperialism and excess, represented so perfectly by the Super Bowl. Like many aspects of Can-Am relations, however, the Super Bowl experience is not a simple narrative. Many Canadians have long been fascinated with the American entertainment industry, of which sport is part, and have not only integrated the Super Bowl into their sporting calendars but prefer it to the domestic product. The growing cultural influence of the Super Bowl north of the border made national headlines in 2015 when ratings revealed that more Canadians, per capita, watched the Super Bowl than Americans.[5]

Traditionally the attitudes reflected in Canadian media demonstrate a clear bias that favoured the Grey Cup over the Super Bowl. Canadian sports journalists have sanctimoniously championed the competitive drama of the Grey Cup, the purported superior design of the Canadian game and applauded the off-field festivities. They characterized the Super Bowl, by contrast, through its lack of excitement, supposed inferior rules and flawed commercialism. The Super Bowl's prominence in Canada was written by Canadian sports scribes as regrettable and undeserved while the virtuous Grey Cup, they asserted, went under-appreciated, not just globally but increasingly domestically. This chauvinistic rhetoric supports and adds to the existing research that focuses on Canadian reaction to American mass culture.

To understand the historical treatment of the Super Bowl by Canadian media, it is important to explore prevalent attitudes that explain how American mass culture has been absorbed north of the border. Media scholar Richard Collins argued in *Culture, Communication, and National Identity* that Canadian intellectuals were negatively predisposed towards American mass culture.[6] In part, Canadian intellectuals judged American culture in unflattering terms as a means of maintaining national superiority. Historian Paul Rutherford wrote that from a Canadian's eyes,

> Americans were seen as excitable, even 'childlike', 'money-mad', lawless, 'more-corrupt', and 'less moral', boastful and 'less cultured', although they were credited for being 'daring and enterprising' or generous. By contrast, Canadians appeared more honourable, law-abiding, and conservative, and their society, 'quieter, slower, in tempo and saner in quality'.[7]

Aniko Bodroghkozy, media scholar, argued this distaste of American mass culture extends to the Canadian leftist press that view domestic cultural products as undeservingly disadvantaged to the mass culture sourced from the powerful United States.[8] Consistent with the concepts described above, through the examination of Canadian media treatment of sport, American mass culture (represented by the Super Bowl) was denigrated as corrupted by commerce, backward by design, and dangerous to Canadian culture (represented by the Grey Cup) through its powerful popularity. Canadian sport writers described the Grey Cup, contested in 'manly' weather and under high-minded rules, as a better, but unfairly endangered, product.

The Canadian media's rejection of the Super Bowl relies on a long-rooted anti-American sentiment. Renowned American sociologist Seymour Lipsett remarked, 'Canadians are the world's oldest and continuing anti-Americans'.[9] With such a mighty neighbour, Canadian nationalists were concerned about being suffocated by American influence on their economy and culture, or worse, invasion and annexation. In 1812 Americans made an attempted invasion, and though they failed to capture Canada, notions that their northern neighbour belonged within their sphere of 'manifest destiny' persisted in the United States. In 1869, shortly following Canadian Confederation, US Senator Zachariah Chandler fulminated that Canada was 'a mere speck on the map', a 'nuisance', and 'a standing menace ... that we ought not tolerate'.[10] While open animosity was reduced over the years and yielded to friendship, the past cannot be forgotten.

For the sake of context, it is also critical to understand that rejection of American sporting culture by Canadian media did not begin with the Super Bowl, but instead is part of a deeper tradition. Baseball in Canada was met with hostility in certain circles in the late nineteenth and early twentieth century, largely because of its ties to American culture. Canadian baseball promoters seldom drew notice to the sport's privileged place within American society, but its detractors' criticism often mentioned the game's Americanism. As baseball's popularity in Canada surpassed that of cricket and lacrosse, those who saw baseball as an unwanted American influence and voice of an unruly working-class culture questioned the game's respectability. Rowdiness, gambling, thrown games, and the consumption of alcohol by fans and sometimes by the players themselves were among their concerns.[11]

The Canadian media often led the charge against perceived American cultural intrusion. In the early twentieth-century, influential newspapers such as Toronto's *Mail and Empire* as well as the *Toronto Globe* were apprehensive about the heavy influence of American news and society on Canadian culture and suggested that it was destroying any domestic culture. They lamented that American culture promoted lesser morals.[12] In all likelihood, some of their anxiety stemmed from their own industry's bleak economic outlook. American publications dwarfed those of Canada and, by 1912, imported American and British periodicals outsold domestic publications in Canada ten to one.[13] Nevertheless, some Canadian newspapers saw it as their duty to assail cultural infringement from the south – of which baseball, they believed, was a key element. The *Hamilton Spectator* warned about Canadian baseball's subservience to American leagues and the *Hamilton Times* complained about the American-style professionalization of the Canadian game when it remarked:

> The question of the championship was a mere question of dollars and cents, and by this manner London [Ontario] has come to the fore. Baseball is meant to develop the muscle of the youth, and not the gambling speculation for roughs. Cricket has steered clear of this. Why shouldn't baseball?[14]

The negative press suffered by baseball, however, had little impact on the sport's momentum. Its popularity, to some, seemed unstoppable. The *Victoria Times* remarked: 'In sport, the continent is rapidly becoming "Americanized". It would appear to be useless to attempt to stem the tide, even if it were desirable to attempt such a thing.'[15] While some newspapers bemoaned the game's prominent presence in Canada, others were key players in the dissemination of baseball's happenings. Samuel Moffett, American intellectual and journalist, declared in *The Americanization of Canada* (1907):

> The Canadian newspapers print fuller telegraphic accounts of the great baseball contests of the National, the American and the Eastern Leagues than they do of the proceedings of the British Parliament. The American baseball language, which would be entirely unintelligible to an English reader, is fully familiarized in the Canadian press.[16]

For their part, some Americans seemed glad that their sport had been successfully transplanted beyond their borders. In an attempt to demonstrate the existence of genuine American culture around the world, legendary baseball promoter, sporting goods tycoon and nationalist, Albert G. Spalding, toured the New York Giants and Chicago White Sox across the western United States, Japan, China, Hong Kong, Manila, Australia, Egypt, Italy, France, and Britain from October 1913 to February 1914. In 1924 the Giants and White Sox made a smaller, less successful tour.[17] The American press portrayed the ballplayers as semi-religious figures. The magazine, *Time*, commented, 'Instead of Bibles and hymn-books, these missionaries carry with them balls, bats, mits [*sic*]. Instead of love and light, these missionaries shed baseball fanaticism all over Europe'.[18] American enthusiasm for the global spread of baseball, real or imagined, mirrors the modern day aspirations Americans have for the Super Bowl as a global sporting phenomenon.[19]

While baseball's global success was the ultimate goal for promoters and patriots such as Spalding, Americans had cheered baseball's presence in Canada. Moffett proclaimed:

> It is no trivial matter that baseball is becoming the national game of Canada instead of cricket. It has a very deep significance, as has the fact that the native game of lacrosse is not able to hold its own against the southern intruder. 'It has not one player in Canada', regretfully observed the Toronto *Mail and Empire*, 'where baseball has a score. Thousands of people will quit work of an afternoon to applaud two contending gangs of salaried aliens at Diamond Park, while as many hundreds would not be induced to attend a lacrosse match'.[20]

These laments were echoed decades later when America's Super Bowl emerged as prominent fixture in the Canadian sporting calendar. The *Globe and Mail's* Scott Young, whose son Neil went on to musical fame and fortune in the United States, was a leading opponent of Canadian glorification of an American football championship. In 1977, Young criticized undue media attention devoted to the Super Bowl.

> It is a dumb, overplayed U.S. sports story that no Canadian news organization should spend five cents, or more than 12 inches of type, to cover …. That's okay for the Americans if they want to punish themselves that way …. The Super Bowl is the sport world's greatest fertilizer factory.

Young was adamant that media coverage of the Super Bowl was based on false assumptions about Canadian intrigue.

> I'm convinced that if a survey were done, it would return an overwhelming answer that the Canadian public thinks the Super Bowl is grossly over-covered in all media, and should be cut down considerably in coverage, or eliminated. Anyone interested, let'em watch it on U.S. TV. Let'em buy the *New York Times*.

Young concluded that overdone coverage of the Super Bowl was 'cheating the youth of Canada' and that the resources should be directed at covering Canadian sport. Young stopped short of a demand that restricted all coverage of American sport because, in his mind, the World Series, big prize-fights and horse racing were at least entertaining.[21] Still, Young's column represents a common Canadian nationalist's plea to ignore the Super Bowl.

Young was far from alone. Among the Canadian sports media cohort, the Super Bowl was reduced to rubbish, particularly when compared to the Grey Cup. Jim Taylor's column in the *Vancouver Province* placed the Grey Cup upon a pedestal.

> It is not the Super Bowl. For this, we make no apologies. The Super Bowl is a football game dropped in the middle of a week-long party-cum-brainwashing, a marvellous melding of marketing and technology screened around the world for fees that could bankroll emerging nations. Some day they'll forget to play the game. Hardly anyone will notice. The Grey Cup game is … well, ours.

Taylor went on to lambaste Canadians who refused to get behind his message and wrote that it was a 'national curse' not to properly support domestic inventions. He finished his column, locked in-step with his Canadian sport reporter fraternity as the last bastions of a noble tradition against those who would ignore or export the CFL brand. 'Canadian football as we know it is over. Oh, we'll fight, some of us. We'll stand on the ramparts throwing editorial darts while the people who run our game continue to sell it down the river'.[22]

Canadian media depicted the Grey Cup as an important national event with unifying properties for a country split along cultural and linguistic lines. Located in the nexus of French–English divide, the *Montreal Gazette* remarked that the Super Bowl, 'supposedly the *ne plus ultra* of professional football' was meaningless to Canadians while the Grey Cup was culturally relevant: '… but trite as it sounds, the East-West Grey Cup rivalry has contributed to national unity'.[23] Beyond its ability to bring the country together in shared experience, the Grey Cup had a particularly nationalistic flair in an increasingly globalized world. In an editorial, the *Windsor Star* remarked:

> Despite the changes that will happen anyway because of the economy and our evolving society, the Grey Cup will remain one of the times during the year when, as a nation, we can let our hair down and just celebrate our uniqueness, and yes, maybe our silliness … Anything that faintly smells of American imperialism gets Canadians riled up faster than it takes a wide receiver to run a post pattern. … The Grey Cup is, was, and always will be our game, even if most of the players are American, and even if both teams, heaven forbid, someday are American. It's all ours and we'll keep it, thank you very much.[24]

Canadian roots and sentiments of vaguely or non-defined 'pure Canadiana' peppered many of the articles and columns that addressed the Grey Cup's value to national culture and served as powerful persuasion that it was more than simply a football game; more than simply a trophy. This loaded messaging was an appeal for Canadian sport fans to embrace the CFL, and by extension, the Grey Cup, for the sake of the league's survival. The implication was to value Canada's meritorious sport and to avoid the dazzling deception offered by the Super Bowl's glitz. Chris Zelkovich of the *Toronto Star* contended that

> while the fact that almost every Grey Cup is a thriller is a major factor in drawing viewers, there's another factor at work. In an era when Canadian institutions are crumbling, it's still comforting to take part in a game that is played nowhere else in the world. It's truly ours.[25]

What could cause the CFL and the Grey Cup to crumble? The obvious answer from the Canadian sport media was NFL-aligned Americans with aspirations of expansion into strategic Canadian marketplaces.[26] It was a familiar narrative, as old as the American Revolution. American concepts were inherently threatening. A significant reason why the NFL, and by extension the Super Bowl, was met with hostility by some Canadians was that it appeared as a threat to the CFL. As early as 1960, concerns of NFL expansion into Canada were publicly reported.[27] Loyalists to Canadian football, sport media chief among them, were as obstinate as they seemed baffled. Long-time *Globe and Mail* columnist Marty York looked to the future with despair:

> And so some day, if the NFL does indeed invade Toronto and other Canadian markets, there likely will be no more CFL football to kick around. In the meantime, though, the CFL is still breathing and it is desperately clinging to life. And, for all its zaniness, silliness, inept marketing and image problems, the plain truth is that it still provides considerably more entertainment than NFL football.[28]

In the early 1990s, the American threat to the CFL was not limited to possible NFL expansion. In a move that proved temporary and unsuccessful, the CFL expanded into several American markets that the league believed to be underserviced by the NFL.[29] The *Washington Post* speculated that the CFL would be wise to lose its Canadian-content rules for the sake of positive league attendance and increased media exposure, 'but the old-guard Canadian fans – who waved upside-down American flags and pelted Baltimore players with snowballs in Winnipeg – view Baltimore's success as a precursor to the demise of the CFL as they know it'.[30]

When possible NFL expansion into Canada was rumoured, Canadian scribes bemoaned the death of the CFL. When speculation of CFL southern expansion arose, the same media decried such plans out of fear that the Canadian game would become Americanized. As far as Canadian media were concerned, any involvement with the United States was a threat. Scott Feschuk of the *Globe and Mail* warned his Canadian readership in 1991 that reliance on the United States for the CFL's survival came with significant costs. Among them, the Canadian content of rosters would be disappear and that the Grey Cup game would no longer be played on Canadian soil.[31]

Notions of the Americanization of football in Canada became particularly acute at historical moments that emphasized or stressed the Can-Am relationship. Over the course of the North American Free Trade debates in Canada in the late 1980s, special attention was paid to the status of cultural industries in Canada and what assurances they would receive that would ensure their survival. While the discussion centred on the subsidies and protections that should be dedicated to the struggling television, film, music, and publishing industries, the *Montreal Gazette* wondered about the CFL:

> Back in the mid-'70s, Canadian cultural and economic nationalists flew up in arms over the attempt to bring a World (i.e. U.S.) Football League team to Toronto. Marc Lalonde and the federal Liberal government blocked that insidious attempt to undermine Canadian culture. But in the very week Canada was again succumbing to Super Bowl hype, Canadian nationalists who were worried about free trade never uttered a peep about the possible demise of the CFL.[32]

Media outlets argued that the CFL, and the Grey Cup by extension, not only needed protection, but also deserved it. Canadian sports writers espoused a common narrative that the Grey Cup provided a far higher entertainment value than the Super Bowl. These statements were usually based on style of game, total offence and narrower margins of victory. One of the first mentions of the Grey Cup advantage was the *Globe and Mail's* Andy O'Brien's column in 1973, conveniently titled 'Canadian Football is Better', which boasted the 1972 Grey Cup in Hamilton was 'vastly superior' to the 1973 Super Bowl in Los Angeles. O'Brien wrote that this realization surprised some Canadians who had been 'brainwashed' into thinking the 'grossly exaggerated' NFL game was better.[33] O'Brien's labour was typical of the Canadian sport reporter on this debate – one of proselytization. The Canadian sport fan, plagued with national cultural insecurity, required a gridiron conversion to understand that their national game was more worthy.

Canadian media also believed that their audience should not simply take the word of the press corps as the only proof that the Canadian version was better. It enlisted players from the CFL to help with the conversion. 'If people would just sit back and assess what they are seeing, fewer Canadians would be professing preference for the NFL brand of football', Sean McKeown, a Canadian-born offensive tackle with the Toronto Argonauts, told the *Toronto Star*. The newspaper reported that

> he [McKeown] also made the obvious comparison between the Super Bowl Bore and the Grey Cup nailbiters. But McKeown knows the downside of the CFL all too well. He was a first-round draft choice of the Calgary Stampeders in 1984 and was with them in '85, when the Stampeders came within a blocked kick of folding.[34]

This message was a familiar refrain for the Canadian sport media who so staunchly supported the CFL. Their nation possessed a league cursed with a superior but underappreciated and underfunded product.

The Canadian media reinforced this message by the addition of other voices that supported its cause – particularly American ones with NFL experience. The *Toronto Star* used the words of Heisman Trophy winner Doug Flutie after his Toronto Argonauts captured the 1996 Grey Cup:

> Absolutely the truest statement about Sunday's wonderful Grey Cup game was uttered by Doug Flutie moments after Toronto's stirring 43-37 victory over Edmonton. Flutie's sentiments, echoed continually by others, suggest Super Bowls are never like this, that the NFL could never produce a championship spectacle that begins to compare. Absolutely bang-on correct .... It has been this way for 10, for 20, probably for 30 years.[35]

Three years after Flutie's remarks, the *Toronto Star* boasted the

> Grey Cup is a national treasure, the one sporting event we can count on to live up to the hype, a wondrous escape at the onset of winter. The Super Bowl – that much-ballyhooed event south of the 49th – is an overblown, all-bark-and-no-bite imitation of the real thing. The Super Bore, Super Blowout.

To substantiate its claims, the *Star* used the Grey Cup's smaller margin of victory as statistical proof that the game was better than the Super Bowl. While only eight Super Bowls have been decided by seven points or fewer, nearly half (15 of 33) the Grey Cups since 1966 have been won by a converted touchdown or less.[36] Jim Taylor of the *Vancouver Province* also leaned on statistics as quantifiable proof of Grey Cup superiority.

> Personally, I loved Super Bowl XXIV. It was the best advertisement Canadian football could ever get, and it didn't cost even one of the dollars the CFL doesn't have. San Francisco 55, Denver 10. ... The past three Super Bowl games have produced 153 points, with winning margins of 32, four and 45 points. The last three Grey Cup games have produced 200 points, with winning margins of two, one and three points. Two of the three Super Bowls were settled shortly after, 'Oh, say, can you see'.[37]

On the occasions when the Super Bowl provided an entertaining game, Canadian media attributed it to some sort of astronomical fluke. The *Hamilton Spectator* opined after Super Bowl XXX in 1996:

> The moon must be in in the seventh house and Jupiter aligned with Mars. How else to explain what happened on every television in America last night? People tuned in to the Super Bowl and a Grey Cup broke out. Hold enough of the darn things, and throw enough billion-dollar hype at innocent bystanders and every once in a while, you get something that lives up – if only partially – to advance notice.[38]

To add to the echo chamber, newspapers printed letters to the editor that matched their claims of Grey Cup supremacy. Reader John Velchak wrote the *Toronto Star*: 'If, as some people claim, the NFL is so much better than the CFL, why then is the Super Bowl always such a boring, predictable Sleeper Bowl? …. Give me the excitement of the unpredictable Grey Cup.'[39] Fellow reader Scott Rehill supported those thoughts in the *Star*:

> I just felt I had to write to let it be known how bored I was watching the supposedly superior NFL's Super Bowl …. The playoffs might be exciting, but isn't the Super Bowl supposed to be climactic and not anticlimactic?[40]

High school student Craig Skinner complained to the *Ottawa Citizen* about the lack of excitement provide by Super Bowl XXIX: 'This year, the game was about as predictable as a WWF wrestling match … Basically, the Super Bowl is a Super Bore'.[41] In a letter to the editor printed in the *Globe and Mail*, Clint Wood wrote:

> The Canadian Football League is not a bad league, but when the media started embedding the idea that it is poorly played, the people frowned upon it. We aren't Americans, so let's stop being influenced by them so heavily. We need a culture we can call our own!'[42]

The criticism is insightful as it faults Canadian news media for the perpetuation of the Super Bowl hype at the expense of the Grey Cup. In some ways, the reader's comments were aligned with individual sports reporters, most notably Scott Young, who felt newspaper editors created Super Bowl ballyhoo and did not merely satisfy reader interest.

The Super Bowl clearly cannot be claimed by Canada but domestic sport media has found methods over the years to find Canadiana in the American championship – even if the connections appear somewhat tenuous. It has been standard practice over the years in Canadian sport reportage to provide extra exposure for not only Canadian-born players and coaches for making it to the Super Bowl, but also any former CFL players or coaches, whatever their nationality. This interest was particularly evident with the 1969 version of the Minnesota Vikings that were defeated by the Kansas City Chiefs in Super Bowl IV. Upon the defeat of his Edmonton Eskimos in the CFL playoffs, head coach Neill Armstrong resigned and assumed a defensive consultant's role with the Vikings who were in mid-season. Under the headline, 'More Canadiana for Minnesotans' the *Globe and Mail* pointed out how Armstrong had joined general manager Jim Finks (former general manager, head coach and player with the Calgary Stampeders), head coach Bud Grant (former head coach and player with the Winnipeg Blue Bombers), and quarterback Joe Kapp (formerly of the British Columbia Lions) as the Canadian contingent on the Vikings. That none of the four former-CFLers were actually Canadian either escaped the notice of the newspaper or was deemed too unimportant to mention.[43] Support for Kapp was particularly strong in Vancouver after he led the British Columbia Lions to their only Grey Cup win in 1964. In advance of his Super Bowl start, more than 3,000 Lions fans contributed 25-cents each to have their name attached to a telegram of well wishes to Kapp with the proceeds donated to a local Vancouver charity.[44] Through the promotion of players and coaches with a CFL past that had blossomed in the NFL, the insinuation was that the CFL was a worthy league with great talent that required further observation and appreciation.

The Canadian game was not simply one of underestimated talent, its media supporters chimed, but also owed some of its greatness to the enlightened design of the game. The Canadian-style three-down approach favoured more passing plays and the wider field ensured that receivers were more difficult to cover. Again, the Canadian media used the words of a well-regarded American to spread the word. Marv Levy, who coached in two Grey Cups with the Montreal Alouettes and four Super Bowls with the Buffalo Bills was referenced in the article as a 'widely experienced and erudite observer of the game', lauded the Canadian rules – including the rouge, a scoring play unique to Canadian football that awards a single point to the kicking team for punts and missed field goal attempts that are not returned from the end zone.[45]

The rhetoric of superior design was heightened during discussions of CFL expansion in the United States for fear the game would become more Americanized and the Grey Cup would more closely resemble the Super Bowl. In an open letter to CFL Commissioner, Donald Crump, Jim Taylor of the *Vancouver Province* wrote:

> Stop talking about changing CFL rules so the game will look more like the American version. I know you mean well and you're looking at it dispassionately as a route to survival. I know you're telling yourself that a little tinkering won't change Canadian football life as we know it …. That ours is the better game with the better rules and the better field …. Besides, who made the U.S. rule-makers God? …. I think that's the part that riles me most, Don, this idea that somehow we must tailor our game to fit America's perception of how the game should be played. The CFL started before the NFL. The Grey Cup is old enough to be the Super Bowl's great-grandfather. If there's so much American interest in joining the Canadian league, let them play our rules. Tell them to widen their field, put in a 55-yard line, extend their end zones and play three-down football. If they say no, tell them to take a hike. Just once, let's be proud enough of something that's uniquely Canadian to keep it that way.[46]

Still not convinced of the Grey Cup's superiority to American mass culture? The media steered the conversation towards the bawdy, perpetuating a myth that was true in the mid-1980s but not in 2003 when *CanWest News* printed a thinly veiled reference to genitalia: 'So what if our balls are bigger?'[47] To be fair to the report, the CFL, as a league, was guilty of extending this misinformation when, upon hard financial times in 1996, the league adopted the edgy slogan *Our Balls Are Bigger* – a desperate, if inaccurate, appeal to gutter masculinity.[48]

Beyond the rules, the media in Canada spoke too about the weather conditions that added mystique to their Grey Cups and tested the fortitude of the players – something the Super Bowl could not boast since those games were almost always played in sunny or domed environs. Their identity as a nation of hardy Northerners became a central theme in the development of a Canadian national identity in the mid-nineteenth century. Nationalists employed climate and geography as more than simply national unifiers. There was also an exclusivity created by the Canadian environment. The Canadian 'Northerness' was continually, and favourably, compared with the 'Southerness' of the United States.[49] The *Edmonton Sun's* Terry Jones, who had covered 31 Grey Cups and 15 Super Bowls at the time of this pronouncement,

We take some kind of perverse pride in our bad weather. You talk to old-timers and they'll tell you about the Fog Bowl, the Mud Bowl, the Ice Bowl. It's really remarkable. It's a celebration of the sport, the event, the culture, everything.[50]

Canadian sport media insisted that the Grey Cup was not only a better game than the Super Bowl, but a better event. Dave Perkins of the *Toronto Star* praised the folksy appeal of the Grey Cup and criticized the Super Bowl for it out-of-touch lavishness.

Take it from someone who has been to about 10 of the overblown U.S. championship games, seldom leaving impressed. The Grey Cup, bless its Canadian heart and soul, is the fans' game. The Super Bowl is all about corporations and excess.

Perkins recommended the tradition-laden Calgary Pancake Breakfast as well as the inexpensively priced nightspots such as Riderville and Tigertown (at a modest $5 or $10 to get in, Perkins wondered, who can resist?). Perkins declared: 'This is the one big difference between Canada's game and the big one down south. Fans will always be front and centre at the Grey Cup, rather than a necessary afterthought.'[51]

The *Globe and Mail's* Stephen Brunt, at the time of his comments an attendee of 15 Super Bowls and 15 Grey Cups, remarked that the seeming grassroots nature of the Grey Cup was part of its charm, which was particularly evident if the game was hosted on the prairies (in Canadian terms, due to fan dedication, a football holy land). 'The Super Bowl, they put on all these bells and whistles, it's like a carnival coming to town. The (Grey Cup) is different. It's smaller obviously, it's more modest. It honestly kind of grows out of the local culture.'[52] Brunt's comments are steeped in judgement – smaller is better – which contradicted the enormity and extravagance of the Super Bowl.

The Canadian media wanted readers to know about this stark contrast, which was apparent even from the early years. Bud Grant, who coached in six Grey Cup games with the Winnipeg Blue Bombers and four Super Bowl with the Minnesota Vikings, was quoted in the *Globe and Mail*: 'In Canada, it was always good to be a real part of the action. But here, except for news conferences – and they are only with reporters – there's no contact with the general public. It's just too big.'[53]

'Too big' was not a worry at the Grey Cup. Matthew Sekeres of the *National Post* referred to it as 'charmingly small potatoes' in comparison to the Super Bowl. Sekeres wrote about easy and affordable access to Canada's main football celebration: 'Without much effort, you can share a beer with commissioner Tom Wright in a downtown tent or mosh dance with Hamilton Tiger-Cats quarterback Danny McManus at one of the many free parties put on by the league's nine franchises'. He cautioned Canadians that the Super Bowl experience was very expensive and the best events were invitation-only and off-limits to the average fan.[54]

The media continued to keep the monetary comparisons in print as a way of highlighting the differences between the two sport showcases. The high-priced Super Bowl, however, was not given a narrative of envious opulence as much as outlandish expense. Ed Willes of the *Vancouver Province* reported in 2004 that a fan paid $25,000 for his Super Bowl experience. 'You couldn't spend $25,000 at a Grey Cup unless you purchased a minority share in one of the teams', Willes criticized. To further explain how the CFL's pricing and salaries were more in step with reality than those stateside the reporter quoted British Columbia Lions President Bob Ackles: 'I think fans identify with the guy who's making sixty grand a year and who's busting his ass. I think they get tired when they hear people complaining about making $1.8 million.'[55]

When it came to the scale of the festivities, however, there was mixed messaging from Canadian media that, on one hand, lauded the folksy appeal of the Grey Cup when compared to the mass hysteria of the Super Bowl but, on the other hand, looked to the party to the south with envy. In 1995, the *Vancouver Province* chastised CFL personnel for their delay in embracing Super Bowl tactics. When a small contingent from the Argonauts, led by President Bob Nicholson and director of communication Dave Watkins, visited Miami for Super Bowl XXIX, the *Province* criticized their measure as 15 years too late.

> It is one of football's great mysteries that as successful as the over-bloated Super Bowl has become, the ever-struggling CFL has never seen the need to come down to one and find out what the NFL is doing to sell itself and its normally boring championship game. Surely, even the folks who can't get the National Football League's initials out of their mouths without it becoming a snarl, could see some value in borrowing one or two of the less outlandish things the NFL does to entertain people.[56]

Perhaps the most pronounced discrepancy in the competing football celebrations was in the musical acts that performed at the festivities. In 1999, for example, the *National Post* defended the lack of star power at the Grey Cup. The Canadian championship featured bands little known south of the border, including the Parablegics, Hawg Wild, Skruj MacDuhk, the Arrogant Worms and Big Dave McLean (only the latter three even have Wikipedia entries)[57] while the Super Bowl featured music legends recognizable not only in the US but in Canada and everywhere else in the world – Kiss, Stevie Wonder, and Cher. The newspaper suggested that in their musical choices for halftime fanfare, Canadians were 'true to their roots' and not swayed by style over substance.[58] Earlier that decade, Stephen Brunt of the *Globe and Mail* was certain that the CFL was on the brink of selling its soul in the name of Super Bowl-like promotion. Brunt's accusations were largely levied at the Argonauts, who were set to host the 1992 and 1993 Grey Cups, their monstrous new state-of-the-art SkyDome and cosmopolitan Torontonians who Brunt felt saw themselves as too refined for the folksy appeal of Grey Cup traditions.

> Like the Super Bowl, it will become primarily a television-driven exercise, a 'culmination event' (as the WWF calls Wrestlemania), an excuse to squeeze the maximum exposure and maximum dollars out of a single football game. Unfortunately, there aren't enough Winnipegs left for it to be any other way. The CFL can evolve or die. Doing things the way they've always been done, counting on the rest of the country to again feel the way they do here, just isn't an option for a league struggling to survive. The Argonauts' brass, the people who brought you Mariel Hemingway and the Blues Brothers for the season opener, have already begun booking acts for Grey Cup week, 1992. It promises to be a star-studded, world-class, high-gloss kind of affair, just the ticket to make the jaded denizens of the metropolis aware that something's doing. Maybe they'll stick in a pancake breakfast, or a pep rally, or put Mariel on a horse just for nostalgia's sake. But everyone there will know from the start that Grey Cup LXXX represents a whole new ballgame.[59]

Perhaps the starkest difference between the two national fan-bases resides in the almost complete American ignorance of the existence of the Grey Cup. For all of attention Canadians devote to the Super Bowl – either as unabashed fans, jingoist detractors or curious onlookers – Americans spend very little effort in their consideration of the Grey Cup. In some ways the pro-Grey Cup chauvinism espoused by Canadian sport journalists counter American ignorance and arrogance about the CFL and its title game. The *New York Times*, in an attempt to educate its readership about football in Canada, referred to the Grey Cup in 1969 as 'Canada's Super Bowl'.[60] At the time of the article, the Super Bowl had been awarded three times and the Grey Cup game had been played 60 times. It is doubtful supporters of the Canadian game viewed their storied national football championship as an emulation of its American counterpart, still in its infancy. Jake Gaudaur, CFL commissioner 1968–1984, told the *Globe and Mail* that Super Bowl organizers learned from the established Grey Cup rather than the other way around.[61] The descriptor 'Canada's Super Bowl' has been frequently used by the American press in the years that followed and demonstrates a lack of understanding of nuance to Canadian culture and sensitivities.

Some Canadian media members bristled at the extended honorific of Super Bowl victory – world champion. Veteran *Globe and Mail* columnist Dick Beddoes commented on the 'gall' of his American counterparts for their reference to the Super Bowl as the 'world's championship' in 1970. Beddoes suggested that the winner of the Super Bowl (who turned out to be the Kansas City Chiefs) should have to defeat the Ottawa Rough Riders, defending Grey Cup champions, before such a boast had merit.[62]

In 2001, sport scholars Christopher R. Martin and Jimmie L. Reeves argued in an essay titled 'The Whole Word Isn't Watching (But We Thought They Were): The Super Bowl and U.S. Solipsism,' that claims of the American football title game qualified as a global spectacle had been wildly exaggerated. They insisted that while the game had immense importance within the United States, hardly anyone outside of the US watched the game or cared about the spectacle. They concluded it did not meet the criteria necessary to qualify as a global mega-event. Whether or not that remains valid 15 years later is up for debate. What is clear from ratings and other indicators of cultural phenomena, however, is that Canadians have fully embraced the Super Bowl. In 1992, Larry Humber wondered in the *Globe and Mail*, 'Are Canadians losing interest in the Grey Cup? And is that interest swinging to the Super Bowl?'[63] It was not the first or last time that those questions were posed. Perhaps counter to the musings and fears of Canadian sport journalists there is no or little correlation between the two questions. Why does the Super Bowl have to triumph at the Grey Cup's expense? There is some season overlap, but could not a Canadian football fan have room in heart and mind for both games, spaced more than two months apart? Academics and theorists believe it is possible. Historian Paul Rutherford argued that mass culture from the United States 'in itself does not pose, and never has posed, a direct threat to the Canadian identity, because consumers have "read" its message through a special lens made in Canada.'[64] To further that point, Aniko Bodroghkozy insisted that 'rather than seeing Canadian audiences of American mass entertainment as duped by and subjected to the imperializing strategies of these texts and their producers, audiences negotiate with and struggle against the texts in active and self-interested ways.' Ultimately, Canadian sport reporters have not credited Canadian sport fans with the ability to absorb the Super Bowl intelligently. Instead the media outlets generously polish the Grey Cup with praise and caution anyone who will listen that the Super Bowl is little more than fool's gold. In doing so, Canadian media continue a tradition of denigration of American mass culture. More than a century ago Canadian media lamented baseball's unwarranted popularity in Canada as an agent of corruption from the south. The press of that day saw it as their national duty to divert sport-minded Canadians away from American trifles and towards pursuits more deserving of their attention and admiration. The Canadian sport press corps of more modern times have pursued a very similar path as they assailed the Super Bowl and championed the Grey Cup.

Despite warnings from domestic media, it is undeniable that Canadians want to watch the Super Bowl. 'Canadian viewers appear to crave myths and ritual experiences that encourage a sense of cultural collectivity whether such experiences are created at home or not', Bodroghkozy concluded.[65] The Super Bowl certainly qualifies in that respect. Media scholar John Fiske wrote that people are skilled at taking *their* commodities and turning them into *our* culture.[66] Canadians are well-practised Super Bowl revellers and it is reasonable to assume their national cultural sensibilities have allowed them to make the Super Bowl their own.

The Canadian Super Bowl experience, however, moves ever closer to that of the United States. Against the wishes of Canadian broadcasters who will see revenues limited, the Canadian Radio-Television and Telecommunications Commission (CRTC) have sided with viewers who lodged a complaint in regard to the simultaneous substitution practice employed by Canadian broadcasters carrying foreign content. 'Simsub', as this practice is known, allows for the airing of revenue-generating Canadian-sourced commercials in place of those aired in the United States. Only about 100 of the 9 million Canadian Super Bowl viewers felt their Super Bowl experience was harmed by not witnessing the American commercials that have become part of the larger Super Bowl experience, but it was enough to move the CRTC in their favour. Bell, who owns the Canadian broadcast rights in English (CTV) and French (RDS), has said they will file an appeal.[67]

What perhaps gets lost in the Super Bowl's standing as a mega sporting event in Canada is that the CFL, in some meaningful ways, appears as healthy as it has ever been. The findings of an Angus Reid survey focused on sport fan interest in Canada was reported by the *Halifax Chronicle-Herald* shortly after the 2014 Grey Cup. The poll revealed that 47% of those surveyed agreed 'the Grey Cup is an important part of Canadian culture and identity'. A further 6% were more enthusiastic, agreeing that it 'defines Canadian culture and identity'. The CFL trailed only the NHL in Canadian interest. The NHL carries support of 40% and the CFL 21%. The number became impressive when it is considered that Major League Baseball was third at 18% and the NFL only fourth at 17%.[68] Perhaps it is time that Canadian sport media realizes that the Grey Cup does not need to be rescued and it can coexist alongside its American counterpart, the Super Bowl.

Notes

1. It is worth noting that the CFL attempted American expansion in the 1990s with several short-lived American franchises. For a variety of reasons that ranged from 'quirky' rules to unknown players, the league never gained a foothold in the United States, despite its willingness to go into what it believed were underserved markets. Readers interested in learning more information on the expansion efforts should consult Craig Greenham and Ben Andrews, *Canadian Football on the World Stage*, http://theallrounder.co/2016/09/29/canadian-football-on-the-world-stage/. The NFL has had brief flirtations with Toronto as a possible expansion or relocation destination. Toronto served as surrogate host for Buffalo Bills home games but the second five-year hosting contract was terminated early by the Bills. Please consult the CBC news story (http://www.cbc.ca/news/canada/toronto/buffalo-bills-to-cease-playing-home-games-in-toronto-1.2858780) for more details.
2. Harvard University and McGill University played a series of games in 1874 that are believed to be, if not the source, certainly instrumental to development of football in both countries. Reader interested in more information are directed to Frank Cosentino, *Canadian Football: The Grey Cup Years* (Toronto: Musson, 1969), 13. This reference is cited by more recent sources, including Don Morrow and Kevin Wamsley, *Sport in Canada: A History* (Toronto: Oxford University Press, 2013), 222.

3. For an updated version of CFL roster regulations as it applies to foreign players, please consult http://www.cfl.ca/game-rule-ratio/.

4. Readers interested in learning about the NFL's financial success are directed to Michael Oriard, *Brand NFL: Making and Selling America's Favorite Sport* (Chapel Hill: University of North Carolina Press, 2010). Richard Crepeau, *NFL: A History of America's New National Pastime* (Urbana: University of Illinois Press, 2014) also explores the NFL's emergence from a relatively obscure football organization to an economic titan.

5. John Kryk, 'More Canadians watched the Super Bowl per capita than Americans,' *Toronto Sun*, 7 February 2015. http://www.torontosun.com/2015/02/07/more-canadians-per-capita-watched-super-bowl-than-americans.

6. Richard Collins, *Culture, Communication, and National Identity: The Case of Canadian Television* (Toronto: University of Toronto Press, 1990), 205–14.

7. Paul Rutherford, 'Made in America: The Problem of Mass Culture in Canada,' in David H. Flaherty and Frank E. Manning (eds), *The Beaver Bites Back? American Popular Culture in Canada* (Montreal: McGill-Queen's University Press, 1993), 270.

8. Bodroghkozy further argues that the Canadian media has been heavily influenced by the political economy writings of historian Harold Innis whose metropolis-hinterland thesis suggests that Canada (the hinterland) is culturally and economically dependent on the United States (the metropolis). Innis' thesis is well-known in Canadian historical circles and has been heavily utilized. It is unclear why Bodroghkozy believes, however, that the Canadian media was/is staunch supporters of Innis. Aniko Bodroghkozy, 'As Canadian as Possible: Anglo-Canadian Popular Culture and the American Other,' in Henry Jenkins, Tara McPherson, and Jane Shattuc (eds), *Hop on Pop?* (Durham, NC: Duke University Press, 2003), 571.

9. Seymour Lipset, *Continental Divide* (New York: Routledge, 1990), 53.

10. Ibid.

11. Colin Howell, *Blood, Sweat and Cheers: Sport and the Making of Modern Canada* (Toronto: University of Toronto Press, 2001), 42.

12. J.L. Granatstein, *Yankee Go Home? Canadians and Anti-Americanism* (Toronto: HarperCollins Publishers, 1996), 76.

13. Reginald C. Stuart, *Dispersed Relations: Americans and Canadians in Upper North America* (Baltimore: Johns Hopkins University Press, 2007), 30.

14. Humber, *Diamonds of the North: A Concise History of Baseball in Canada*, 32.

15. *Victoria Times*, 13 May 1905.

16. Samuel E. Moffett, *The Americanization of Canada* (Toronto: University of Toronto Press, 1972), 109–10.

17. A detailed account of this tour can be found in James Elfer, *The Tour to End All Tours: The Story of Major League Baseball's 1913–1914 World Tour* (Lincoln: University of Nebraska Press, 2003).

18. *Time*, 22 September 1924.

19. Readers interested in learning more about athletic and cultural phenomena in the United States should consult Mark Dyreson and Jaime L. Schultz, eds., *American National Pastimes – A History* (London: Routledge, 2015).

20. Moffett, *The Americanization of Canada*, 109.

21. Scott Young, 'Let's Button Up on the Super Bowl,' *Globe and Mail*, 12 January 1977, 31.

22. Jim Taylor, 'Today Marks CFL Change of Heart,' *Vancouver Province*, 27 November 1994, A83.

23. Dick Bacon, 'The Grey Cup: From the Mud Bowl to the Fog Bowl, There's Nothing Quite like it,' *Montreal Gazette*, 29 November 1986, D1.

24. 'Whither the CFL?,' *Windsor Star*, 29 November 1994, A6.

25. Chris Zelkovich, 'Grey Cup a Special Affair,' *Toronto Star*, 25 November 2000, C1.

26. 'NFL Commissioner Rozelle Lists Toronto as site for Franchise in Expanded League,' *Globe and Mail*, 4 June 1965, 39.

27. 'U.S. League Expansion Plans Fail to Ruffle CFL Officials,' *Globe and Mail*, 12 May 1960, 29.

28. Marty York, 'Zany CFL should be Enjoyed while it Lasts.' *The Globe and Mail*, 21 July 1995, C12.

29. Notions of CFL expansion into the United States dates back to 1972 when New York real estate developer Robert Schmertz petitioned the CFL for an expansion franchise to play out of Yankee Stadium. Schmertz owned the New England Whalers of the renegade World Hockey Association (WHA) and co-owned the Boston Celtics of the National Basketball Association (NBA). Previous to that investment, however, he was a founding co-owner of the expansion Portland Traiblazers in the NBA in 1970. Schmertz threatened the CFL that if they did not grant him an expansion franchise that he would simply create his own league and put them out of business.
30. Saul Wisma, 'Grey Cup is a U.S.-Canada Border War,' *Washington Post*, 27 November 1994, 1.
31. Scott Feschuk, 'Grey Cup Weathers U.S. Touches,' *Globe and Mail*, 29 November 1991, A1.
32. Nick Auf Der Maur, 'Our Cultural Nationalists Lost in Super Bowl Hype,' *Montreal Gazette*, 27 January 1986, A2.
33. Andy O'Brien, 'Canadian Football is Better,' *Globe and Mail*, 8 July 1973, A18.
34. Milt Dunnell, 'CFL Homebrews Prefer Their Brand to NFL,' *Toronto Star*, 2 July 1990, D4.
35. Dave Perkins, 'Great Grey Cup Games no Help to CFL's Plight,' *Toronto Star*, 26 November 1996, C7.
36. Rob Klovance, 'Grey Cup Usually the Super Game,' *Vancouver Sun*, 24 November 1999, F12.
37. Jim Taylor, 'Stop Apologizing and Start Celebrating,' *Vancouver Province*, 30 January 1990, 53.
38. Steve Milton, 'Finally, a Super Bowl Game that's Really Super,' *Hamilton Spectator*, 29 January 1996, D12.
39. 'Sleeper Bowl no Match for Exciting Grey Cup,' *Toronto Star*, 31 January 1987, B3.
40. 'Who Needs American TV?' *Toronto Star*, 27 February 1988, S3.
41. 'Nothing "super" About it,' *Ottawa Citizen*, 2 February 1995, B4.
42. 'Cultural Integrity,' *Globe and Mail*, 9 February 1981, S9.
43. 'More Canadiana for Minnesotans as Neill Armstrong joins Vikings,' *Globe and Mail*, 16 December 1969, 35.
44. 'Canadians Back Kapp,' *Washington Post*, 11 January 1970, D2.
45. O'Brien, 'Canadian Football is Better.'
46. Jim Taylor, 'Don't Allow the CFL to Lose its Identity,' *Vancouver Province*, 24 January 1991, 71.
47. Greg Harder, 'Grey Cup Uniquely Canadian,' *CanWest News*, 14 November 2003, 1.
48. The CFL has an extensive website devoted the ball size and its history throughout the league. Readers who would like more information about CFL balls should consult https://cfldb.ca/faq/equipment/.
49. Readers interested in a synthesis of the northern character component in early Canadian national identity should consult Craig Greenham, 'Outfields, Infields and Battlefields: How the Great War Influenced Professional Baseball in Canada,' (PhD diss., The University of Western Ontario, 2010), 68–71.
50. Harder, 'Grey Cup Uniquely Canadian,' 1.
51. Dave Perkins, 'Grey Cup is a Super Event for Canadians,' *Toronto Star*, 20 November 2007, S1.
52. Harder, 'Grey Cup Uniquely Canadian,' 1.
53. Christie Blatchford, 'Bud Says Game "Scary,"' *Globe and Mail*, 7 January 1977, 26.
54. Matthew Sekeres, 'Super Bowl? Yes, but it's Super Exclusive,' *National Post*, 31 January 2004, S1.
55. Ed Willes, 'Grey Cup has Human Face; Super Bowl does Not,' *CanWest News*, 18 November 2004, 1.
56. Kent Gilchrist, 'CFL Missing the Showboat,' *Vancouver Province*, 29 January 1995, A71.
57. Those sites can be found at https://en.wikipedia.org/wiki/Scruj_MacDuhk; https://en.wikipedia.org/wiki/The_Arrogant_Worms and https://en.wikipedia.org/wiki/Big_Dave_McLean.
58. Scott Burnside, 'In the Battle for TV Ratings Supremacy, the Grey Cup and Super Bowl Fight to the Finish,' *National Post*, 30 January 1999, B2.
59. Stephen Brunt, 'Say Farewell to Traditional Grey Cup,' *Globe and Mail*, 20 November 1991, C6.
60. 'Canada's Super Bowl,' *New York Times*, 2 November 1969, 29.
61. Murray Campbell, 'Hype Surrounding Super Bowl Game Knows no Bounds,' *Globe and Mail*, 24 January 1987, 2.

62. Dick Beddoes, 'Vancouver had AFL Chance,' *Globe and Mail*, 13 January 1970, 30.
63. Larry Humber, 'It's a Super Test with Shades of Grey,' Globe and Mail, 25 November 1992, C7.
64. Rutherford, 'Made in America,' 280.
65. Bodroghkozy, 'As Canadian as Possible,' 574.
66. John Fiske, *Understanding Popular Culture* (Boston, MA: Unwin Hyman, 1989), 23.
67. Peter Miller, 'CRTC's Ruling on Canadian ads During the Super Bowl is a Fumble,' *Globe and Mail*, 6 February 2016, http://www.theglobeandmail.com/report-on-business/rob-commentary/crtcs-ruling-on-canadian-ads-during-the-super-bowl-is-a-fumble/article28615781/.
68. Chris Cochrane, 'CFL's Challenge is to Retain Young Fans,' *Halifax Chronicle-Herald*, 29 November 2014, C3.

Disclosure Statement

No potential conflict of interest was reported by the author.

Amerika: The Super Bowl and German Imagination

Lars Dzikus

ABSTRACT

The Super Bowl has played a central role in the diffusion of American football in Germany, as interviews with the 'founding fathers' of 'gridiron' football clubs and analysis of German media accounts reveal. American football and the Super Bowl have also played an important role in the construction of traditional German *Amerikabilder* – images, ideas, and symbols associated with America. German media rarely covered American football until the late 1970s. At that time, brief highlight shows of the Super Bowl on German television and broadcasts on the American Forces Network significantly contributed to the diffusion of American football and the emergence of an American football league in Germany in the late 1970s. In the process of covering the Super Bowl, German journalists reproduced Germany's double-headed *Amerikabild*: America as a model of modernity on the one hand, and as a violent, cultureless society on the other. The press further invoked historical clashes between German *Kultur* and the dreaded *Zivilisation* of the West. This exploration of the social processes surrounding the reception of the Super Bowl in Germany employs the theories of cultural globalization, migration, and electronic mediation developed by the anthropologist Arjun Appadurai to explain the complexities of contemporary global cultural flows.

Six–and-a-half minutes into the first quarter of Super Bowl 50, the Carolina Panthers, trailing the Denver Broncos by three points, tried to convert on a third and 10 back on their own 15-yard line. As Broncos pass rusher Von Miller sacked and stripped Carolina's quarterback Cam Newton, commentators on Germany's *SAT 1* television station enthusiastically exclaimed, 'Und da haben sie ihn. Das gibt's doch nicht! Touchdown Denver, nach super Defense! Der Showman wackelt! Cam Newton wackelt!' In their one-minute commentary of the live scenes and the ensuing replays, the commentators freely mix German and English, including the words touchdown, defence, show man, tackled, blindside, front side, and playbook, as well as the phrase 'sack-forced-fumble'. Clearly, the expectation was that the majority of the reported 1.78 million people watching the broadcast around 1:00am in Germany would be familiar with these English terms.[1]

Among the television audience were 1.3 million 'marketing-relevant' 14–49-year-old viewers, resulting in an overall market share of 36.1% and almost 50% in the target audience. At the end of the game at 4:22am, the ratings showed that 860,000 viewers – about the

81

population of San Jose, California – were still willing to forgo sleep – or had at least left their televisions on. The viewer ratings for the third quarter of the game, which aired around 3:00am local time, made the Super Bowl broadcast the station's third-highest rating for the day. Only a double feature of the American television series *Castle* attracted more viewers that Monday. Though German viewers added just over 1% to the American audience of nearly 112 million, the ratings caused one analyst to claim, 'America's largest sporting event made the jump from niche interest to fascination for an audience of millions in Germany'.[2] Although sport-media scholars Christopher Martin and Jimmie Reeves are correct in stating that the National Football League (NFL) notoriously, and possibly intentionally, overestimates global Super Bowl audiences – seemingly an effort to place the event and the United States in the centre of the sport universe – American football has developed a devoted niche following abroad.[3]

A number of scholars have pointed towards American exceptionalism and isolationism to explain the lack of popularity of association football in the United States and the marginal status of American football and baseball in Europe.[4] Dutch sport historian Maarten van Bottenburg, for example, discussed 'the cultural insignificance of [American] football in Europe despite the receptiveness of Europeans to American popular culture in general'. In 2003, he argued, 'in terms of players, spectators, and television audience, [American] football remains a minor sport in Europe at the present time'.[5] As of the turn of the twenty-first century, American football made up 1% of total television transmission time in Germany, compared to association football's 15%.[6] Van Bottenburg explained American football's failure in Europe as follows:

> Because football did not become the most popular sport in the United States until the second half of the 20th century, and there were no catalysts of diffusion present to help spread the sport before that time, football only started to gain a foothold in the European sport space after the basic layout of that space had already been determined.[7]

In Van Bottenburg's estimation, the NFL had placed too much emphasis on promoting the game as a commercial product and spectator sport, and not enough on developing active participation in the game, which could later be translated into viewership.

Arguably, Germany represents an exception to Van Bottenburg's thesis. Compared to other European countries, Germany has been quite receptive to American football as illustrated by the relative success of the NFL's spring league in the 1990s and early 2000s (known as World League of American Football, 1991–1992; World League, 1995–1997; NFL Europe, 1998–2005; and NFL Europa, 2005–2007) and grass-roots participation in Germany.[8] In regards to the latter, in 2015, the German Olympic Sports Confederation (Deutsche Olympische Sportbund, DSOB) counted 475 American football clubs and departments with 53,851 members. The sport ranked 36th among the largest 62 organizations under the umbrella of the DSOB. It followed the German triathlon union with close to 55,000 members and led jujutsu by about 3,000 members. The gridiron was clearly dwarfed by the almost seven million members of the German soccer federation (ranked first) and the nearly five million members of the German gymnastics federation (ranked second). The sport also trailed other American sports such as volleyball (430,093, ranked 15th) and basketball (191,882, ranked 18th), arguably the two most global sports with American origin. Yet, American football players outnumbered those who participated in ice hockey (24,722, ranked 40th), baseball and softball (23,364, ranked 44th), and rugby (13,542, ranked 51st).[9] As of 2012, according to the European Federation of American football:

Roughly every second person engaged into [*sic*] American Football within Europe stems from Germany. With 18,000 players Germany according to a recent [International Federation of American Football] IFAF survey is the world's most active nation regarding male senior tackle football behind the U.S. [and] slightly ahead of Japan.[10]

As a measure of achievement on the field, the German men's national team has played in each of the last five finals of the European championships, winning three of those tournaments. Currently, 9 of 22 (40%) European-born players active on NFL rosters are from Germany, outnumbering the contribution of any other European country. In comparison, in 2016, there are 9 German players in the NHL and 11 in the NBA. Two Germans have played in the Super Bowl: Markus Koch played in Super Bowl XXII for the Washington Redskins and Sebastian Vollmer won Super Bowl XLIX with the New England Patriots. In 2016, Moritz Böhringer reached another milestone by becoming the first German player to be drafted into the NFL directly out of the German–American football league without any high school or college experience.[11]

The relative openness of the German market for American football, as well as its resistance, might be explained by regarding (West) Germany as a *Sonderfall*, or special case, of cultural Americanization. Alexander Stephan, a scholar of German literature, summarized the *Sonderfall* argument in five main points. First, in search of a national identity following Germany's late unification in 1871 and the failure of the Weimar Republic, many Germans clung to traditional notions of *Geist* und *Kultur*, thus resisting Western *Zivilisation* and American consumer culture longer than its European neighbours. Second, Nazism, the Second World War, and the Holocaust, left Germany in a political, economic, moral, and symbolic void, as well as subject to an unprecedented re-education programme, which in West Germany was led by the American occupation forces. Third, throughout the cold war, West Germany continued to depend on its new American ally. The alliance brought with it the stationing of hundreds of thousands of Americans and their dependents. In some parts of Germany, this led to intense cross-cultural encounters. Fourth, after 1990 unified Germany had to redefine its former eastern and western allies, in ways not experienced by countries such as France, Britain, or Poland.[12] Arguably, all of these reasons make Germany a particular case to study the reception of the Super Bowl as a particularly American product. Van Bottenburg, too, acknowledged Germany's exceptional status: 'A fairly large audience for football only emerged in Germany, where the largest number of American troops had been stationed in the post-war decades', he observed.[13]

Van Bottenburg's initial analysis leaves many of the mechanisms through which American football diffused into late twentieth-century Germany obscure. In-depth interviews with the 'founding fathers' of American football in Germany and analysis of German media accounts help to illuminate why American football attracted, and repelled, particular German demographic cohorts. These sources also reveal the Super Bowl and *Amerika* as 'imagined worlds', to apply globalization scholar Arjun Appadurai's useful concept.[14] *Amerika*, in this context, is America as a locally imagined by Germans through the construction of a German *Amerikabilder*, or images, ideas, and symbols associated with America. Appadurai's conceptualization of the global cultural economy underscores the locally situated, fluid, and irregular reception of the Super Bowl in Germany.

The Super Bowl and *Amerikabilder*

Since the middle of the nineteenth century, Germans have developed dualistic conceptions of the United States as both a global peril and a promised land. A German newspaper correspondent in an 1837 story in *Augsburger Allgemeine Zeitung* trenchantly captured the negative view:

> What we Europeans dislike the most about the Americans are usually three things: that they don't have poetry, they love money, and they don't abolish negro slavery despite their principals of freedom and equality.[15]

According to this account, lack of *Kultur*, greed, and hypocrisy were three common stereotypes Germans harboured about Americans at the time. These notions became firmly woven into the tapestry of how Germans have viewed America ever since. Kaspar Maase, a German *Volkskunde* expert, asserts that the basic stereotypes appearing in the German imagination of America in the late twentieth century were already formalized by 1850. He identifies two major positions. In the early twentieth century, the educated middle class felt threatened by what it perceived as a levelling effect of the commercial orientation in American society deficient of real *Kultur*. On the other hand, the impression of the lower classes was characterized by a fundamentally hopeful attitude about the quality of life in the United States, a notion inherited from the previous century.[16]

Educated elites in Germany have had a history of praising German *Kultur* and its high esteem for intellectual and artistic work. The roots of the antithesis between *Zivilisation* and *Kultur* reach as far back as Emmanuel Kant (1724–1804), the German philosopher and founder of critical idealism, and Wilhelm von Humboldt (1767–1835), the reformer of Prussia's educational system.[17] Since the late eighteenth century, various forms of Romanticism in art and poetry expressed sentiments against the ideas of the Enlightenment juxtaposing fate, destiny, intuition, faith, and tradition, on the one side, against natural law, reason, logic, and progress, on the other.[18]

Historically, a number of German cultural critics have shared an aversion to liberalism, an ideology that they blamed as the principle cause for the coarsening of modern society and the source of such evils as materialism, democracy, and lack of political leadership. All of these maladies were seen as products of Western *Zivilisation*. While Germans believed that the character of *Kultur* was permanent, the qualities of Western *Zivilisation* were seen as transitory.[19] In the process of covering the Super Bowl, German journalists reproduced and reinforced Germany's double-headed *Amerikabild*. They depicted America as an ideal model of modernity on the one hand, and as a violent, cultureless society on the other. The press further invoked historical clashes between German *Kultur* and the dreaded *Zivilisation* of the West through Super Bowl commentaries. It is in this broader context that American football and the Super Bowl emerged in Germany.

The Super Bowl as Catalyst for the Diffusion of American Football in Germany

Super Bowl broadcasts were an instrumental catalyst in the relatively recent diffusion of American football to Germany. Although post-Second World War re-education measures had led to the incipient introduction of American sports of football and baseball in Germany, these efforts proved to be anaemic and did not result in the establishment of these sports.[20]

Ultimately, the introduction of gridiron football was the outcome of coincidences and personal initiatives. It was not until the late 1970s and early 1980s that the presence of American military personnel became a factor in the formation of permanent structures of American football in the form of clubs and federations. The proximity of most of the initial American football teams to large American military facilities indicates the significant role Americans had in the process.[21] Interviews with the German 'founding fathers' of American football reveal the critical roles the first broadcasts of Super Bowl highlights on German television, the increasing press coverage, and football programmes on the American Forces Network (AFN) played in the growth of the sport in Germany.[22]

In 1977, a chance encounter between German Wolfgang Lehneis and an American Alexander Sperber led to the formation of the first significant German–American football club in Frankfurt am Main. Both were in their early to mid-twenties when they started the *Frankfurt Löwen*. Subsequently, television broadcasts of Super Bowls in 1977 and 1979 sparked the formation of other clubs in a number of West German cities. At the initiative of Holger Obermann, German television brought Super Bowl highlights to German viewers. Formerly a professional goalkeeper in Germany, Obermann had done 'pioneer work' in American soccer in the 1960s and apparently was motivated to do the same for American football in Germany.[23] The German public broadcasting system, *ARD*, at the time operating one of only three channels available to most German viewers, showed a summary of Super Bowl XI between the Oakland Raiders and Minnesota Vikings on Wednesday 12 January 1977 from 10:50 to 11:35pm. Despite the three-day delay and the late hour, the programme 'received enormous response', according to one newspaper.[24] On Tuesday 30 January 1979, Obermann hosted the *ARD*'s second Super Bowl summary, which aired from 11:00 to 11:45pm. Over 20 years after these broadcasts, several of Germany's football pioneers remembered vivid details of the game between the Pittsburgh Steelers and the Dallas Cowboys and described these first images as instrumental to their getting involved in American football. One player referred to Obermann as 'the midwife of American football in Germany'.[25]

The 'midwife' and 'the founding fathers' were also involved in a television moment that gave birth to a number of *Frankfurt Löwen* offspring. In January 1979, Obermann invited Sperber and Lehneis to promote their team during a live television interview. Sperber pulled off a winning bluff, when Obermann asked him on the air about football's popularity in Germany. Although Sperber knew of only one other German team, the *Düsseldorf Panther* founded in 1978, he observed that clubs already existed in every major city in West Germany.[26] Following the programme, the station passed on numerous phone calls and letters it had received from people wanting to get in touch with the purported clubs in their hometowns. Caught in a bind, Sperber reacted with another white lie when he told interested parties that the supposed club founders in the respective city had been involved in a car accident and would be unable to continue their work. In their place, Sperber and Lehneis offered help in setting up a new team or advised callers to start their own club.[27]

The ripple effects of the Super Bowl and the agency of Sperber and Lehneis can be exemplified with the origin story of the *Ansbach Grizzlies*. In the late 1970s, Ansbach, the capital of Middle-Franconia, was home to a residential population of about of 40,000 people plus a major American military community with about 10,000 soldiers and their families. The Grizzlies owed much of their dominance on the gridiron during the first decade of football in Germany to this American presence. Between 1979 and 1986 Ansbach reached every national championship game winning the title three times. The pigskin and the gridiron were familiar objects to many Germans in Ansbach. Chiefly responsible for the formation of the Grizzlies was Erich Grau, who had spent almost every summer vacation in America during the 1970s and had brought back several footballs from his trips. Other Germans attended games of the successful local American military high school team or watched games on AFN. Grau watched his first Super Bowl on AFN in 1976 at the age of 21. The next day, it turned out that the majority of his fellow physical education majors had tuned into the game on AFN as well:

> At the time, nobody was listening to anything but AFN radio. By using a cloth hanger in the back of your TV set you were also able to receive AFN on television. You needed a different kind of antenna. In fact, the signal was so strong that you had to unplug your antenna and use a metal hanger instead, which immediately gave you great reception. You really needed an NTSC decoder, which, of cause, nobody had at the time. That means we watched the football games without sound. However, the Super Bowl was also broadcast live on [AFN] radio.[28]

With such exposure, Grau had no problem motivating a group of his friends, who were competitive athletes in other sports, to start a team of their own after they had learned about the existence of the clubs in Frankfurt and Düsseldorf through a television report of a game between the two in 1978. On 3 April 1979, Grau invited the public to an informational meeting after which 15 more players signed up and a group order for equipment went out to Sperber and Lehneis. Less than eight months later the Ansbach Grizzlies held their own against the much more experienced Frankfurt Löwen in the first German championship game, losing by only a touchdown.[29]

Among the six original *Bundesliga* 'gridiron' football teams, Bremerhaven was located the farthest north. The team owed its football know-how to the fact that the city had been part of the American enclave in British-occupied northern Germany, which had given the American troops a strategically important seaport. Already in the 1950s, Germans attended the home games of the Bremerhaven Blue Devils in the American military leagues. However, as it did elsewhere, the idea to form a German team did not mature until the Frankfurt Löwen made the national news and the Super Bowl aired on television. In February 1979, Americans and Germans together founded the '1. Deutsch-Amerikanischer Sport- und Football-Club e.V. "Bremerhaven Seahawks"'. At the age of 21, Thorsten Schultz joined the club during its first year of existence when he followed the lead of his girlfriend who was a cheerleader for the team. As in other cities, American football on AFN and particularly the Super Bowl ignited German imaginations. In 1975, AFN Bremerhaven had become the first AFN television station to broadcast in colour.[30] By the early 1990s, the station's main intended audience were about 8,600 soldiers and family members stationed in Lucius D. Clay Kaserne located between Bremerhaven and Bremen.[31]

Schultz shared that watching football on AFN fostered close ties between the American and German players on the Seahawks team:

> [AFN] television and radio, you could receive everything. Smart ones could turn their antenna just the right way to receive a clear picture. That's why there was a lot of uproar when they closed down the station. After that you needed a satellite dish with a secret code from the US Army. We still watch the original [i.e., American] football program in the German-American club via satellite here … That's also where we watch the Super Bowl, instead of the German broadcast. That way you get the original commentators with quality comments instead of the rubbish you get from [German commentators] … Most of us understand English, and those who don't enjoy the pictures. The good thing about it is that we make it 'American'. For years

now we have our club party on that day with barbeque and a round of free beer for every touchdown scored.[32]

Franz Bayer was among those who joined the *Munich Cowboys*, whom he led as quarterback during their premier season in 1979. At the time the 26-year-old businessman had already spent a year and a half in America for his employer Phillip Morris. Bayer's first introduction to football came through a friend who was already fascinated with American sports and listened regularly to basketball, baseball, and football broadcasts on AFN radio in Munich. Without ever having seen football himself and simply going by the American commentary, the friend imagined what the game looked like and explained the rules to Bayer. 'Because of his explanation, the way he described it to me, I got into it', he remembered. 'I liked the rules and the flow of the game, the way he had explained it to me. I found it incredibly fascinating'. Next, Bayer discovered by coincidence that he was able to receive AFN television. He bought a special TV set, and started to watch college football. Being able to actually see the action on the screen, Bayer was most impressed by the physical contact. However, he said he could not appreciate the impact of two players colliding until he saw his first game in person at a game played on the campus of the American University in Munich. Even though he knew the calibre of game was low, he admitted: 'That was the final piece. You realized that it crashes a good deal, and that impressed me a lot in the beginning'. After watching Terry Bradshaw's heroics in Super Bowl XIII on Germany's *ARD* and seeing the number for the *Frankfurt Löwen* on screen, Bayer heard that people in Munich were looking to start a football team and were seeking players. At that point, Bayer recalled, he knew his days playing soccer were over.[33]

On 12 February 1979, a group of young fans founded West Berlin's first American football club, the *Berlin Bären*.[34] As a teenager in West Berlin during the mid-1970s, Dieter Hoch first experienced American football while watching AFN television in his home in the southern part of the city, which had been part of the American Occupied Zone after 1945 and where many of the American military installations were still located. While AFN radio was more widely available throughout the city, the reception of the American television programme was mostly restricted to the districts of Zehlendorf and Steglitz, traditionally the home of educated middle-class families.[35]

Although the reception was often poor, Hoch regularly watched football with a group of 6–10 classmates. Spending the night of the first to the second day of the year watching New Year's Day bowl games became an annual fixture for the group. Later, he and his friends also followed the NFL when AFN added professional football to its line-up. Twenty-five years, later he fondly remembered how late-night television sessions first led to playing eight years for the *Berlin Bären* and *Adler*, and later to a career as a football journalist:

I saw that these padded people were fighting around on the screen. Naturally, I didn't know exactly what that was at the time. I stayed with it, got interested, and it developed from there up to the point when the team was founded in '79.[36]

AFN became an important part many other German youths' conversion to American football. Frank-Peter Schmidt's football experience began, like others, when he went to extraordinary lengths to make sure he could receive the programme. While looking at a new Berlin apartment in 1980, Schmidt found out by coincidence that a television set that had been left by the previous owner was able to receive the American station. He kept the apartment and the television, for which he had extra parts installed for colour and sound at a local shop that specialized in such updates. In the early 1980s, Schmidt had access to a pilot programme that introduced cable television to Berlin and which, much to his delight, included AFN as part of the cable package on a trial basis from 1981 to 1984. According to Schmidt, the station was removed at the request of the American broadcaster CBS, when an employee of network by coincidence noticed that their shows were part of the public cable access in Berlin. Apparently, CBS was providing programming to AFN for little to no cost to entertain the American troops abroad. The assumption was that most people in Berlin were able to watch AFN. In reality, however, it still required some technical ingenuity to receive the signal. By mid-October 1984, AFN was no longer available via cable in Berlin. After that, Schmidt got an extra antenna to ensure he would still be able to watch football on AFN.[37] Although AFN was only one catalyst responsible for the diffusion of football, it is an important aspect of the larger influence the American military presence in Germany had on the process.[38] The interception of AFN airwaves is a prime illustration for the fact that the arrival of the Super Bowl and American football in Germany was to considerable degree a product of unintended and unforeseeable consequences.

Whether in Berlin, Bremerhaven, or Munich, interviews with the founding members of other American football clubs kept repeating the same refrains of AFN, *ARD*, and the Super Bowl. Every one of them recalled the first images of American football on television and it made a lasting impression on them.[39] Televised images, however, were not the only source that fed the imaginations of young German gridiron enthusiasts. Newspapers and magazines also shaped the way Germans read the Super Bowl and *Amerika*. In 1979, Germany's most popular TV guide, *Hör Zu*, announced *ARD*'s 45-minute highlight show of Super Bowl XIII by writing,

> These football warriors plunge into the mayhem like armored knights … Just about anything is allowed in doing so: battering, kicking, and fist blows. Hence, the 'list of casualties' is long during the four-month season. About every fifth player gets seriously injured – and there are even deaths.[40]

This emphasis on American football as a violent and bewildering phenomenon dominated much of the initial print coverage in Germany.

Super Bowl XV–XXIII on the Pages of the *Frankfurter Allgemeine Zeitung*

An analysis of the Super Bowl coverage of a leading German newspaper, *Frankfurter Allgemeine Zeitung* (*FAZ*), in the 10-year period from 1981 to 1990, reveals additional layers in the story of German reception of American football. This timespan covers the time of initial growth of American football as a participant sport for Germans and ends the year before the arrival of the NFL's *World League of American Football* (WLAF). Published in Frankfurt am Main, the cradle of American football in Germany, the *FAZ* became Germany's first truly national newspaper after the Second World War. By devoting itself 'totally to coverage of events throughout Germany and the world', the paper gained a reputation as among the most influential in West Germany.[41]

Prior to the 1980s, *FAZ*'s sport coverage had little to say about American football. In 1976, for example, it published a picture of a ball carrier skilfully escaping his defender. The illustration was simply captioned 'Pas De Deux' and was not accompanied by any article.[42] In the following years, *FAZ* continued to sporadically publish pictures from the NFL without providing additional information beyond the image itself and a caption. Often, the images and the captions highlighted the confusing and exotic characteristics the sport. In February 1979, the paper showed a scene from the previous month's Super Bowl captioned: 'Subjected: Thomas Henderson of the Dallas Cowboys, an American pro-football team, triumphs; the opponent (Larry Anderson of the Pittsburgh Steelers) lies in the dust in front of him'.[43]

In January 1981, on the occasion of Super Bowl XV, *FAZ* published a major article under the headline 'Violence according to the needs of a large audience: The more blood, the more spectators'. Next to an ad, this piece filled an entire page with its six columns and two pictures. The story focused around two themes that highlighted the apparently foreign character of American football for the newspaper's readers: the degree of violence and sport as big business. The opening paragraph outlined the magnitude of the upcoming Super Bowl. Almost as many journalists would cover this 'American media spectacle par excellence' as the entire soccer 1974 World Cup in Germany. Black market ticket and hotel prices seemed equally impressive to the German observer. The article then focused on American football as a serious business in which the end justifies any means. Anecdotes of late hits and personal fouls completed the picture. With head coaches acting like generals and players awarded stars on their helmets, the parallels between war and football seemed all too obvious for the writer. To support this notion, unidentified observers of the American sports scene were quoted explaining the rising popularity of American football in the United States. One of the sources asserted that the American passion for football 'only proves once again the violent character of this country and the inability of the country to cope with social and economic shifts'. Further unnamed sources pointed to American football's alleged function to distract domestic attention away from the consequences of the Vietnam War. The text did mention an honourable but hopeless opposition formed by concerned parents, a couple of players who played by the spirit of the rules and refused to take cheap shots – and were thus exceptions to the rule, and a few honest politicians seeking protective legislation. The tenor of the report, however, was that all of these people were basically fighting for a lost cause, since 'those for whom the American football sport is just regular business, believe that the commercial value of the game increases with the bloodshed. The more blood, the more spectators'.[44]

In the ensuing years, the newspaper sporadically and briefly reported on signs that American football was budding in Germany. For the most part, the accounts reflected three stereotypes of America in general and football in particular: violence, militarism, and materialism. However, by 1984 *FAZ*'s football coverage shifted its focus from the violence on the field to the spectacle surrounding the game – and especially, the Super Bowl. In 1984, the newspaper published two short articles with pictures from Super Bowl XVIII. Ten days before the game, one article pointed out that the excitement and media attention made the Super Bowl the 'sport event of the year', outshining the US Open tennis tournament in New York City and even the summer Olympics in Los Angeles. In another story following the game, the reporter marvelled over the magnitude of the Super Bowl as documented in figures. The story included the factoids that players of the winning team earned 100,000 *Deutsch marks*, with half of that sum going to the losing side; that 150 million television viewers in the United States, Canada, Japan, and Great Britain tuned into the game; and that a one-minute commercial sold for 1.3 million *Deutsch marks*. For the first time, the text mentioned the actual game result and commented on players' performances. Running back Marcus Allen of the Oakland Raiders, the game's most-valuable-player, received particular attention.[45]

In 1985, the paper devoted half a page to Super Bowl XIX. Once again, the spectacle rather than the athletic event that impressed the reporters. One article. probably based on official press releases, offered the standard ingredients for what was to become the dominant narrative of the football coverage for the years to come. The reporter observed that the Super Bowl had grown so immense that it was 'overshadowing every other event in the United States'. This story also covered bonus payments for players; international TV ratings (reported 150 million viewers in 30 countries); the price for a one-minute commercial and broadcast rights; attendance in the stadium; black market price for tickets; and the number of journalists present. A correspondent in San Francisco wrote a piece that described the celebrations and festivities following the 49ers' win. The only attention the game itself received was a mention of the result and an action shot of 49ers' running back Roger Craig, incorrectly identifying Craig as a wide receiver. The text also mentioned quarterback Joe Montana as the game's outstanding player. The fact that the terms 'wide receiver' and 'quarterback' were translated into German in parentheses suggests that the editors expected the average German reader to be unfamiliar with the terms. In a shift from previous practices, the sportswriters referred only once to violence on the field, when they labelled football as 'America's most brutal sport'.[46]

In 1986 and 1987, the annual Super Bowl reports added more substance to the standard descriptions. In 1986, one journalist made an attempt to explain the game itself to the readers after watching the Super Bowl in Germany until 3:30am on AFN. The author also commented on the perceived parallels between the American way of life and American football: 'Football is not only a sport, football is more, a perspective on life that projects life's struggle on the green rectangle. Only the strongest, the truly strongest, make it through'.[47] The awkward formulations used to describe Chicago Bears lineman William Perry's touchdown run revealed how foreign the game still was to German eyes. 'American football is less widely spread in Europe than the American way of life', a correspondent commented. 'The rules of the latter are easier to understand'. In 1987, for the first time, the summary included some statistical information comparing New York Giant quarterback Phil Simms' and Denver Broncos quarterback John Elway's completion rates.[48]

An article in 1988 followed the trend towards more detail with most of the story line focusing on the underdog win of the Washington Redskins and their quarterback Doug Williams against quarterback John Elway and the favoured Denver Broncos. The text pointed out that Williams was the first black quarterback to lead his team to the championship. This tendency towards more substance and detail may indicate a growing interest in and familiarity with the game, as well as an extended publicity push from the NFL. By 1988, the NFL's market expansion towards Europe was well underway. Great Britain had been the first target of this drive. London hosted the first American Bowl exhibition game in 1983, and then staged the game annually beginning in 1986. NFL games began to be shown regularly on British television since 1982.[49] By 1988, the Super Bowl was reportedly broadcast in 55 countries, up from only four in 1984 and 30 in 1985.[50]

By 1989, the Super Bowl had become important enough for *FAZ* to produce an article before and after the game. Super Bowl XXIII was also the last before the NFL began to promote the intercontinental professional World League of American Football – founded that same year considering a franchise location in Frankfurt. One article demonstrated that German journalists were by no means taking an uncritical approach towards this latest American export product or succumbing to an all-powerful American influence. A pre-game article focused on the fact that the Super Bowl would be played despite three days of riots that cost the lives of three people in a predominantly black district of the host city of Miami. 'The climax of the football season is much too important and much too profitable to become a victim of the expression of social abuses', the reporter sarcastically observed. The writer acknowledged that the Super Bowl had become a sporting event with international importance. According to the author, global fascination with the Super Bowl could not be attributed to the sport itself but rather to the perfectly staged spectacle that engulfed the game and to the images of machismo demonstrated by the gigantic athletes on the field.[51]

The first year the *Frankfurter Allgemeine Zeitung* paid attention to games leading up to the Super Bowl was 1990. *FAZ* covered the AFC and NFC championships in a 'results' section accompanied by pictures. An article published before the Super Bowl once again paid tribute to American football as an astonishingly profitable multi-billion-dollar business. In fact, Super Bowl XXIV was available live to viewers in Germany via two cable stations, *Tele 5* and *Sportkanal*. According to the author, the fees for television licences in German professional soccer looked like pocket change by comparison. The reporter stressed that unlike in Germany, NFL franchises had been run like business entities for a long time in America. The correspondent also pointed out that American football and with all of its glitz and glamour was on its way to Germany. The article foreshadowed the arrival of professional football in Germany by mentioning for the first time the development of the 'Weltliga' (world league) and informing is readers about the possibility of locating a team in Frankfurt.[52]

Besides the commercial aspects, the article highlighted the match-up between the San Francisco 49ers and the Denver Broncos as well as the success of 49ers' super-star Joe Montana. The exceptional role of San Francisco's quarterback at a time when American football garnered more exposure to a broader audience in Germany made Montana the first recognizable NFL hero for many Germans. The article following the game exemplified the change in commentaries that had occurred since 1976. Instead of describing American football as a form of legal assault, the reporter depicted it as 'a rough contact sport that required a mixture of the toughest physicality and the agility of a ballet dancer'. Much like in later World League coverage, the author praised the thrilling essence of the sport, with the game itself accompanied by a spectacular sideshow with 'music, ballet, and girls', as well as an emotional performance of the national anthem, 'culminating in spectacular indoor fireworks'. Whereas, reports 10 years earlier had not even mentioned the Super Bowl's final score, two-thirds of this 1990 article consisted of an actual account of the game itself.[53]

In summary, the analysis of the *FAZ*'s reporting about the Super Bowl in the 1980s reveals that American football was not at first a regular part of this newspaper's sports coverage. In the early years of this period, scattered reports painted a grim picture of the sport that reinforced German stereotypes of rampant violence and materialism in America. By the mid-1980s alternative narratives emerged as annual reports about the spectacle of the Super Bowl increasingly introduced positive stereotypes that associated the game with entertainment and economic success stories. Towards the end of the 1980s reporters increasingly commented on the game itself, as scores, statistics, and stars slowly entered the narratives. This expanded coverage was partially due to increased public relations efforts to expand the NFL's international visibility and to tap into new markets. Yet, to assume that this shift in German perspectives was solely due to 'brain-washing' Americanization would neglect the agency of German consumers and ignore decades of experience in adapting American popular culture to German life.

Imagined Worlds: The Super Bowl in Germany

As one of the leading scholars of the globalization of sport, Joseph Maguire, has suggested, the work of anthropologist Arjun Appadurai provides a rich theoretical framework for the analysis of media-sport production complex, including American football in Europe.[54] Addressing the cultural sameness/difference debate, Appadurai pointed out that homogenization arguments, including Americanization theories, often fail to account for indigenization. The prospect of indigenization relates to a question raised by Martin and Reeves in their assessment of the Super Bowl's global impact: 'what happens when a ritual originating in one regime of experience is applied to a very different set of historical conditions?'[55] Opposing centre-periphery or push-and-pull models, Appadurai characterized late twentieth-century global cultural economy as 'a complex, overlapping, disjunctive order'.[56] As a framework for exploring this condition, Appadurai proposed 'five dimensions of global cultural flow … : (a) ethnoscapes; (b) mediascapes; (c) technoscapes; (d) finanscapes; and (e) ideoscapes'. He understood these -scapes to be 'deeply perspectival constructs', which means they are contextual in the same way that how one views a landscape depends on one's position within the vista. He insisted that how these various 'scapes' play out varies by 'historical, linguistic and political situatedness'.[57] Seeing and understanding the global cultural economy from the perspective of social actors on the ground, Appadurai invoked the concept of 'imagined worlds', or 'the multiple worlds which are constituted by the historically situated imaginations of persons and groups spread around the globe'.[58]

Applying Appadurai's idea of 'scapes' to the Super Bowl and international imaginations, requires and understanding of the specific historical, linguistic, and political contexts of the audiences in various countries and within those countries. In the case of West Germany, given the long-term US occupation and re-education efforts, the German relationship with American popular culture has been exceptionally intense.[59] Relating Appadurai's understanding of 'scapes' reinforces the idea that these local imaginations are fluid and irregular. Appardurai's methodology treats the Super Bowl and America as imagined worlds. Thus, the German 'imagined world' of *Amerika* represents a locally imagined America in Germany.

Appadurai defined the cultural flows of globalization as follows. First, an ethnoscape represents

> the landscape of persons who constitute the shifting world in which we live: tourists, immigrants, refugees, exiles, guestworkers and other moving groups and persons constitute an essential feature of the world, and appear to affect the politics of and between nations to a hitherto unprecedented degree.[60]

This aspect relates to human movement, as 'more persons and groups deal with the realities of having to move, or the fantasies of wanting to move'.[61] Second, a technoscape denotes 'the global configuration, also ever fluid, of technology, and of the fact that technology, both high and low, both mechanical and informational, now moves at high speeds across various kinds of previously impervious boundaries'.[62] Third, a finanscape is an increasingly 'mysterious, rapid and difficult landscape' involving the flow of global capital through international currency markets and national stock exchanges'.[63] Fourth, a mediascape relates to 'both to the distribution of the electronic capabilities to produce and disseminate information' and 'the images of the world created by these media'.[64] Fifth, an ideoscape involves the flow of political discourses rooted in the Enlightenment era and employed to ideologically support or counter state power, including concepts and images of freedom, rights, sovereignty, representation, and, especially, democracy.[65]

The study of the Super Bowl in Germany illustrates groundbreaking changes in cultural flows between the 1970s and 1990s. In the post-1970s information age transnational companies and individual entrepreneurs (e.g. media moguls such as Ted Turner and Rupert Murdoch) capitalized on the development of fibre-optic cables, along with direct broadcast satellites and personal computers. These changes in the technoscape catalysed a revolution in the global telecommunications market. *ARD*'s and AFN's American football coverage in the 1970s predated the media- and finanscape of what the American historian of international relations Walter LaFeber called 'the new global capitalism'.[66] Gradually in the 1980s and 1990s, the Super Bowl became more accessible to German audiences. While German television coverage of the game in the late 1970s was limited to brief highlights days after the event, by 1990 German viewers were able to watch Super Bowl XXIV live on their choice of two cable stations. This immediacy arguably contributed to *FAZ*'s expanded reporting, corresponding changes in the commentary, and how Germans imagined *Amerika*.

The appropriation of the AFN Super Bowl broadcasts by some Germans further serves as an example of the unstable relationship between ethnoscapes, technoscapes, mediascapes, and ideoscapes. Originally, AFN had been designed as a diasporic medium intended as a vehicle to keep American soldiers stationed abroad connected to their families and homes – and also their nation-state and to particular notions of nationalism, freedom, and democracy.[67] In the post-Second World War era, as a historian of the AFN, Stephen Craig, has contended, 'sports programming [on AFN] was felt to have an important role in keeping young soldiers in touch with home'.[68] Yet, the Super Bowl on AFN also became a means for some Germans to create their own imagined worlds of *Amerika* through American football. In post-Second World War Germany, AFN radio had already been a key facilitator of the diffusion of American music genres, especially rock 'n' roll and Dixieland jazz.[69] AFN Radio started airing the Super Bowl with its inauguration in 1967.[70] In Frankfurt, AFN television first aired the Super Bowl live in 1971, while the programme showed taped-delayed in Berlin.[71] In the early 1980s, the network reached a target audience of about 500,000 American military and civilian personnel as well as their families via seven AFN studios located mostly in West Germany. A weekly estimated 'shadow audience' of one million mostly Germans also tuned to the radio broadcasts. This means that unintended audience considerably exceeded AFN's intended target audience.[72] Some scholars have contended that relatively few Germans were able to receive AFN television. Indeed, in order to avoid 'signal spillover' to local civilian audiences and associated contract disputes with American distributors, AFN had opted for a low-powered television network operated on the US television system NTSC. In a case study in military broadcasting, Craig concluded, 'although Europeans also can obtain such [compatible TV] sets, few live close enough to U.S. installations to pick up the low-powered AFN television signal'.[73] As the oral histories with the founding generation of American football clubs in Germany demonstrates, however, industrious Germans found access to American football images on AFN, which in turn sparked their interest to form their own local structures to play the sport. As Craig argued, 'Attracted by the upbeat style, popular music, and straight-forward news, these shadow listeners [and viewers] have received large doses of American culture and ideology'.[74]

The ingenuity and agency of the Germans who rigged their radio and TV sets illustrates the constant fluidity and uncertainty between the global cultural flows. As they redirected the flow of radio and television signals, the 'founding fathers' of German American football also redirected the media-, techno-, and ideoscapes of the Super Bowl, thus disrupting their former relationships. Inadvertently, the actions of these media pirates eventually would also influence ethnoscapes. On the one hand, it allowed these young Germans to fantasize about moving to the United States or creating their own imagined *Amerikas*.[75] On the other hand, by starting their own American football clubs, they developed the structures for the bidirectional movements of American and German football players, coaches, and fans.

Through AFN's signals mediascapes and ideoscapes reached German audiences relatively unfiltered. Unlike services such as the Voice of America (VOA), Radio in the American Sector (RIAS), or Radio Free Europe (RFE), AFN had not been conceived as a propaganda tool to reach local audiences. Its content was designed as 'authentic' programming for Americans. According to Craig, 'for the shadow audience of Germans, AFN provided a welcome alternative to the pervasive postwar radio propaganda'.[76] As early as 1956, the former chief of AFN's Music Production Department Walter Shepard, warned against efforts to turn the network into an overt tool to influence local 'eavesdroppers',

> AFN would then be labeled as a propaganda instrument, an onerous label in European minds.
> I am convinced that AFN is the most effective broadcast propaganda for the United States in
> Western Europe today for the very reason that it is not conscious propaganda ... By continuing
> just as it has in the past, AFN will go on making friends for the United States until the American
> forces leave Europe.[77]

The spread of American football in Germany makes Shepard's assertion seem prescient. After imbibing American football on AFN, Germans created their own versions of the game. On the playing fields of the *Berlin Bären* or *Bremerhaven Seahawks*, as well as on the pages of national newspapers like the *FAZ*, Germans produced and consumed their own interpretations of American football, thus adding to the mediascapes and ideoscapes of the Super Bowl. Though the *FAZ*'s Super Bowl reports in part echoed American discourses from structural-functionalist analyses to critiques of violence and commercialism, the newspaper's narratives represented national readings of the Super Bowl as they were written by German journalists for German readers.[78] As such, the resulting *Amerikabilder* were, at times, similar to those produced for and by Americans (e.g. on AFN), but they were also distinctly German interpretations.

It should be noted, however, that such a view of agency is far more optimistic than Appadurai's original notion of 'the fetishism of the consumer', which only creates an illusion of consumer power. For Appadurai, real agency rests not in consumers, but producers. He perceived consumers to have been duped by advertising and merchandising into thinking of themselves as social actors, when they are at best merely selectors of limited alternatives offered by global economic conglomerates. Yet, Appadurai's own discussion of the decolonization of Indian cricket suggests the potential of local social agents to create cultural hybrids. Although 'cricket is a hard cultural form that changes those who are socialized into it more readily than it is itself changed', Appadurai concluded, 'counterintuitively, it has become profoundly indigenized and decolonized' by Indians. Contributing to vernacularization of the game, according to Appadurai, was the confluence of indigenous patrons, state support, commercial interests and a variety of identity politics, which together, 'permitted the gradual unyoking of cricket from its Victorian value framework and its animation by new forces associated with merchandising and spectacle'.[79] Though it seems quite difficult to imagine that American football in Germany will ever rise to the cultural significance of cricket in

India, Appadurai's discussion of sport suggests that consumers can become producers of meaning and thus contributing to a vernacularization of the Super Bowl.

The Past and Future of the Super Bowl in German Imagination

The period between the mid-1950s and late-1980s marked the NFL's ascent from a marginally profitable enterprise to a leader in the US sporting industry. That rapid rise led the NFL to cultivate global ambitions for market expansion. During this process, rapid changes in the global flows of mediascapes and technoscapes made images and depictions of the Super Bowl increasingly available to German audiences. This exposure triggered the construction of imagined worlds and the beginning of American football as a participation and spectator sport in Germany. An analysis of the Super Bowl's depiction in the *Frankfurter Allgemeine Zeitung* in the 1980s shows a shift from violence to spectacle. Both themes reproduced long-standing notions of *Amerika* in Germany, which involved America as a model of modernity and as a violent society that lacks *Kultur*. Finally, studying the historically contextualized *Sonderfall* of the Super Bowl's reception in Germany illustrates the analytical power of Appadurai's conception of global cultural flows.

In the first decade of the twenty-first century, the NFL scrapped its plans to expand markets and develop talent via a European-based professional farm league. When NFL Europa closed after the 2007 season, five of the six remaining teams were located in Germany. In 2003, this concentration on the German market had prompted *FAZ*'s American football expert Frank Scheffler to comment on the development. His own coverage of the *Frankfurt Löwen* had helped to sow the seeds of the German grass-roots gridiron in the late 1970s.[80] Scheffler argued that a more appropriate title for NFL Europe would be 'NFL Germany'.[81] The journalist wondered why American football worked in Germany, even though it had 'failed in the rest of the world'. By his own admission, Scheffler was unable to provide convincing reasons for why the Germans had 'so much love for an athletically questionable American spectacle'. Possibly hinting at the political climate of the Iraq War, Scheffler concluded: 'When it comes to football, Germany is almost the last one standing faithfully by America's side'.[82]

Perhaps the last faithful American ally, then, was England. The same year that the NFL Europa folded, the NFL announced plans to host a regular season game in London.[83] This change in the league's international strategy consisted of not only a shift from minor league to 'the real deal', but also a retreat to the NFL's original bridgehead in England and its primary overseas target in the 1980s.[84] Between 2007 and 2016, the league staged 18 regular-season games in London as part of the 'NFL International Series'. During that period, the NFL's British fan base had reportedly tripled or quadrupled to 13 million.[85] Meanwhile, commentators have been discussing the likelihood of an NFL expansion franchise in England's capital.[86] The NFL's momentary popularity in England demonstrates that although the German reception of American football must be read in a broader historical context of German-American relations, Germany's niche following of gridiron football might not be a unique *Sonderfall*. Early into the twenty-first century, Germany's faithful followers of American football have not abandoned their fascination with *Amerika* and the Super Bowl. After a slight dip in the early 2000s, viewership of Super Bowl broadcasts on *SAT 1* have steadily increased from 0.58 million in 1999 to 0.95 million in 2013 and 1.7 million in 2016.[87] In an increasingly fragmented mediascape and 'imagined communities' sustained by social media,[88] the Super Bowl has developed into a viable specialty product in a particular market segment where people imagine *Amerika*. In doing so, these consumers will continue a tradition started by Germany's gridiron pioneers, who in the 1970s devotedly followed the Super Bowl on *ARD* and AFN.

Notes

1. The reported viewership was based on an average for all four quarters of the game. Sidney Sharing, '"Super Bowl" punktet auch mitten in der Nacht', http://www.quotenmeter.de/n/83688/super-bowl-punktet-auch-mitten-in-der-nacht (accessed 20 May 2016); and Fabian Müller, 'Super Bowl 50: Neuer Quotenrekord in Deutschland – aber nicht in den USA', http://www.horizont.net/medien/nachrichten/Super-Bowl-50-Neuer-Quotenrekord-in-Deutschland---aber-nicht-in-den-USA-138703 (accessed 19 October 2016).
2. Sharing, '"Super Bowl"'.
3. Christopher R. Martin and Jimmie L. Reeves, 'The Whole World isn't Watching (but We Thought They Were): The Super Bowl and United States Solipsism', *Culture, Sport, Society* 4, no. 2 (2001), 213–36.
4. Andrei Markovits and Steven Hellerman, *Offside: Soccer and American Exceptionalism* (Princeton, NJ: Princeton University Press, 2001); and Stefan Szymanski and Andrew S. Zimbalist, *National Pastime: How Americans Play Baseball and the Rest of the World Plays Soccer* (Washington, DC: Brookings Institution Press, 2005).
5. Maarten van Bottenburg, 'Thrown for a Loss?: (American) Football and the European Sport Space', *American Behavioral Scientist* 46 (2003), 1550, 1552.
6. Ibid.
7. Ibid., 1560.
8. Lars Dzikus, 'American Football in West Germany: Cultural Transformation, Adaptation, and Resistance', in Annette Hofmann (ed.), *Turnen and Sport: Transatlantic Transfers* (Münster: Waxman, 2004), 221–39; Lars Dzikus, 'American Football, Deutschland und der Unternehmer: Amerika in unseren Köpfen und Stadien', *Sportwissenschaft* 32 (2004), 50–64.
9. Deutscher Olympischer Sportbund, *Bestandserhebung 2015* (Frankfurt am Main, Germany: Deutscher Olympischer Sportbund, 2016).
10. European Federation of American Football, 'GFL versus X League', http://www.efaf.info/index.php?News=1467 (accessed 20 May 2016).
11. Dave Campbell, 'Vikings Pick WR Boehringer, a European First for NFL Draft', http://bigstory.ap.org/article/ad57ce4b72bb4442a744b4fc5b9cd585/vikings-enter-final-day-draft-6-picks (accessed 19 October 2016).
12. Alexander Stephan, *Americanization and Anti-Americanism: The German Encounter with American Culture after 1945* (New York: Berghahn Books, 2005).
13. van Bottenburg, 'Thrown for a Loss?', 1561.
14. Arjun Appadurai, 'Disjuncture and Difference in the Global Cultural Economy', *Theory, Culture & Society* 7, no. 2 (1990), 295–310.
15. The author went on to reconsider the first two notions. The relative lack of poetry could be excused: 'since they still fight with nature they can't serenade her yet'. Slavery, however, could not be rationalized. Mebold, 'Über die Lage der Vereinigten Staaten', *Augsburger Allgemeine Zeitung* 1837. My translation. Reprinted in: C. Sommer, G.A. Mattox, W.C. McDonald, & U. Müller (eds), *Was die Deutschen aus Amerika Berichteten, 1828–1865* (Stuttgart: Akademischer Verlag, 1985), 63.
16. Kaspar Maase, *BRAVO Amerika: Erkundung zur Jugendkultur der Bundesrepublik in den Fünfziger Jahren* (Hamburg: Junius Verlag, 1992), 45. For an excellent source of what German immigrants and correspondents reported about America to newspapers in Germany during the period from 1828 to 1865, see: Sommer et al., (eds), *Was die Deutschen*.
17. Fritz Stern, *The Politics of Cultural Despair: A Study of the Rise of Germanic Ideology* (Berkley: University of California Press, 1974), 196.

18. The work of the Romantic painter and avid nationalist Casper David Friedrich is an example for the effective use of symbols of Germanic mythology of nature, and veneration of the sacred forest. The Romantics tried hard to trace Teutonic symbolism back to Roman Times. Friedrich's *Traveler Overlooking a Sea of Fog* and *The Cross and Cathedral in the Mountain*, painted around 1812, suggested a religious theme of resurrection were an expression of resistance against Napoleonic domination, and anticipation of Germany's national renewal of a mythical past. 'Schama's Landscape: Symbolism a Romantic Vision', *Times Magazine*, 8 April 1995, 13.

19. Stern, *The Politics of Cultural Despair*, xiii, 196.

20. For more on attempts to bring American football to Germany in the aftermath of the Second World War, see: Lars Dzikus, 'From Violence to Party: A History of the Presentation of American Football in England and Germany' (PhD diss., Ohio State University, 2005).

21. Ibid.

22. These interviews were originally conducted for a larger project on the history of American football in Germany; see: Dzikus, 'From Violence to Party'.

23. According to a newspaper interview, Obermann played for S.C. Elizabeth in the German–American Soccer League in New York 'for $25 a game' and got a semi-professional soccer league of the ground in Florida. He also wrote for the *New Yorker Staats-Zeitung* and did work for ABC. Oskar Beck, 'Mister Holger und das Fernweh', *Welt am Sonntag*, 7 February 1999.

24. For the response to the *ARD*'s Super Bowl summary, see: Harald Stenger, 'Die Avantgardisten vom Grüneburgpark dem Ziel nahe', *Frankfurter Rundschau*, 2 February 1977. *ARD* stands for *Arbeitsgemeinschaft der öffentlich-rechtlichen Rundfunkanstalten der Bundesrepublik Deutschland*.

25. 'American Football', *Hör Zu*, 27 January–2 February 1979, 54. Holger Korber referred to Obermann as 'the midwife of American football in Germany'. Holger Korber, translated interview by author, e-mail, 03 October 2002. In 1979, the *ARD*'s regional programme in Hesse, *Hessisher Rundfunk* (HR), had brought a total of six football-related stories. In 1980, Obermann cited the programme's high cost as a reason for the *ARD*'s decision not to air a Super Bowl summary that year. Holger Obermann in a letter to Holger Korber dated 15 January 1980.

26. Graham Bradley, 'Germans Punting, Passing: Soccer Fields Sites of Games', *Washington Post*, 24 August 1980, F4.

27. Alexander Sperber, translated interview by author, tape recording in the author's possession, Laufach, Germany, 24 October 2002.

28. Erich Grau, translated telephone interview by author, tape recording in the author's possession, Ansbach, Germany, 10 June 2001.

29. Ibid.; and Wolfgang Scheffler, 'Schlußpunkt einer deutschen Meisterschaft in einer amerikanischen Sportart', *Frankfurter Allgemeine Zeitung*, 12 November 1979, 17.

30. Barbara Fulenwider, 'Bremerhaven Will Get Color TV', *Stars and Stripes (European Edition)*, 21 August 1975, 27.

31. John Brooks, 'LDCK Provided the Comforts of Home', *2AD Dispatch*, 12 June 1992.

32. Thorsten Schultz, translated telephone interview by author, tape recording in the author's possession, Bremerhaven, Germany, 28 June 2001.

33. Franz Bayer, translated phone interview by author, tape recording in the author's possession, Munich, Germany, 16 July 2002. Bayer became the quarterback of the Munich Cowboys and the German national team and played until 1987, after which he became Munich's head coach. 'Munich Cowboys', *Huddle*, 11 April 1991, 16.

34. The *Berlin Bats* may be considered the city's first football team, although there is no evidence that they ever played a different team or formerly established a club. In January 1978, nine football enthusiasts looked for teammates through an article in the *Berliner Zeitung*. The group reportedly practiced on Saturdays at 2pm on a field with artificial turf on Siebenendenweg. About a dozen young ranging from in age from about 16 to 23 continued to meet on weekends throughout 1978. Several of the Bats eventually joined the Bären in the winter of 1979. 'Wer will American Football spielen?', *Berliner Zeitung*, 5 January 1978. Andreas Schreck, translated

telephone interview by author, tape recording in the author's possession, Berlin, Germany 26 July 2002.

35. Only after the transmission power of the station was increased in 1983 was it possible to receive the signal in the northern part of the city. Dieter Hoch, translated interview by author, tape recording in the author's possession, Berlin, Germany, 4 July 2002.

36. Dieter Hoch, translated interview by author, tape recording in the author's possession, Berlin, Germany, 4 July 2002.

37. Frank-Peter Schmidt, translated interview by author, tape recording in the author's possession, Berlin, Germany, 29 June and 4 July 2002.

38. Independent from each other both Hoch and Schmidt had witnessed their first American football game in person in June 1976, when NAIA Division I teams Texas A&I and Henderson State, Arkansas, met in Berlin's Olympic Stadium to celebrate the American Bicentennial with American troops and their families. Dieter Hoch, translated interview by author, tape recording in the author's possession, Berlin, Germany, 4 July 2002. Frank-Peter Schmidt, translated interview by author, tape recording in the author's possession, Berlin, Germany, 29 June and 4 July 2002. Dieter Hoch, 'Jubiläum', *Huddle*, 27 June 1996, 12; and 'Texas-Fußball! Hübsche Mädchen, heiße Burschen', *Bild-Zeitung Berlin*, 2 June 1976.

39. Several interview partners identified the two programmes as instrumental to either their own getting involved in football in the late 1970s or the foundation of their club: Franz Bayer (associated with Munich Cowboys; interview on 16 July 2002), Markus Becker (Düsseldorf Panther; 16 December 2002), Erich Grau (Ansbach Grizzlies; 10 June 2001), Holger Korber (Berlin Bären; 19 July 2002), Angelo Leichtenstern (Munich Cowboys; 16 July 2002), Walter Rohlfing (Düsseldorf Panther; 20 July 2001), Alexander Sperber (Frankfurt Löwen; 29 July 2002), Udo Thimian (Berlin Bären; 25 July 2002).

40. 'American Football', *Hör Zu*, 27 January–2 February 1979, 54.

41. *All About the Newspaper: Frankfurter Allgemeine Zeitung*, (Frankfurt am Main: Frankfurter Allgemeine Zeitung, 1979), 1, 2, 73.

42. Frankfurter Allgemeine Zeitung, 3 January 1976, 18.

43. Frankfurter Allgemeine Zeitung, 11 October 1979, 22.

44. Erich Vogt, 'Gewalt nach den Bedürfnissen eines großen Publikums: Je mehr Blut, desto mehr Zuschauer', *Frankfurter Allgemeine Zeitung*, 23 January 1981, 20.

45. Deutsche Presse Agentur Sport Informations Dienst, 'Die Super-Bowl - ein super Geschäft', *Frankfurter Allgemeine Zeitung*, 24 January 1984, 19. The article was based on texts from *Sport Informantions Dienst* (sid, sport information service) and *Deutsche Presse Agentur* (dpa, German press agency).

46. Wolfgang Scheffler, 'Reagan spielt mit', *Frankfurter Allgemeine Zeitung*, 22 January 1985, 18; and Rod Ackermann, 'Das Football-Herz von San Francisco: Eine Stadt ausser Rand und Band', *Frankfurter Allgemeine Zeitung*, 22 January 1985, 18.

47. Note that the German journalist's reflections echo similar assessments in the United States. See: Michael R. Real, 'Super Bowl: Mythical Spectacle', *Journal of Communication* 25, no. 1 (1975), 31–43.

48. 'Die Bärenstarke Nacht von New Orleans', *Frankfurter Allgemeine Zeitung*, 28 January 1986, 23; and Sport Informations Dienst, 'Die New York Giants sind die Größten', *Frankfurter Allgemeine Zeitung*, 27 January 1987, 23.

49. Joseph A. Maguire, 'American Football, British Society, and Global Sport Development', in Eric Dunning, Joseph A. Maguire, and Robert E. Pearton (eds), *The Sports Process: A Comparative and Developmental Approach* (Champaign, IL: Human Kinetics, 1993), 209.

50. The rapid expansion of the NFL would continue through the beginning and middle of the 1990s. Super Bowl XXX was reportedly broadcasted to a record 187 countries. Even more telling than the one-time-event Super Bowl was the growth of regular season games. By 1996, weekly telecasts reached 174 countries, compared to 47 in 1991. The World League of American Football, *The Official 1996 World League of American Football Record & Fact Book*, 6. Wolfgang Scheffler, '"Super Bowl" im American Football: alles andere als ein Eiertanz', *Frankfurter Allgemeine Zeitung*, 2 February 1988, 26.

51. The translation does not do justice to the assessment in the German original: 'Längst hat nämlich das rauhe Spiel der geposterten Muskelmänner um den ovalen Schweinslederball die Grenzen Nordamerikas überschritten und ist zu einem Sportereignis von internationaler Bedeutung geworden. Einem Ereignis, dessen Faszination weniger im Sportlichen selbst liegt, als vielmehr in seiner Ausstrahlung vom wonnig demonstrierten Machismo hühnenhafter Athleten'; Rod Ackermann, 'Das Finale im Lieblingssport der Amerikaner in Miami: Unruhen schaden dem Football-Geschäft nicht', *Frankfurter Allgemeine Zeitung*, 21 January 1989, 24; and Rod Ackermann, 'San Francisco und das Fernsehen die Sieger in der Super Bowl: Spannung, Knochenbrüche - Football aus dem Lehrbuch', *Frankfurter Allgemeine Zeitung*, 24 January 1989, 23.
52. Frankfurt was not awarded a World League team until 18 June 1990; Benedikt Fehr, 'American Football - vom Millionengeschäft zum Millardengeschäft', *Frankfurter Allgemeine Zeitung*, 26 January 1990, 31; and Benedikt Fehr, 'Mehr als einhundert Millionen Menschen sehen den vierten Football-Triumph der Kalifornier: Joe Montana und San Francisco sorgen für Superlative', *Frankfurter Allgemeine Zeitung*, 30 January 1990, 26.
53. Case in point, on 26 January 1990, the paper brought a picture showing Montana confidently looking forward to the game. The picture was not linked to an article and the subtitle contained very little information. Yet with this, American football made a record total of four appearances surrounding the Super Bowl that year. Fehr, 'American Football - vom Millionengeschäft zum Millardengeschäft', 31; and Benedikt Fehr, 'Mehr als einhundert Millionen Menschen sehen den vierten Football-Triumph der Kalifornier: Joe Montana und San Francisco sorgen für Superlative', *Frankfurter Allgemeine Zeitung*, 30 January 1990, 26.
54. Appadurai, 'Disjuncture and Difference'; and Joseph A. Maguire, 'The Media-Sport Production Complex: The Case of American Football in European Societies', *European Journal of Communication* 6 (1991), 315–35.
55. Martin and Reeves, 'The Whole World isn't Watching', 215.
56. Appadurai, 'Disjuncture and Difference', 296.
57. Ibid., 296.
58. Ibid., 296–7.
59. Netherlands Institute for Advanced Study in the Humanities and Social Sciences, 'Questions of Cultural Exchange: The NIAS Statement on the European Reception of American Mass Culture', in Rob Kroes, Robert W. Rydell, and D.F.J. Bosscher (eds), *Cultural Transmissions and Receptions: American Mass Culture in Europe*, (Amsterdam: VU University Press, 1993), 330–1.
60. Appadurai, 'Disjuncture and Difference', 297.
61. Ibid., 297.
62. Ibid., 297.
63. Ibid., 298.
64. Ibid., 298–9.
65. Ibid., 299.
66. Walter LaFeber, *Michael Jordan and the New Global Capitalism*, 2nd edn (New York: W. W. Norton, 2002).
67. Stephen R. Craig, 'The American Forces Network, Europe: A Case Study in Military Broadcasting', *Journal of Broadcasting & Electronic Media* 30, no. 1 (1986), 33–46.
68. Stephen R. Craig, 'American Forces Network in the Cold War: Military Broadcasting in Postwar Germany', *Journal of Broadcasting & Electronic Media* 32, no. 2 (1988), 312.
69. Richard C. Helt, 'A German Bluegrass Festival: The "Country-Boom" and some Notes on the History of American Popular Music in West Germany', *Journal of Popular Culture* 10, no. 4 (1977), 821–32; and Tamara Domentat, *Coca-Cola, Jazz und AFN – Berlin und die Amerikaner* (Berlin: Schwarzkopf & Schwarzkopf, 1995).
70. 'Dial Day: Your Guide to Good Listening in the EC', *Stars and Stripes (European Edition)*, 15 January 1967, 23.

71. 'Super! It'll Be Live on AFTV and Radio', *Stars and Stripes (European Edition)*, 17 January 1971, 21 In Berlin, AFN television showed the Super Bowl live first in 1972. 'AFN to Air Super Bowl', *The Berlin Observer*, 14 January 1972, 1.
72. Craig, 'American Forces Network in the Cold War'.
73. Craig, 'The American Forces Network, Europe', 44.
74. Craig, 'American Forces Network in the Cold War', 308.
75. Marco Butzkus remembered his first impressions of America growing up as a teenager in Bremerhaven, 'We listened to AFN Radio and dreamed of travelling to America someday or even of living there'. Marco Butzkuks, *16 Years-16 Lives: Americans in Bremerhaven* (Bremerhaven, Germany: aikon media, 2014), 9.
76. Craig, 'American Forces Network in the Cold War', 317.
77. Walter Sheppard, 'AFN at Work', *Saturday Review*, 13 October 1956, 45–6.
78. For a range of American readings of American football see, for example: Peter Gent, *North Dallas Forty* (New York: Morrow, 1973); Michael Oriard, *Reading Football: How the Popular Press Created an American Spectacle* (Chapel Hill: University of North Carolina Press, 1993); and Real, 'Super Bowl'.
79. Arjun Appadurai, 'Playing with Modernity: The Decolonization of Indian Cricket', in C.A. Brackenridge (ed.), *Consuming Modernity: Public Culture in a South Asian World* (Minneapolis: University of Minnesota Press, 1995), 23–48.
80. Dzikus, 'From Violence to Party'.
81. Wolfgang Scheffler, 'Kleine Football-Welt', *Frankfurter Allgemeine Zeitung*, 5 November 2003, 33.
82. Ibid., 33.
83. Jackie Bamberger, 'Here's where we are 10 years into NFL's grand UK experiment', http://sports.yahoo.com/news/heres-where-we-are-10-years-into-nfls-grand-uk-experiment-231157933.html (accessed 19 October 2016).
84. Maguire, Joseph A, 'More Than a Sporting Touchdown: The Making of American Football in England 1982–1990', *Sociology of Sport Journal* 7 (1990), 213–37.
85. Bamberger, 'Here's Where We are'.
86. Gregg Doyel, 'Doyel: London is Not Getting an NFL Team', http://www.indystar.com/story/sports/columnists/gregg-doyel/2016/10/01/doyel-london-not-getting-nfl-team/91326044/ (accessed 20 October 2016); Piers Edwards, 'NFL vs. NBA: The Battle for World Supremacy', http://edition.cnn.com/2016/10/20/sport/nfl-nba-twickenham-london-china/ (accessed 20 October 2016); and James Palmer, 'Indianapolis Colts: Irsay on Potential London Expansion', http://www.nfl.com/news/story/0ap3000000716346/article/doug-pederson-perfect-for-eagles-realities-of-london-expansion (accessed 20 October 2016).
87. Müller, 'Super Bowl 50'.
88. Anatoliy Gruzd, Barry Wellman, and Yuri Takhteyev, 'Imagining Twitter as an Imagined Community', *American Behavioral Scientist* 55 (2011), 1294–318.

Disclosure Statement

No potential conflict of interest was reported by the author.

A Century of British Readings of America through American Football: From the *Fin de Siècle* to the Super Bowl

Iain Adams

ABSTRACT

This paper examines the development of American football and the Super Bowl in the British imagination utilizing data from the British press. Divergent images of America have been present for centuries in British minds, and American football became intertwined with these images in the nineteenth century. Initially presented as a brutalized version of British varieties of football, once American football was seen live in Great Britain and it became a familiar subject on newsreels, some commentators interpreted it as a spectacle and a synonym for American life–modern, exciting, fast, and fun. Others viewed it as a threat that could undermine the British cultural heritage. The regular broadcasting of the NFL by Channel 4, including the Super Bowl live, was a watershed with the game swiftly gaining audience numbers whilst English association football was in a dour period. The increased popularity resulted in more media coverage, including negative images of unbridled capitalism, fixed games, and drug use. By the 1990s, audience numbers declined as English football was rehabilitated and American popularity waned, mainly through unpopular foreign policies. Today, many Britons regard watching the Super Bowl in the same way as a trip to Disney, an one-day holiday to a 'foreign' culture.

> It is bad enough to agree to have cruise missiles here in England, but to have American football as well must surely herald the end of our ancient and revered civilisation.[1]

America has fascinated the British for over 500 years. As scholars of British visions of America have observed, Britain has been 'assailed with two quite distinct images of America'. These divergent views were established in the colonial period by settlers, typically from the lower economic classes, and visitors, usually middle or upper class. The former enjoyed greater economic opportunities and political freedom away from hierarchical Britain, but the latter, enjoying the privileges of British society, portrayed the American colonies as a philistine society plagued by both natural and human dangers.[2]

By the late nineteenth century, America had been transformed from an agrarian colonial society into an independent industrial and urban nation that was beginning to politically and economically challenge European countries and their empires. The shared language, cultural ties, and historical traditions ensured the impact of the United States (US) was greater on Britain than elsewhere in Europe and British interest in America blossomed.[3] Britons relied upon the burgeoning print media for information, and newspapers catering to all social classes regularly featured America and American life as settlers and travellers inevitably recorded their experiences. In an 1869 letter to possible emigrants, Daniel Archer, a settler who had landed in New York in 1850, wrote:

> America, with all its difficulties and defects, is the most prosperous and highly-favoured country to emigrate to on the habitable globe. There can be no place where the poor working-man can so easily obtain subsistence for himself and family, and where the intellect of all classes is, or may be, highly cultivated, or where man is more highly appreciated according to his real value. Success is certain to the man of energy and good repute.[4]

Others, defending the culture they enjoyed, depicted British society as led by cultured gentlemen, whereas America was dominated by a boorish middle class; 'robber barons's rapaciously exploiting their workers leaving inner cities as areas of unemployment and poverty whilst producing a shallow and degraded society in which materialism subsumed high culture.[5] The US was seen as the crucible of a mass culture characterized by democratic mediocrity, barbarism, and scant respect for tradition rather than the progressive processes of industrialization and urbanization. British critics of the US conveyed this viewpoint through stories of violence, corruption, and poverty. As the English writer Rudyard Kipling once quipped: 'I have struck a city – a real city – and they call it Chicago … Having seen it, I urgently desire never to see it again. It is inhabited by savages'.[6]

The Image of American Football, 1887–1909

This *milieu* explains the tone of British newspaper reports that a meeting of the Inter-Collegiate Football Association had amended American football rules due to the 'unanimity among the representatives present in expressing the opinion that the old roughness and brutality of the game should be done away with'.[7] Over the following two decades, most British press stories concerning American football focused on its brutality. In response to concern about unruliness in rugby, a Welsh newspaper commented that 'rugby footballers in England, though sometimes blamed for rough play, must be lamb-like in their actions compared to a typical American footballer. The football reports of American newspapers are a perfect catalogue of horrors'. Frequent accounts of American football's 'butcher's bill', outlining the fatalities and serious injuries occurring, were promulgated.[8] Elite university games were no exception. The 1894 Harvard-Dartmouth match was 'brutal and cowardly', one report noted, adding how the object of the game seemed to be 'knock out' the opposition. After watching the teams 'lining out' with each man going for the man opposite and bringing him down 'by any means in his power', the correspondent concluded: 'I left disgusted with the exhibition. Brute force was accepted as a substitute for skill and science, and there was little, if any, real sporting spirit shown by the players'.[9] Another story in the British press marvelled that the number of casualties sustained in traditional Thanksgiving Day games

> was enormous, and the recent match between Yale and Harvard almost assumed the proportions of a small massacre … To return with his shield or on it would almost seem to be required as a motto by the modern footballer.[10]

British newspapers reported other negative aspects of the American game. As British conservatives battled to maintain amateurism in sport, they insisted that the evils of professionalism had already penetrated into American university sport. The *Manchester Guardian* recorded that the 1893 Yale-Princeton match had brought in $50,000 in gate receipts and that these profits were being used to recruit students solely for their football talents.[11] Positive views were occasionally offered. In 1895, the US defender of American amateurism Caspar Whitney reported the impressions he garnered on his pilgrimage to study English sport. Whitney expressed disappointment with English football although he could identify where American 'scientifically developed play' originated:

> Our own American university game is so superior in point of scientific preparation and skilful play that I felt exactly as though, for instance, I had gone to see the Princeton 'Varsity team, and, instead, the scrub slaves had been brought out for my entertainment. I could not help the feeling, as I stood on the side lines, that I was a spectator of an undeveloped game – that there were so many ignored opportunities. One who knows American football must, on first seeing a Rugby Union match, feel he is watching an elementary game.[12]

At the end of the nineteenth century, despite sporadic efforts to portray American football as a product of a modern, sophisticated, and cultured society, the overarching British portrayal depicted vulgar Americans remaking a tough, manly British sport into a degenerate game–the product of a coarse and deteriorating culture.[13]

The Game Arrives, 1910–1918

In April 1910, the British press informed the public that American football rules had been materially changed again to increase safety, 'but without eliminating the spectacular side of the game'. However, in November of that year, British newspaper readers were informed about the death of West Virginia University quarterback Rudolph Munk from 'concussion of the brain'.[14] Five days later, the media announced that an American football match was to be played in London by the visiting US Navy's Atlantic Fleet. The USS *Idaho* of the fleet's Third Division, moored in the Thames estuary, had challenged the USS *Michigan* of the First Division lying at Portland.[15] The press stressed that the initial challenge had been issued by wireless over a distance of approximately 130 miles, buttressing the view of America as a developing naval and technological power. Ultimately, a three match tournament was organized, starting with one game for the Third Division in London and a further match for the First Division in Weymouth, both on Thanksgiving. The winners were slated to meet for the fleet championship. The day before Thanksgiving, the newspapers revealed that the team representing the battleship *Idaho* would play the squad from the battleship *Vermont* at Crystal Palace. Reports promised that 'American sailors will appear on the field with a full complement of the necessary football "armour," including head-guards, shin-guards, and well-padded clothing. British reporters anticipated a keen display of their much-discussed American "College" game'.[16]

In light of the established image of American football, it is not surprising that the *London Daily News* account of the USS *Vermont* versus USS *Idaho* clash led with the headline: 'Nobody was killed at the American football match at the Crystal Palace yesterday'. The London correspondent observed that the game attracted widespread interest 'mainly because of its novelty to an English crowd, and partly because of the appalling casualty lists from the States that so frequently bring the American game into derision on the English side of the Atlantic'. The curious English crowd of 12,000 enjoyed 'a rousing struggle' which the *Idaho* won 19–0.[17] *The Times* reported that the slippery ground, a greasy ball, and the ineptitude of the *Vermont* team had prevented an object lesson in American football, 'the first of the kind ever given in this country'. In the view of *The Times*, the majority of spectators left the American exhibition convinced that Rugby Union was 'superior in every respect, better to play, and better to watch'. *The Times* did admit that it was a clean match played with keenness and good humour and casualties were few and not serious. The London daily opined that the 'yearly "butcher's bill" of which so much is heard in the United States' must be the result of those who deliberately indulged in foul and brutal play. Nevertheless, even when played in a sporting spirit and to the letter of the laws, the game was rough. In fact, *The Times* contended that 'an ill-tempered game of Rugby football in the Celtic twilight is a Sunday school picnic in comparison'. The report concluded that the game was a:

> Direct descendant of the all-in football of our ancestors (but we) shall stick to our preference despite the Crystal Palace object-lesson in an antiquarian pursuit, a fossilized form of football. But one must needs feel amazed and a little amused that the Americans should be playing 16th century football in the 20th century. Really it is rather unprogressive.[18]

In the next contest, the USS *Connecticut* beat the USS *Michigan* at Weymouth, setting up a contest against the *Idaho* for the championship. In the lacklustre final, 'the only score was the winning try gained by the Idaho team'. The victory signalled the *Idaho*'s band to make great demonstrations of enthusiasm. 'The hurricane-like tactics of the players is reflected in the attitude of the spectators, who follow the game with a nervous energy and vociferous enthusiasm which must be rather exhausting', *The Times* marvelled. The game produced, from the vantage of elite London daily, 'an exhibition which, if to a great extent incomprehensible to the English football expert, was nevertheless interesting by reason of its mystery and contrast'.[19]

American football left Britain with the fleet until the outbreak of the First World War when sporting events began to be used for charity. In November 1915, two American teams played an American football match for the benefit of the Prince of Wales's and the Red Cross Funds during the Christmas holidays.[20] Once the US joined the Allied cause and American troops began to arrive, charity matches were played around the country. Two US Navy units drew 0–0 at Stamford Bridge, Chelsea, in aid of the St. Dunstan's Blind Servicemen charity. *The Times*, after trying to explain the game's rules, concluded by describing the many 'concomitants, which we are accustoming ourselves to hear in many American games', including the marching band, an airship, and dancing by spectators. In 1918, the Liverpool Hospital Cup final was held on the American Thanksgiving holiday at Goodison Park between the USS *Leviathan* and a team of engineers from the Knotty Ash American Army rest camp. The event featured the usual entertainment: the ship's band, organized cheering and displays, and a trophy presented by the Lord Mayor of Liverpool.[21]

Significantly more people, however, were introduced to American football through a 45 s, silent, black and white Pathé newsreel of the Harvard-Yale game in 1916 than through charity gridiron contests in England. Although the newsreel did not include pre-match or half-time entertainments, the film narrative captured essential elements of pageantry of American football, including the vast crowd emphasized through an opening panning shot, the speed of the game revealed by a long distance view of a down, and the intensity of the action captured from a side-line camera. Audiences enjoyed a longer exposure in the comedy short *Won by a Foot*, released to good reviews in 1917, a year when over 20 million people a week went to the cinema. One critic labelled it 'a rattling comedy in which the remarkably strenuous American game of football was vividly illustrated'.[22]

The First World War irrevocably changed the relationship between Britain and America as the US realized its potential as a world power and Britain's self-confidence declined and a slow retreat from empire began. Significant numbers of British citizens must have wondered if the America portrayed on the cinema screen, in American novels and comics, and in American versions of team sports offered a better future. American football departed with the troops but significant numbers of the public had now either seen it, live or on film, or read match reports. The game was different, not British, but nevertheless an entertaining spectacle generating excitement. To many, this alternative version of football offering modernity, dynamism, and fun represented a microcosm of the possibilities of American styles of life.

The Interbellum

Post-war, newspaper reports of American football declined, becoming mainly restricted to the results or 'sports in brief' columns. Occasionally, more detailed stories appeared with the press continuing to illuminate the differences between American football and British games. However, with the public having seen the game, the images of brutality and violence were curtailed and the sport as spectacle emphasized. In 1929, a syndicated story described attending a match in America:

> Just as you cannot fool all the public all the time, so the game would not persist, nor enjoy its wonderful popularity, if it were not actually a great game … the band and cheer leaders fan a flame, and thus when a sensational incident does occur, lo! One is on one's feet with the rest of them … you too are yelling at lung limit, and what you are yelling, and why you are yelling, you don't quite know – nor do you care; you've been bitten by the football bug.[23]

The enthusiasm of the vast crowds was accentuated in the newsreels which, by the 1920s, were widely popular and audiences felt that no cinema programme was complete without them.[24] Pathé showed the opening game of the 1921 season in a story entitled 'U.S.A. Some Game! … the game, although a little more strenuous than ours, – attracts many "fans"'. The film sets the format for broadcasting American football to British audiences for the period, starting with an opening long shot of the action including the large stadium crowd, then cutting to a medium shot showing a fast-moving down, and then inter-cutting views of a happy boisterous crowd, including a smartly dressed band in this instance, followed by close-ups emphasizing the power and intensity of the action. By 1929, the newsreels included the pre-game show as well. The newsreel of Notre Dame's 7–0 defeat of the Army highlights the vast crowd and the drilling cadets on the field with a group of male cheerleaders forming a pyramid. The Army-Navy game became an annual staple and followed the well-established format of an enticing title. In 1930, British audiences were heralded with 'Excitement! … 100% plus!!'. The clip then presented pre-game shots of drilling army and navy cadets, and close-ups of players emphasizing their ruggedness in a similar manner to the heroes of Westerns of the period. Once the game starts, the action is interspersed with close-ups of the excited cheering crowd and streamers being thrown into the air when a touchdown is scored. Outside of the areas where the cadets congregated, the cameras captured a high proportion of well-dressed women.[25]

The newsreels also featured children's and prison football games, as well as women training and playing. The newsreel narratives stressed the modernity of the game through the training equipment in use, the precision manufacture of equipment, and even a clip of a scientist demonstrating a new helmet design by running head first into a brick wall. American football also introduced slow motion to British viewers. The 1926 Princeton victory over Harvard followed the standard format until an inter-title, 'Going for it "hammer and tongs ... in slow motion"', emphasized the athleticism of a running back and the power of the tackling and blocking through slow-motion footage.[26]

While cinema audiences were declining from the 1917 peak, the 1920s and 1930s saw a steady growth in middle-class cinema goers although the most frequent customers were the young urban working-class, especially women. There was an accompanying increase in the proportion of American films shown and to many in the audiences America seemed glamorous, sophisticated, and romantic; a 'Promised Land' away from their own dull jobs and financial struggles. British audiences copied clothing styles and saw the progenitors of rock music in films. A cinema correspondent observed:

> The plain truth about the film situation is that the bulk of our picturegoers are Americanised to an extent that makes them regard a British film as a foreign film, and an interesting but more frequently irritating interlude to their favourite entertainment. They go to see American stars ... They talk America, think America, and dream America. We have several million people, mostly women, who for all intent and purposes are temporary American citizens.[27]

With the arrival of 'talkies' in 1929, the weekly audiences recovered reaching 18 million per week in 1930 and increased dramatically through the Second World War to peak at 31 million in 1946. Throughout the 1920s, 1930s, and 1940s, American films dominated the screens with their stories of ambition, competition, conflict, tension, and moral and emotional intensity, and American football was integral to stories that showcased these themes in such films as *The Freshman*, *Horse Feathers* and *Easy Living*.[28] Although live games had disappeared from Britain, the silver screen image of American football represented fun, speed, excitement, and spectacle in a dynamic, wealthy, egalitarian, and developing America.

The interwar period also intensified British critiques of American culture and influence. As travel improved, more writers crossed the Atlantic and the diverse opinions of America intensified. H.G. Wells, the prolific English writer, believed American influence would help the world be freer and more stable and J.B. Priestly, a social commentator, was impressed by the collective developments of 'The New Deal' whilst joining other critics in worrying that the worst of monopoly capitalism was fuelling a superficial and vulgar mass culture that could undermine Britain's cultural heritage.[29] As the 1930s ended, a larger invasion by American mass culture approached.

The Second World War

Cinemas remained open throughout the Second World War and newsreels continued to show American football, even on the deck of the USS *Wasp* at sea. In 1940, Pathé introduced a story with consecutive titles, 'Exclusive!', 'Special Release!', 'The FIRST Newsreel subject ever presented in color', 'The Tournament of Roses – The Rose Bowl Game'. Stirring music accompanied the headline barrage. This story ran for nearly six and a half minutes and featured the Rose Parade with horsemen carrying the American flag, two-piece swimsuited girls waving from a float accompanied by wolf whistles on the sound track, marching majorettes, and the Grand Marshal in an open-topped car. The Rose Bowl game followed, utilizing the formula of interspersed takes of the action and the crowd, who, at half time, made a US flag by holding up coloured cards. In blacked-out and ration-book Britain, the event must have appeared highly glamorous, fun, and seductive. The colour and mixed crowd of men and women would have made a vivid contrast to the male working-class throngs in dour football stadiums in Britain.[30]

In 1942, the first of three million American servicemen arrived and live games re-emerged, often, once again, for charitable purposes. Despite having reported on the games of 1910 and 1918, *The Times* inaccurately asserted that 'the first game of American football ever to be seen in this country will be played at the White City Stadium on Saturday, May 8'. The match was in aid of the Red Cross Prisoners of War Fund and the teams competing were 'The Crimson Tide' and 'The Fighting Irish', a field artillery unit and an engineering unit. The London daily announced that complete regulation equipment was to be worn, two US Army bands would attend, and there would be cheerleaders and reserved cheering sections for soldiers. On the morning of the game, *The Times* outlined the main features of the game, once again mistakenly asserting that the exercise was necessary because 'American football … has often been seen on the films but never in the flesh in this country'. It noted that the game was being played as a gesture of gratitude for the hospitality shown to American troops in Britain and every attempt was being made to make the match like 'an inter-collegiate game back home'. The post-game story revealed that most non-American spectators thought there were too many delays, that the game was slow, 'almost, at times, to the point of becoming tedious', and that most British spectators missed a number of the finer points of the American version of football. Some spectators no doubt missed all of them.[31]

The game that stirred up the most media interest was the 'Tea Bowl' at the White City stadium in February 1944. This pitted a Canadian Army team against an US Army team. The crowd of 30,000 had the additional entertainment of the Canadian pipe bands and an US army band. The first half was played under American rules and the second half under Canadian rules. The Canadians won 16–6 and the Americans demanded a rematch. A month later, the White City hosted the 'Coffee Bowl' in front of 50,000 people which the Americans won 18–0.[32]

The Cold War

At the end of the Second World War, as Britain's economy lay in ruins, America's position as the world's leading military and economic power was confirmed. In February 1946, Soviet Premier Joseph Stalin announced that capitalism and imperialism made future wars inevitable and in March, British Prime Minister Winston Churchill delivered his speech in the USA asserting, 'an iron curtain has descended across the continent'.[33] The American government committed itself to the defence of Europe and some 50,000 American service personnel remained in Britain.

The permanent basing of American troops meant that more American football was being played than ever before in Britain, although mainly out of the public eye on military bases. The United States Air Force in Europe (USAFE) established an American football league with an United Kingdom Sports Conference. Although newspaper coverage of American football declined, Pathé news continued their frequent film stories featuring the occasional professional game, the customary Army-Navy games, the Cotton and Rose Bowls, as well as intermittent oddities such as a 1958 feature of a women's water skiing team passing a football.[34]

In December 1952, the USAFE American football season championship match was played at Wembley. On the morning of the game, *The Times* reported that 'This afternoon promises to be full of astonishing sights and sounds – that is to British eyes and ears – as it will be unique for the Americans themselves'.[35] The programme featured massed bands, cheerleaders, drum majors, and majorettes 'along with all the other concomitants of a football match of the first magnitude on the other side of the Atlantic'. The post-game story provided a summary of the match and noted 'an astonishing number of colourful formalities' in which the famous drum majorettes played their part before the appearance of the teams. At half-time, there was a memorable exhibition of drill by the Honour Guard from Heidelberg who conducted at a quick step with rifle drill that could only 'be described as juggling … a truly remarkable performance'. Newsreel footage the following week emphasized the 'girl cheerleaders', close-ups of the ferocious action, and the enthusiastic crowd of 20,000.[36]

The prevalence of American service personnel and the continued preponderance of American films and TV programmes resulted in millions becoming infatuated with American popular culture. A minority reviled the obsession with America. From their vantage, it felt as if the military occupation of the Second World War was being replaced by an occupation of the mind. However, many Britons identified with and desired the lifestyles projected at the movies and on television, the freedom of the open road, modern cities with sky-scrapers, shopping malls, clean highly automated factories, and well-laid out suburbs where good-looking men and women had nice houses and luxury cars. America offered a vision that anyone could be talented and become successful, even if they were from unfashionable working-class communities. Women and girls copied American clothing and hairstyles whilst using or wanting make-up by American brands, and James Dean and Marlon Brando equally impressed young men. Popular culture depicted life as exciting, glamorous, and romantic in America, and all that made life pleasurable in Britain seemed to come from the US.[37]

American football newsreels strengthened this view. The highlights enhanced the excitement of the action and of the crowds, including close-ups of beautiful women and glamorous celebrities. The British press began to emphasize star players. Cut-ins of the 1959 Baltimore Colts defeat of the New York Giants showed packed stands, including Vice President Richard M. Nixon, and close-ups of the Colt's dynamic quarterback, Johnny Unitas, underlining his rugged masculinity in a manner reminiscent of Western heroes, a force for good, and the prototype modern heroic quarterback.[38] Some politicians and intellectuals believed that 'having a good time' was being emphasized rather than the necessary ethos of hard work with plain living and unsophisticated leisure, qualities now perceived by many to equate to a life of boredom and banality. Critics continued to believe that American mass culture was not only levelling down high culture, but also lowering the morals of the young. Although little graphic violence or sex was portrayed through film or the TV, some developed the impression that American cities were in the thrall of gangsters and dope addicts.[39]

The increase in TV ownership through the 1950s and the development of nightly news broadcasts sounded the death knell for the newsreel with the result that American football faded in the consciousness of the general public.[40] By the 1960s, America was no longer the place of dreams to most Britons. Britain had been transformed into a more liberal society set in its own modern landscape whilst enjoying increased ownership of the modern conveniences of life. British popular culture garnered global admiration as America's international prestige declined. The assassination of President John Fitzgerald Kennedy and the Civil Rights Movement received widespread coverage alongside bleak TV images of urban decay. Still, the spectacular and sometimes disputed nature of American football games captured some newspaper attention. *The Times*, for example, reported on the battle by some University of Chicago students to enforce the 1939 ban on American football at their institution because they felt that the game was a symbol of all that was undesirable in American education, 'a brutish throwback to barbarism'. *The Times* noted that as Chicago was a small university, it could not organize 'a big time' college team since the public 'still demand spectacular games, with marching bands, drum-majorettes and other half-time attractions'.[41]

The Super Bowl Arrives

Through the 1970s, the British view of America became darker as rising murder and crime rates were widely reported. The Watergate scandal exposed corruption in society's upper reaches and a new wave of films, such as *Dog Day Afternoon,* and TV programmes such as *Starsky & Hutch* showed violence as part of everyday American life.[42] Nevertheless, America still fascinated the world and its popular culture was admired and copied. In 1971, Britain's commercial network, Independent Television (ITV), telecast a 'World of Sports' programme that used Super Bowl highlights to entertain and amuse its audience between two of its featured horse races. The Super Bowl fit among other between race fillers, including archery, gymnastics, and table tennis as well as international events such as log rolling from Alberta or cliff diving from La Quebrada.[43] ITV's innovation proved successful and the programme showed annual Super Bowl highlights until 1980. Awareness of the Super Bowl developed through these annual glimpses, initially through happenstance. In 1971, *The Times* reported that the lead news item of the morning in New York was not the safe return of Apollo 15 from the moon but an injury to Joe Namath's knee, the quarterback of the New York Jets and one of America's most glamorous sportsmen. 'Broadway Joe' illustrated how sportsmen had become international celebrities, known as much for their activities off the football field as on it. He featured in glossy magazines and his name and image regularly appeared in the newspapers, on television, and on advertising billboards. Namath helped to change the image of the American footballer from a 'beautiful physical specimen, abstemious and not noted for his intellect', to a man who was not only a Super Bowl winning quarterback but admitted liking strong drink, pretty girls, fast cars, and fast talk.[44]

British journalist Ian Wooldridge, was in New Orleans reporting on the Joe Frazier versus Terry Daniels world heavyweight title fight the day before Super Bowl VI. He noticed that the Super Bowl generated far more interest than the heavyweight title bout. Woolridge observed that the Super Bowl spectacle was 'the craziest razzamatazz event in the entire calendar of American athletic entertainment', attracting 65 million American television viewers in 1971 and generating more than 1,200,000 words cabled by the media from the stadium.[45] Woolridge noticed that American football had replaced not only prize-fighting but baseball as the most passionately followed sport in the US. As soon as the Super Bowl finished President Nixon phoned the winning coach offering congratulations 'in precisely the same emotionally throaty tones that he uses for Apollo splashdowns', Woolridge trenchantly observed.[46] British correspondents noted how the interest of politicians signalled an increase in the game's importance and glamour. *The Times* reported on the rising passion for football sweeping America making it 'the national obsession which, however briefly, leaps across the barriers of class, race, and even sex'. Those enamoured included President Nixon who even telephoned tactical suggestions to football coaches 'more often than to his military commanders'. Indeed, military operations had code words chosen from football, such as the 1972 'Operation Linebacker' in the Vietnam War. *The Times* contended that the

> meticulously calculated applications of brute force and opportunism and the gladiatorial passions these arouse do reflect a uniquely American aspect of character ... The glory of the game is the soaring, artillery-shell forward pass, which in its brief grace can compensate for all the dour slogging.[47]

The *Economist* revealed that Mrs. Patricia Nixon advised football widows to watch the game themselves; if the President was called away to the phone, she regarded it 'as her duty to report to him what he had missed'. The *Daily Mail*'s Dermot Purgavie noted that America was prepared to come to a halt for the Super Bowl, but the main philosophical question was on which side was God as both teams, Washington Redskins and Miami Dolphins, held locker-room services before a game. The Redskins also benefited from the prayers of the president.[48]

By 1974, the British newspapers had begun an annual fascination with the Super Bowl environment. Super Bowl finances especially captured interest. The *Daily Mail* reported that the advertising slots had been sold out in April, 10 months before the game and before anybody knew who was playing. At £84,000 a minute, the lucrative deals netted Columbia Broadcasting System (CBS) £1,596,000. The *Economist* contemplated on the idea that television had done more for professional American football than the forward pass: 'In fact, the Super Bowl has become so attractive that advertisers who use television only occasionally paid $210,000 a minute to put their message over in 30 million homes'.[49] In 1977, the *Daily Mail*'s Anthea Disney revealed that America was in the throes of 'the Six Million Dollar Hype, otherwise known as the Super Bowl'. She argued that if Britons imagined it 'as a simple athletic event you are very wrong'. She reported on the media frenzy, the well-behaved athletes who answered the same inane questions two hundred times, the fact that there was more gambling on Super Bowl Sunday than the rest of the year combined, and the fact that researchers have concluded 'that the Super Bowl is only slightly less popular than sex'. The following year Disney focussed on the competition for catering rights and the enormous efforts required to provide for the needs of the 75,000 fans lucky enough to get tickets.[50] Disney's *Daily Mail* colleague, Liz Hodgson, underpinned the importance of the game to America by noting that whereas 2000 reporters covered the summit between US President Ronald Reagan and Soviet leader Mikhail Gorbachev, 2400 were accredited to the Super Bowl, outnumbering players by a 40 to 1 ratio.[51]

In 1981, Super Bowl XV became the first championship spectacle transmitted live to Britain. Beamed to an audience at the Odeon Theatre in London's Leicester Square, the event drew a crowd numbering about 2500, most of whom were Americans.[52] Post-game *The Times* reported:

> There was a corner of Leicester Square the other night that was, for three hours at least, American. Cowboy hats, football shirts, cheerleaders, hot dogs and whooping cries were the scene as the Odeon cinema audience prepared for the Super Bowl, the United States version of the FA Cup Final ... (however) long before the end, those arrayed in green walked away from inevitable defeat and out into the reality of a cold London dawn.[53]

The Channel 4 Years, 1982–1998

In November 1982, Channel 4, with a remit to provide alternative programming for tastes not served by mainstream TV, began broadcasting in Great Britain. The network appointed Adrian Metcalfe the commissioning editor for sport. An experienced sportsman and a 1964 Olympic silver medallist in the 4x400 metre relay, Metcalfe had also worked in sport television production for London Weekend Television and in the US on CBS 'Sports Spectacular'.[54] Metcalfe wanted to not only report on sport but surround broadcasts with the event atmosphere. If Channel 4 broadcast an event, it would be covered well and production companies would be carefully selected.[55] Metcalfe admired the way US broadcasters handled NFL football and decided to emulate the American model in his new venture.

He selected Cheerleader Productions to produce the programme and purchased an NFL video and commentary package which he believed to be appealing to advertisers and the British audience. Channel 4 re-packaged NFL games into edited highlight shows accompanied by carefully selected music and vivid graphics. The remit for commercial broadcasting permitted experimentation and attracted funds from American brewing giant Anheuser-Busch to glamorize the product whilst providing a strategic marketing opportunity to develop the British taste for American football and Budweiser beer.[56] Cheerleader's managing director, Derek Brandon noted:

> The televising of sport in America is simply stunning. They make it fun, they make it stylish, and they make it a family occasion. These are all things we've lost from British sport. If LWT had done American Football ... they'd have been back to the presenter in the blazer with the glass of water.[57]

Shortly before broadcasting began, the *Economist* related that more Americans watched the Super Bowl than any other TV programme and it was attracting young, affluent and well-educated fans. It noted that the three US national networks had agreed to pay the NFL $2 billion over the next five seasons to broadcast the games because the NFL had more 'razzmatazz than baseball or basketball'.[58]

Channel 4 broadcast its first American football show three days after the station went on air, 5 November 1982. Early programmes included an 'idiot's guide' to the game. In the same vein, *The Times* added,

> to the uninitiated American football is covered with as many technical phrases as there are bits of padding on the dozens of players in each team, and the sport is as bewildering to the Englishman as cricket is to the average American.

Still, *The Times* remarked, 'the spectacular sport is ablaze with glittering colour, awash with deafening noise and alive with a vibrant atmosphere rarely found in an English stadium ... At times the sport is bruisingly brutal; at others as delightfully delicate'. An estimated 750,000 people watched the first 75-min programme, more than had viewed rugby union earlier in the evening.[59] The broadcast slot, across 6.00 p.m. on Sundays, was traditionally a TV dead spot for British youth given that the 'BBC and ITV were showing religious programs' in that time slot. American football allowed Channel 4 to corner the youth market in that broadcast slot. Up until this point, American football had been considered a 'zany' pastime which most Britons did not understand. Channel 4 would soon change that.[60]

To introduce the programme the multi-coloured Channel 4 logo morphed into a smoke-snorting American football helmet-wearing figure accompanied by the score of the 'Montagues and Capulets' from Prokofiev's Romeo and Juliet.[61] Then Jeremy Isaacs, the Channel 4 CEO noted Cheerleader Productions 'gave it the works to the sound of pop hits – quarterbacks threw, wide receivers leaped, tight ends crashed, running heroes touched down for glory and bounced, signalled and postured in celebration'.[62] Channel 4's first season ended with a live broadcast of Super Bowl XVII, and the success of the coverage increased reportage of American football across the media. The *Daily Mail*, previewing the National Football Conference playoff, announced that 'for the first time in ten years something *really* important is happening in Washington ... today at 12:30 the Redskins begin combat against their arch rivals, the Dallas Cowboys'. The correspondent noted that the American capital city was 'certifiably crazy' over the game and awash in burgundy and gold. When the Redskins won, qualifying for the Super Bowl, the London daily reported that Secretary of State George Shultz and his party had arranged a live feed of the game during their diplomatic tour of Tokyo. Commenting on the following unexpected Super Bowl win by Washington, the *Economist* reported that President Reagan, sporting a Redskins cap, saluted the team's heroic running back, John Riggings, by rechristening his financial policy 'Rigginomics', in an effort to restore its popular appeal.[63]

In its first season Channel 4 averaged an audience of over one million viewers for its Sunday programme. Nearly three quarters of a million tuned in for the Super Bowl, which began at midnight in the British Isles. In a pre-match commentary for Super Bowl XVIII, the second to be shown live by Channel 4, *The Times*' Simon Barnes suggested 'American football is becoming a fact of British life, and if you are not going to a Superbowl [*sic*] party on Sunday night, you really aren't making it'. He knew that many people thought the game would not catch on because Britons

> could not understand who was doing what to whom and what the rules are. Perhaps that is no hindrance after all; as a San Francisco 49er recently remarked, half the American audiences don't really understand the rules, and we've got a few players like that as well.[64]

More than twenty years later, in 2007, The *Guardian* reminisced that people went to Super Bowl parties in the 1980s barely knowing which teams were playing, 'hadn't the foggiest notion of the rules ... stayed up to three in the morning drinking weak beer (Miller Lite, anyone?) vaguely staring at a screen'.[65]

By Super Bowl XVIII, Channel 4's American football telecast was regularly one of its top ten shows and also in the top ten sports shows on British TV. In August 1983, *Touchdown*, a British-based magazine devoted to the sport debuted. It soon sold over 25,000 copies per issue. Britons began to play as well as watch the American version of football. Over 30 British American football teams were regularly playing at that time, albeit mainly flag-football as many of the squads had no kit.[66] The NFL benefitted from British interest as sales of officially licensed products rose from £125,000 in 1983–1984 to over £25 million in 1987.[67] Miles Kington wrote a tongue-in-cheek commentary in *The Times* on why American football was attracting a growing audience in Britain. He opined that whilst American football was boring, it was less boring than rugby and enlivened by dancing girls and the interesting drawings on the players' helmets. In essence, Kington contended, the audience felt they were watching American foreign policy in action and were fairly sure that Americans were going to win for a change.[68]

American football remained Channel 4's sports flagship for the next ten years, but viewing figures peaked in 1986 with a weekly audience of nearly 3¼ million and over 3½ million watching Super Bowl XX.[69] The growth years coincided with English association football seemingly condemned to terminal decline following stadium tragedies at Bradford and

Heysel that killed scores of fans, intransigent and ingrained traditions of hooliganism, and the domination of the game by tedious and dreary tactics. In addition, English football was blacked-out from TV for over four months due to arguments over rights-fees.[70] Into this TV void came American football, with fun-filled features including 'cheerleaders, "Hail Marys" and sophisticated touchdown celebrations'.[71] Even the stadia in which American football was played seemed universally comfortable, attractive and, usually, sun-filled, symbols of modernity compared to the decayed state of British football stadia.[72]

Market research for the 1985–1986 and 1987–1988 American football seasons identified Channel 4's audience as being affluent and principally from the middle and upper classes, as well as being predominantly male and in the younger age groups.[73] As *The Sunday Times* observed:

> Cheerleader have clearly found the advertisers' nirvana – a young, rich and enthusiastic audience … It's almost as if the yuppies of the world were waiting for a spectator sport they could feel was theirs – something that was at its best when watched on the small screen in the warmth of their home.[74]

The media continued to report the astronomical sums paid per minute of air time during the Super Bowl and in 1999 the *Economist* concluded that 'the Super Bowl, which attracts around 90 m viewers, the largest audience of the year, is the ultimate brand-building slot, and Super Bowl advertisements are the most talked about of the year'.[75] However, British Channel 4 viewers could not see the much-hyped advertisements unless they sought them out on the internet.[76]

Super Bowl XVIII in 1984, reinforced the image of American wealth, glamour and excitement shown in programmes such as *Dallas*, a national obsession in Britain. It featured two university marching bands of well-scrubbed youngsters in extravagant uniforms with glittering instruments performing a stunning and fun display before Barry Manilow, a highly popular artist in Britain, sang the national anthem. The half-time show harkened back to a nostalgic and romantic American past through a musical 'Salute to the Superstars of the Silver Screen'.[77]

In contrast to the razzmatazz of the Super Bowl, TV programming, newspapers and movies of the mid-1980s painted a bleak picture of the US in the British imagination, depicting cities as squalid and awash in crime fuelled by an epidemic of drug abuse. In 1985, Sue Mott of *The Times* broached the issue of drug problems in American sport. She revealed a litany of disturbing incidents. Tulane University players had shaved points for gambling syndicates in return for cocaine; a Pittsburgh drug trafficking ring involved baseball players; and Steve Courson of the NFL's Tampa Bay Buccaneers' estimated that 95 per cent of football players had tried drugs. 'You've got to get on drugs if you want to survive', Courson confessed. In America, Mott ventured, the athlete is perceived as a 'coke snorting, dope-pushing, steroid popping zombie, who would sell grandma and the furniture for a Porsche convertible and a spot on a television beer commercial'. She noted that evidence suggested that drugs were prevalent in sport from high school to the professionals. In 1986, Michael Binyon penned *The Times* report on Don Rogers, the Cleveland Browns football star, who died from a cocaine overdose. Rogers' death led to questions about the NFL Players Association protests against mandatory random testing as an invasion of privacy. Binyon depicted drug usage in American sport and society as rampant, noting that 'one in six has tried cocaine in high school … and more than half of all crime in the United States is now related to drugs'.[78]

Covering American football led Mott to explore not only drugs but the impact of unbridled American capitalism, a different reading of *Dallas* that focused on the excesses of American materialism, greed, and self-interest buttressing themes also showcased in movies such as *Wall Street*. Mott examined franchising problems in American sport following the attempt of the Philadelphia Eagles owner to move the franchise to Phoenix. She concluded her investigation with a quotation from a Brooklyn Dodgers baseball fan who was still bitter about the flight of his team to Los Angeles more than 25 years before: 'it made me realize that all sport is strictly business and to hell with the fans'.[79]

This split view of America as either a glamorous and exciting place that rewarded individual effort or a squalid and dangerous place where the poor had no effective safety net, led to enigmatic imaginings of America as the 'land of the free' or 'the great Satan', divergent interpretations both supported by American football.[80] In the *Daily Mail*, Dermot Purgavie in his previews of Super Bowl XX recognized the Super Bowl as a cultural rite celebrating the blessed trinity of sport, television, and free enterprise in front of America's biggest TV audience. Purgavie insisted that the trinity's importance was most clearly acknowledged by President Reagan tossing the coin via satellite from Washington where he was being inaugurated for his second presidential term. Two days later, Purgavie prodded beneath the gladiatorial armour to reveal the pain of the game to the 'journeyman' player shown in the HBO documentary *Disposable Heroes*. Jim Otto, a former Oakland Raiders centre, suffered from arthritis in 'every joint in his body' alongside a multitude of other health problems following thirty concussions, 25 broken noses, a detached retina, nine knee operations and 150 facial stitches.[81]

Sporting heroes had been in short supply in 1980s Britain, and the NFL and its teams made individuals available to the British press to help prospective fans identify stars and develop the narrative around the game. William 'the Refrigerator' Perry quickly became a celebrity and 'a good many citizens swooned over that dandy young Miami quarter back, Marino'.[82] In *The Times* Simon Barnes ruminated that American football stars were heroes in Britain partly because little was known about them. American football was the last refuge of the true sporting hero, and audiences got 'fiendishly tantalizing weekly glimpses throughout the autumn, and we know nothing whatever about them other than they play football'. American football, Barnes argued, was 'an exoticism, the rules obscure, the heroes utterly mysterious. They don't even have faces; they play masked. How doubly and trebly wonderful they are because of their mysteriousness'.[83]

In 1986, Market and Opinion Research International (MORI), a leading social research company, found that over 60 per cent of Britons would not want to live in the US if they had to live outside of the UK although they liked Americans and would like a holiday there.[84] In parallel to the decline of American esteem, Channel 4's American football audience declined through the second half of the 1980s and into the 1990s. Many who had responded to the packaging and enjoyed the sport as an opportunity for 'stylistic self-expression', 'self-conscious display', and an 'ethic of fun' moved on to the next big thing. Very few Britons had taken up participating in the American variety of football, resulting in an insignificant number of people attaining a deep understanding of the game or responding to its fundamental nature. Most Britons were passive viewers 'imperfectly equipped with the specific competence needed to decipher it adequately'.[85] Mick Luckhurst, one of the earliest native Britons to play in the NFL as a kicker for the Atlanta Falcons, became one of Channel

4's NFL broadcast hosts after he retired from American football. Luckhurst explained the problems of meeting the needs of an audience not reared in the traditions of the game:

> It is very diversified. There is a small group, 10% or less, that reads every football magazine and studies every play. Then there is a larger group that has a basic understanding and just likes the game. But I am sure that there is quite a large group that is just entertained by the very large men in crash helmets beating the junk out of each other.[86]

In 1993, control of Channel 4 passed to the Channel Four Television Corporation, which signalled a change in target audience from the fringes of society to the edges of mainstream society. American football was shunted around the schedule and viewing figures inevitably dropped further.

In the 1990s, America was often regarded with hostility through its indifference to world opinion, refusing to sign the Kyoto Climate protocol in 1997 and its unquestioning support of Israel as the rest of world sought a Palestinian state. In Britain, the Louise Woodward affair led to the impression that the US had a barbaric legal system.[87] In the same period English football teams were readmitted to international competition and 'rebranded as the Premier League, brawlers were shoved from the stadiums, ratings began soaring into the global-TV-revenue stratosphere and the global-sports-league ionosphere. The NFL waned'. British American football leagues declined from a peak of six in 1987 with 166 registered teams to one league in 1999 with 30 teams. In 1998, Channel 4 dropped American football whilst acquiring the rights to domestic international (Test) cricket matches.[88] British fans have continued watching live coverage of the Super Bowl and various NFL packages as other broadcasters have negotiated TV rights.

American Football as a Reflection of America

America and American football have been intertwined in the British imagination since the late nineteenth century. Initially when the public's only information about the game was through newspapers, the British press portrayed it as a brutal and unsportsmanlike game form evolving from a barbaric and decivilizing society. Once the game was played in Britain, reported upon by journalists who actually saw the game, and highlights were seen on newsreels, the American football transformed from an atavistic carnival into a modern spectacle.

Over the next several decades, through two world wars, the depression, and the Cold War, Britons continued to make occasional readings of American culture through football. The game remained, however, a rare and exotic experience they encountered in an occasional newsreel clip or newspaper story. In the early 1980s television changed the equation. Channel 4's broadcasting of weekly highlights and live Super Bowls was a watershed when a significant proportion of the public came to imagine the gridiron as a slice of America, that, in the words of a reporter in *The Times*, was

> up there with blue jeans, skyscrapers and pecan pie; as a spectacle, a National Football League game is the distillation of a Springsteen concert, a Las Vegas review and a latter-day *Gunfight at the OK Corral*. Real American stuff as they say.[89]

The *Guardian*'s Jim Shelley thought part of the attraction was the commentators' accents, the cool high-tech space-age uniforms, the referees' 'old American faces taking no nonsense', and the players with names like Plaxico Burress. For Shelley, what ultimately makes American football 'so great is its combination of power and speed, skill and violence, but really, as with most things American, when it comes to the secret of its appeal, it's the size, its scale, the sheer monotony that makes it'.[90]

To Simon Barnes of *The Times*, it was no coincidence that the press headquarters of his first Super Bowl was a 'couple of blocks away from Disneyland' as 'the Super Bowl has become the most gorgeously, sumptuously, ridiculously and splendidly vulgar over-the-top media event in the history of sport'. He cited overhearing an American observer who noted that football was like a cartoon, 'people get hit and smashed and chopped down – and then they get up and do it again'. The same man added that football brought out the worst in American society, violence and committee meetings, 'a load of guys jump on top of someone, and then hold a meeting about doing it again'.[91] Barnes acknowledged that 'the Super Bowl is the America we English can understand; all shiny excess, violence and cosmetics. Baseball is the America that does not get on the screen; the America that people live in. The spiritual home of the Super Bowl is Disneyland; the World Series is part of the heartland of America'.[92]

The 1986 MORI poll revealed that the majority of Britons would like to holiday in America and for several million Britons the Super Bowl has become an annual, themed one-day excursion to a mythic America.[93] The trip provides multiple narratives to its British consumers, Luckhurst's 10 per cent watching it for the game, others watching it as theatre, perhaps reminding themselves of a previous American family holiday or anticipating one, and the majority for whom the event is about partying amidst temporary Americana at home or in a pub. Indeed, two American students at a London pub noticed the TV hosts giving viewers' advice on 'pulling sickies' at the end of the live broadcast in the early hours of Super Bowl Monday.[94]

What all viewers get, even if they do not understand the game or care who is playing, is that instant 'when it all works and the receiver is soaring into the air to pluck the ball from the fingertips of his marker and plunge into the end zone; this sudden explosion of perfection and grace is heart-lifting'. Simon Barnes insists that American football, for all of its nonsense, fires the imagination over the 'miracles that brilliant men can work. And isn't that really the point of sport?'[95]

Notes

1. Anonymous letter to the editor, 'Not Cricket', *The Times*, 11 August 1983, 9.
2. C. Armstrong, R. Fagge, and T. Lockley, 'Introduction', in C. Armstrong, R. Fagge, and T. Lockley (eds), *America in the British Imagination* (Newcastle: Cambridge Scholars, 2007), 2.
3. J.F. Lyons, *America in the British Imagination: 1945 to the Present* (New York: Palgrave Macmillan, 2013).
4. Daniel Archer, 'A Voice from America to Intending Emigrants', *Sheffield and Rotherham Independent*, 22 March 1869, 4.
5. B. Miller, '"The Thousand Glassy Eyes": Britishness and American Culture in Travel Narratives and Cultural Criticism', in C. Armstrong, R. Fagge, and T. Lockley (eds), *America in the British Imagination*, 153–67; and H. Bridges, 'The Robber Baron Concept in American History', *Business History Review* 32, no. 1 (1958), 1–13.
6. V.R. Berghahn , 'The Debate on "Americanization" Among Economic and Cultural Historians', *Cold War History* 10, no. 1 (2010), 107–30; J.H. Wiener, *The Americanization of the British Press, 1830s-1914* (Basingstoke: Palgrave Macmillan, 2011); and Rudyard Kipling, *From Sea to Sea: Letters of Travel* (New York: Charles Scribner's Sons, 1899), 139.
7. 'Football: American Football Rules Amended', *Leeds Mercury*, 9 April 1887, 8.

8. 'Football', *South Wales Daily News*, 23 December 1889, 7. For example 'American Football: A Heavy "Butcher's Bill"', *South Wales Daily News*, 7 December 1897, 7; and 'American Football: Heavy Casualty List', *Sheffield Evening Telegraph*, 11 December 1909, 6.
9. 'Amusements Across the Atlantic', *Exeter and Plymouth Gazette*, 25 October 1894, 2.
10. 'Football', *Dundee Evening Telegraph*, 1 January 1895, 3.
11. 'Editorial', *Manchester Guardian*, 20 December 1893, 5.
12. 'Mr. Caspar Whitney', *The Times*, 1 March 1895, 13.
13. H.A. Bryden, 'Football Sketches: The Game – and Some Reflections', *Surrey Mirror*, 6 December 1901, 7.
14. 'American College Football', *Sunderland Daily Echo and Shipping Gazette*, 14 May 1910, 6; 'American Football Player's Death', *The Times*, 16 November 1910, 22.
15. 'American Football: Game at Crystal Palace', *Dundee Evening Telegraph*, 21 November 1910, 4.
16. 'American Football in London', *London Daily News*, 23 November 1910, 10.
17. 'The American Game: Not an Improvement on the British Rugby Code', *London Daily News*, 25 November 1910, 8.
18. 'American Football: Match at the Crystal Palace', *The Times*, 25 November 1910, 23.
19. 'Americans at Weymouth', *London Daily News*, 25 November 1910, 8; and 'American Football: The Battleships Idaho and Connecticut', *The Times*, 5 December 1910, 20.
20. 'American Football Match', *Sheffield Independent*, 18 November 1915, 6.
21. 'American Football: Interesting Game at Chelsea', *The Times*, 29 November 1918, 3; and 'Hospital Cup Final Replay: The American Football Game', *Liverpool Echo*, 27 November 1918, 4.
22. British Pathé, 'An American Cup Tie', http://www.britishpathe.com/video/an-american-cup-tie/query/American+Football (accessed 29 August 2016); '"Blinkhorns" Picture House', *Banbury Guardian*, 25 April 1918, 8; and S. Hanson, *From Silent Screen to Multi-Screen: A History of Cinema Exhibition in Britain since 1896* (Manchester: Manchester University Press, 2007).
23. 'American Football', *The Times*, 27 November 1933, 5; 'The American Cheer Leaders Get to Work', *Yorkshire Evening Post*, 2 December 1924, 6; 'Sports in Brief', *The Times*, 2 December 1935, 5; and E.J. Sampson, 'American Football: How it Strikes a Visitor to the States', *Yorkshire Post and Leeds Intelligencer*, 3 December 1929, 6.
24. Luke McKernan, 'A History of the British Newsreels', *bufvc.ac.uk/wp-content/media/2009/06/newsreels_long_history.pdf* (accessed 27 August 2016).
25. British Pathé, 'Some Game', http://www.britishpathe.com/video/some-game/query/American+Football; British Pathé, 'Notre Dame Whips Army Eleven 7–0', http://www.britishpathe.com/video/notre-dame-whips-army-eleven-7-0/query/American+Football (accessed 29 August 2016); and British Pathé, 'Excitement … 100%!', http://www.britishpathe.com/video/excitement-100/query/American+Football (accessed 28 August 2016).
26. A search for '"American football"', 1920–1940' on British Pathé brings up 64 films, http://www.britishpathe.com/search/query/american+football (accessed 28 August 2016).
27. J. Richards, *The Age of the Dream Palace: Cinema and Society in Britain 1930–1939* (London: Routledge and Kegan Paul, 1984); and G.A. Atkinson, 'British Films Made to Please America', *Daily Express*, 18 March 1927, 6.
28. Hanson, *From Silent Screen to Multi-Screen*.
29. Armstrong, Fagge, and Lockley, 'Introduction', 1–7.
30. British Pathé, 'The Tournament of Roses – The Rose Bowl', http://www.britishpathe.com/video/the-tournament-of-roses-the-rose-bowl-game/query/American+Football (accessed 28 August 2016).
31. 'American Football: A Match to be Played at the White City', *The Times*, 22 April 1943, 2; 'American Football: Saturday's Game at the White City', *The Times*, 4 May 1943, 2; 'American Football: Today's Match at the White City', *The Times*, 8 May 1943, 2; and 'American Football: Match at the White City', *The Times*, 10 May 1943, 2.
32. 'American Football at the White City', *The Times*, 14 February 1944, 2; 'Americans Take "Coffee Bowl"; Whip Canadians, 18–0, Overseas', *The Gazette* (Montreal), 20 March 1944, 18.

33. J.V. Stalin, 'Speech Delivered at a Meeting of Voters of the Stalin Electoral District, Moscow', 9 February 1946 (Moscow: Foreign Languages Publishing House, 1950); Churchill's 'Iron Curtain' Speech, https://www.youtube.com/watch?v=S2PUIQpAEAQ (accessed 20 August 2016).

34. A search for '"American football"', 1945–1980' on British Pathé brings up 29 films, http://www.britishpathe.com/search/query/american+football (accessed 28 August 2016).

35. 'American Football Final at Wembley', *The Times,* 28 November 1952, 12.

36. 'American Football: An Unusual Final at Wembley', *The Times,* 13 December 1952, 4; 'Eagles Outplay Bullets: American Football at Wembley', *The Times,* 15 December 1952, 2; and British Pathé, 'Wembley –US Air Force Football Final Aka ...', http://www.britishpathe.com/video/wembley-us-air-force-football-final-aka-american/query/American+Football (accessed 28 August 2016).

37. Lyons, *America in the British Imagination.*

38. 'Colts Real "Giant Killers"', http://www.britishpathe.com/video/american-football-league-baltimore-v-new-york/query/American+football (accessed 1 September 2016).

39. Lyons, *America in the British Imagination.*

40. McKernan, 'A History of the British Newsreels'.

41. 'Reports from America: Football versus Greek at the University', *The Times,* 3 December 1963, 11.

42. Lyons, *America in the British Imagination.*

43. 'Broadcasting Saturday', *The Times,* 23 January 1971, 16.

44. Michael Leapman, 'Calamity of Joe's Knee is the Talk of New York', *The Times,* 9 August 1971, 1 & 4.

45. Ian Wooldridge, 'What Makes Millionaires Breaks Marriages and Blows a Mind or Two?', *Daily Mail,* 14 January 1972, 26; Ian Wooldridge, 'I Looked for the End of the Rainbow ... This was Just the End', *Daily Mail,* 18 January 1972, 22.

46. Ian Wooldridge, 'Our Great and Glorious Game hasn't Reached First Base Yet ... and Probably Never Will', *Daily Mail,* 21 January 1972, 26.

47. Fred Emery, 'The Cowboys' Turn to Bite Dust', *The Times,* 2 January 1973, 5.

48. 'Football Crazy', *Economist,* 20 January 1973, 26; and Dermot Purgavie, 'Quite Divine, these Dolphins and Redskins', *Daily Mail,* 9 January 1973, 2.

49. Dermot Purgavie, 'The Wonderful Wizard isn't What He Was', *Daily Mail,* 4 January 1974, 2; and 'Football Hooked Up', *Economist,* 19 January 1974, 51–2.

50. Anthea Disney, 'The Next Best Thing to Love', *Daily Mail,* 7 January 1977, 2; Anthea Disney, 'Feeding of the 75,000', *Daily Mail,* 10 January 1978, 4.

51. Liz Hodgson, 'Dermot Purgavie's America', *Daily Mail,* 23 January 1986, 13.

52. 'American Football', *The Times,* 13 January 1981, 10.

53. Stuart Jones, 'American Football: The Night the Eagles Played like Sparrows', *The Times,* 27 January 1981, 10.

54. Peter Catterall, 'Introduction', in Peter Catterall (ed), *The Making of Channel 4* (London: Frank Cass, 1999), xv–xix; and Dorothy Hobson, *Channel 4: The Early Years and the Jeremy Isaacs Legacy* (London: I.B.Tauris, 2008).

55. Paul Harrison, 'Channel 4 Plans for a Jaded Audience: Playing Loudly in a Minor Key', *The Times,* 10 November 1982.

56. J. Maguire, 'More Than a Sporting Touchdown: The Making of American Football in England 1982–1990', *Sociology of Sport Journal* 7 (1990), 213–37; and J. Maguire, 'The Consumption of American Football in British Society', *Sport in Society* 14, nos 7–8 (2011), 950–64.

57. Jennifer Selway, 'A Whole New Ball Game', *Observer,* 5 October 1986, 38.

58. 'Fun – and Some Games', *Economist,* 11 September 1982, 38.

59. Stuart Jones, 'The Warlords of Thunder Arrive', *The Times,* 14 December 1982, 22.

60. Maguire, 'More Than a Sporting Touchdown', 225; and Catterall, 'Introduction', ix–x.

61. https://www.youtube.com/watch?v=cyyHRoQyIy4 (accessed 28 July 2016).

62. Jeremy Isaacs, Channel 4 CEO, cited by Welsh Gaz *forum.nfluk.com, 29* December 2009, (accessed 28 July 2016). See http://www.youtube.com/watch?v=cOxnS0zZT8c.

63. Dermot Purgavie, 'Redskins on the Warpath', *Daily Mail*, 22 January 1983, 4; Dermot Purgavie, 'Game for a Laugh', *Daily Mail*, 29 January 1983, 4; and 'The Triumph of Rigginomics', *Economist*, 5 February 1983, 46.

64. Simon Barnes, 'American Football in Britain: Crash! Pow! Wow!', *The Times*, 20 January 1984, 8.

65. 'Return of Hail Marys, Late Nights and Weak Beer', *Guardian*, 4 February 2007, https://www.theguardian.com/sport/2007/feb/04/ussport (accessed 24 September 2016).

66. Barnes, 'American Football in Britain'. For overviews of British American football see N. Richards, *Touchdown UK: American Football: Before, During and After Britain's Golden Decade* (Milton Keynes: AuthorHouse, 2009); and Lacey Elaine Wismer, 'British American Football: National Identity, Cultural Specificity and Globalization' (PhD thesis, Brunel University, London, 2011).

67. Maguire, 'More Than a Sporting Touchdown', 228.

68. Miles Kington, 'Moreover', *The Times*, 25 January 1984, 10.

69. 'Punctured Football', *Economist*. However Selway, 'A Whole New Ball Game' cited the Super Bowl XX audience as 6.5 million.

70. Simon Hart, 'Remember the 1985 TV Blackout', *Independent*, 14 August 2010.

71. 'Return of Hail Marys, Late Nights and Weak Beer', *Guardian*, 4 February 2007, https://www.theguardian.com/sport/2007/feb/04/ussport (accessed 24 September 2016).

72. Jeff Powell, 'Where are Our Cathedrals of Sport?' *Daily Mail*, 31 January 1990, 6.

73. Maguire, 'The Consumption of American Football in British Society'.

74. 'Punctured Football', *Economist*; *Sunday Times*, 18 January 1987, 49.

75. 'Super Bowl, Super Ads, Supercostly', *Economist*, 28 January 1984, 70; and 'Old Media's Internet Boom', *Economist*, 22 May 1999, 105.

76. Interview with Bob Mullins, Channel 4 Regional Sales Controller (retired), 1 September 2016.

77. http://www.nfl.com/superbowl/history/entertainment (accessed 2 September 2016).

78. Sue Mott, 'Sport in America: Baseball Chief sets out to Restore some Broken Images', *The Times*, 22 May 1985, 28; and Michael Binyon, 'US Shaken by Death of Athletes', *The Times*, 10 July 1986, 12.

79. Sue Mott, 'Sport in America: Land of the Franchise and Home to No One', *The Times*, 19 December 1984, 19.

80. Armstrong, Fagge, and Lockley, 'Introduction', 7.

81. Dermot Purgavie, 'Letter from America', *Daily Mail*, 14 January 1985, 8; and Dermot Purgavie, 'A Question of Love', *Daily Mail*, 16 January 1985, 8.

82. Chuck Culpepper, 'Many Britons Stuck in the '80s When it Comes to NFL', *Los Angeles Times*, 24 October 2007, http://articles.latimes.com/2007/oct/24/sports/sp-britain24 (accessed 29 August 2016).

83. Simon Barnes, 'Dolphin Relaxes in Goldfish Bowl', *The Times*, 26 April 1986, 36.

84. Lyons, *America in the British Imagination*.

85. Pierre Bourdieu, *Distinction: A Social Critique of the Judgement of Taste* (Cambridge, MA: Harvard University Press, 1984); Barrie Houlihan, 'Sport and Globalization', in Barrie Houlihan (ed), *Sport and Society* (London: Sage, 2008), 553–74; Michael Oriard, *Brand NFL: Making & Selling America's Favorite Sport* (Chapel Hill: The University of North Carolina Press, 2007); and Pierre Bourdieu, 'Sport and Social Class', *Social Science Information* 17, no. 6 (1978), 819–40, 829.

86. 'Punctured Football', *Economist*.

87. Louise Woodward was a 19 year old British *au pair* who was convicted of the manslaughter of a baby in her care in Massachusetts. Much of the debate revolved around her use of the word 'popped' which means different things in Britain and America. Later forensic evidence showed that most of the baby's injuries had occurred before Woodward arrived in the US.

88. Culpepper, 'Many Britons Stuck in the '80s When it Comes to NFL'. Wismer, 'British American Football'; and *Channel Four Television Corporation: Report and Financial Statements 1998* (London: Channel Four Television, 1999), 17.

89. Robert Kirley, 'Behind the Gridiron Curtain', *The Times*, 8 August 1987, 34.

90. 'Jim Shelley's World of Sport', *Guardian*, 25 January 2003, D9.
91. Simon Barnes, 'Giants Rule in a Wonderful World of Make Believe', *The Times*, 27 January 1987, 35.
92. Simon Barnes, 'An Occasion to Stir the Hearts of all Americans', *The Times*, 20 October 1987, 44.
93. Lyons, *America in the British Imagination*.
94. Christopher R. Martin and Jimmie L. Reeves 'The Whole World Isn't Watching (But We Thought They Were): The Super Bowl and United States Solipsism', *Culture, Sport, Society* 4, no. 2 (2001), 214; and Valerie Morgan and Abbey Tingle 'A Cultural Phenomenon: Watching the Super Bowl in the UK', *J. School Magazine,* Missouri School of Journalism, June 2014.
95. Simon Barnes, 'Violent but a Giant of a Game', *The Times*, 4 February 1988, 40.

Disclosure Statement

No potential conflict of interest was reported by the author.

'We Will Try Again, Again, Again to Make It Bigger': Japan, American Football, and the Super Bowl in the Past, Present, and Future

Kohei Kawashima

ABSTRACT

This study is to analyse how the Japanese have traditionally received and currently perceive the Super Bowl, and for this purpose, it aims to locate the position of American football in Japanese history, society, and culture. It explores the game's history and then examine the degree of its spread among Japan's sporting population. A two-dimensional approach of historical study and inter-game comparison gives context to the analyses of reference frequency and contents of news media, followed by speculative discussions of what the near future of Japan's American football would be like. To conclude, it clarifies the ways the Super Bowl has been received and is now being perceived by two groups: The first group is the general people who see the Super Bowl as the convenient and useful medium by which they could learn effectively about American culture through the one-night mania for 'conspicuous consumption'. The second group comprises American football experts and enthusiasts, including 13,000 athletes and their OBs, coaches, trainers, and other staff members of the leagues and associations as well as the general sports fans. For this group, the Super Bowl is the apex of their favourite sport to which only a selected talented few could join.

As the event that crowns the champion of the most popular sport in the United States, the Super Bowl represents undoubtedly the most well-known and broadly publicized sporting event in the United States.[1] To many Japanese, however, the term 'Super Bowl' would most likely be associated with the rubber-made toy ball 'super ball'. Only Japanese who are relatively well informed about global sports, particularly the American professional variety, could associate correctly that it is the championship game of the National Football League (NFL). In turn, many Americans may be unaware that people in Japan play the American version of football. As Kiyoyuki Mori, head coach of the 2015 Japanese national team observes:

> Honestly speaking, the typical American doesn't know that Japan even plays football … Sometimes when we go over to the States and talk with people there, they are surprised to hear we play the game. They often ask things like, 'Do you have the same rules?'[2]

Perhaps, it is safe to say, that many Japanese know football a little better than some Americans think that they do.

An analysis of how the Japanese have traditionally understood and currently perceive the Super Bowl requires an investigation of American football in Japanese history, society, and culture. The game has a longer history and a broader spread in Japan than most observers assume. A two-dimensional approach beginning with a history of American football in Japan and a comparison of the reception of football to other games provides a context for an analysis of how the Japanese news media cover the Super Bowl. These methodologies will shed light on the complex past, present, and future of American football and the Super Bowl in Japan.

The Origins of American Football in Japan

The standard histories of American football in Japan date the beginnings of the game back to 1934 when its first official organization was founded. However, recent research has revealed an earlier starting point when Japanese football aficionado Heita Okabe first introduced the sport to his nation in the early 1920s. Sport researchers and Hitoshi Kawaguchi, the former Standing Director of the National Football Association (NFA) in Japan and author of Okabe's short biography, argue that more attention must be given to his contribution to American football as the first Japanese who played, coached, and wrote about the sport.[3]

Kawaguchi describes Okabe as a 'renaissance-type multi-talented' person, who 'shows his presence far more vividly through a rich accumulation of time even after his death'.[4] Okabe was born in 1891 in Fukuoka, a city on the southern island of Kyushu. In 1917 he graduated from the Tokyo Higher Normal School. As a judo master, he contributed greatly to the development of Japan's traditional martial arts and modern sports. At Kodokan Judo Institute, he was promoted from white belt to second degree black belt by beating five opponents in a row, and then to fourth degree black belt by beating seven rivals consecutively. Okabe also excelled in boxing, sumo, and tennis. He attained fame as a journalist and a writer, and also stood out as a poet of Japanese *waka* – a classical form of Japanese literature.[5]

At the age of 25, Okabe ventured to the United States to pursue graduate studies and played American football under the legendary coach Amos Alonzo Stagg at the University of Chicago. Okabe wanted to take the top position of quarterback, but Stagg assigned the neophyte Japanese player to left end and tackle. He took to the American version of football immediately. He once lamented that it was unfortunate he was not born in America as he discovered that he was born to play football.[6] Another Japanese student, Buichi Otani, also joined the football team at Chicago with Okabe, but Otani became better known as the introducer of softball and handball to Japan. Okabe became the football apostle. Upon returning to Japan in 1920, Okabe taught American football to fourth-year students at the Tokyo Normal School, while at the same time teaching at the Tokyo Higher Normal School as well as coaching the track and field team of the Faculties of Agriculture and Economics at the University of Tokyo. From 1923 to 1924, he left the Tokyo schools and took a position with the South Manchurian Railway where he was assigned to inspect the sporting landscapes in selected Western nations. Okabe published his reports in the magazine *Asahi Sports*, a periodical that had just begun to circulate in March of 1923. In one of his reports, Okabe discussed how American football was played using illustrations and diagrams of the field and offensive formations. His reports were compiled into a book published as *The Sports of the World* in 1925, which is reputed to be Japan's first guidebook on American football.[7]

Okabe's pioneering roles in promoting football in Japan did not lead to a more organized development of the game. An American missionary, Paul Rusch, took the lead in establishing Japan's first American football association. For those efforts Rusch rather than Okabe would be later acclaimed as the 'Father of Japan's American Football'. Born in 1897 in Indiana, Rusch grew up in Louisville, Kentucky, became a devout member of prominent Episcopalian congregation, and served U.S. army during the First World War. In 1923, Rusch responded to calls for aid and went to Japan with a Young Men's Christian Association (YMCA) agency for relief in the immediate aftermath of the Great Kanto Earthquake that inflicted enormous damage to the Tokyo region. While in Japan Rusch made new contacts and in 1926, Rikkyo University Chancellor John McKim, impressed by Rusch's talent in management and his enthusiasm for teaching, hired Rusch as professor of economics. In 1934, Rusch invited a number of faculty members and students to the university's Building No. 5 where his residence was located for a meeting to found the first collegiate league of American football in Japan. Rusch served as the league's chief director who raised funds, while Rikkyo's director of physical education, George Marshall, took over the management of the league. Most students who signed up to play in the new league were second-generation Japanese Americans (*nisei*) born in the United States. Many of these students had not yet adjusted to an unaccustomed new life in Japan. They found their *raison d'être* in spreading American football in Japan, a game already popular as a top college sport in the United States and a pastime that reminded them of their earlier lives in their birth-land.[8]

On 29 November 1934, the burgeoning league of students from Japan's major universities, including Waseda, Meiji, and Rikkyo, were joined by one student each from Hosei University and Keio University, two schools that were preparing to start their own football teams. Comprising 26 members, their composite team confronted the 21-member team of Yokohama Country and Athletic Club (YCAC) at the Jingu Gaien Stadium – pre-war Japan's most sacred ground for modern sport that had hosted the 1930 Far Eastern Games. The contest on the gridiron in the Jingu Gaien Stadium was Japan's first official American football game. The opposing YCAC team consisted mostly of English expatriates with experiences in playing rugby. Although they were physically larger and thus had an advantage, they had not played American football.[9]

Jun Hanaoka, a freshman player from Meiji who would later become the team's head coach, recalled that the Japanese collegians played in a festive mood without much anxiety. The organizers staged the game on Thanksgiving Day of the American calendar – a date that was just a regular day for the Japanese. The game garnered a large audience of about 20,000, suggesting that American football attracted considerable attention among the Japanese at the beginning. The vigorous and youthful Japanese team consistently pushed against the older YCAC squad. The Japanese students scored a touchdown in each of the first and second quarters, and two in the fourth, eventually winning with a score of 26 to 0.[10]

Just one year later, the growing number of Japanese football teams had the chance to play against top-notch American college teams. In spring of 1935, the Asahi newspaper syndicate invited an All-American collegiate team to promote the game in Japan. The invitation aimed not only at developing football but enhancing Japan–US relations. The US team played three games against the All-Japan collegiate team and Meiji University. Japanese football promoters also held 10 exhibition games by two internally divided teams. The All-American team consisted of students from football strongholds, including the University of Southern California, the University of California at Los Angeles, the University of Oregon, and the University of Washington, and Stanford University, among others. The American squad featured 14 college football all-stars. The American side crushed the Japanese team by scores of 71 to 7, 73 to 6, and 46 to 0. Waseda University player Motoyuki Inoue was taken to the hospital after one game due to a stomach injury so memorable that he, in his own words, 'never forgot the severe pain' he suffered. The All-American team praised their Japanese counterpart, declaring that the Japanese had 'played great consistently showing a fierce fighting spirit despite the handicap of not having learnt the basics'.[11]

In the fall of 1936, Japanese students took on the challenge of playing the Americans again. Japanese football leaders selected 20 college players for an All-Japan side and sent them with 3 officials to compete against US teams. The Japanese collegians competed against the All Southern California High Schools as well as Roosevelt High School – Hawaii's top prep team of that season. The All-Japan team lost 19 to 6 to the California contingent but managed to tie the Hawaiian powerhouse in a scoreless game.[12] In January of 1938, the Japan American Football Association (JAFA) became the first nationwide official body governing the sport. Paul Rusch served as its first chief director. Two months later, JAFA staged the first East-West Exchange Game between Japanese teams. A crowd of about 25,000 spectators watched the East routed the West by 21 to 0.[13]

In 1940, the JAFA was renamed Japan Armor Ball ('Gaikyu') Association as Japan began to consider the US as its main enemy in the impending war. The new name was derived from the players' uniforms, which the Japanese associated with traditional samurai defensive wares. On 29 March 1943, as the Japan–US war entered its third year, the Ministry of Education prohibited the football as well as outlawing baseball, and ice hockey – games that they labelled as 'enemy sports'. Universities attempted to continue playing the game by transforming the sport to something they call 'Navy Fighting Ball', a game that they planned to introduce as an element in training naval personnel. However, in July of the same year, the Imperial Army and Navy prohibited all college sports activities through and official edict.[14]

Post-War Institutional Development and Limited Popularization

After the war ended, American football returned to Japan. In the midst of recovery efforts from the war, the General Headquarters of the Allied Occupation of Japan led by General Douglas MacArthur encouraged sports, especially American sports, as a mechanism for reviving the defeated nation. In January 1947, the US military authorized the reinstatement of the National High School Baseball Championship at the Koshien Stadium, one of pre-war Japan's most popular sporting events.[15] Inspired by this policy, Japan's leading promoters of American football, particularly those in the Mainichi newspaper syndicate in Osaka, made efforts to host the East–West College Championship. The first post-war football tournament was named the 'Koshien Bowl' and also held at the Koshien Stadium. Keio University won over Doshisha University by a score of 43 to 0.[16]

The American football leaders in Tokyo were inspired by Osaka's success in the Koshien Bowl and revived the all-star game between the East and the West on 17 January 1948. They dubbed the tournament the 'Rice Bowl' after the Japanese staple food. It was held at the Jingu Gaien Stadium. Rusch attended the opening ceremony. He had returned to Japan after living as a refugee in the US during the war. He presented a congratulatory address, declaring: 'Here we are again'. Rusch then ceremoniously made the first kick-off of the game. The East crushed the West, 33 to 0. In 1984, the 50th anniversary of the foundation of Japan's first football organization, the Rice Bowl evolved into a championship game between the victors of the college and the corporate leagues. In the first new Rice Bowl, the college champion Kyoto University Gangsters beat corporate champion Renown Rovers in a tight game of 29 to 28.[17]

While Japan's institutionalization of American football gave birth to the Koshien Bowl and the Rice Bowl, the NFL launched the American Bowl as a pre-season game for its global expansion. The NFL first held the game in London in 1986, and then staged it in 12 major global cities, including Berlin, Mexico City, Dublin, Montreal, Barcelona, and Vancouver, and the Japanese metropolises of Tokyo and Osaka. In the same era, the NFL also extended its reach into Europe with the establishment of the World League of American Football (WLAF) in the spring of 1991. Japanese corporate league players frequently participated in this European league, which would be later named the NFL Europe League, as they saw it as a short cut to the NFL. The first American Bowl between NFL franchises in Japan took place in Tokyo in 1989. This event has been held 12 times in Tokyo and once in Osaka, making Japan the world's most hospitable city to the NFL. In 2005, however, the NFL's strategic shift to China brought an end to the American Bowl. In 2007, NFL Europe collapsed as well.[18]

Japan's association with American football cannot be fully appreciated without mentioning the International Federation of American Football (IFAF) World Championship or World Cup, at least for the first two tournaments. Founded in 1998, Japan has been a key member of the IFAF. Eiji Sasada, then Chief Director of the Japan American Football Association, served as the IFAF's first president. Sasada reflected Japan's high status in the global American football community – a position that in part could be attributed to Japan's victory on 3 August 1998, over Finland, a three-time consecutive winner in the European championship.[19] Italy hosted the first IFAF championship in Italy in 1999, with the Italy, Japan, Mexico, Sweden, Finland, and Australia as the participants. The US declined to participate due to the Kosovo war. Japan defeated Mexico in the finals to win the first championship. The second championship was held in Germany in 2003, again without the US team. Japan defeated Mexico in the finals for the second time. In the third championship, which Japan hosted at the city of Kawasaki, the US team participated for the first time – without brining NFL players. The United States defeated Japan in the finals. The US team also triumphed in the fourth (2011) and fifth (2015) IFAF championships.[20]

In spite of Japan's success on the field and leadership role off the field in the IFAF, American football is not currently thriving in Japan's diverse sporting cultures. Among the important concerns for Japan's over 80-year-old American football community is the shrinking of its playing population. According to IFAF foundation surveys, in 1998 Japan had approximately 20,000 American football players, the world's second largest population after the US.[21] That population decreased to about 19,000 in 2011, and further dropped to 14,700 in 2013.[22] According to a 2011 research by Japan's Ministry of Internal Affairs and Communications, the playing population of a game and its proportion to the total population aged 10 or older was 9.24 million (8.1%) for golf (including practice at driving ranges), 8.12 million (7.1%) for baseball (including playing catch), and 6.38 million (5.6%) for soccer (including futsal). The enormous gap between Japan's most popular sports by participation rates and American football, 19,000 (0.017%), were obvious.[23]

The foregoing surveys on history and institutional development as well as inter-game comparison provide a context for understanding the state of American football in Japan. Three observations are central in the discussion. First, viewed as a foreign-born sport introduced later in Japan, American football is a newcomer compared with the other major games. For instance, Japan's two major team sports, baseball and soccer, have much longer histories. Baseball originated in 1872, whereas soccer first appeared in 1866 or 1873, (depending on the sources). Even basketball, which originated in the USA later than American football, was introduced to Japan in 1908 – nearly a decade earlier than Okabe's encounter with American football at the University of Chicago. Its newcomer status may also reflect in the failure of the game's Japanese name in circulation among Japanese people, as a later section of the paper will reveal. Second, owing to post-war American football leaders' effort, including the opening of national championships such as the Koshien Bowl and Rice Bowl, Japan is now internationally recognized in American football. The country's national team has played superbly in tournaments and emerged as two-time victors in the IFAF world championships since 1999. Third, in spite of those successes, American football in Japan remains a minor sport at the national level in terms of the size of playing population.

Super Bowl Coverage in Major Japanese Dailies

An analysis of media coverage of the Super Bowl in the major Japanese newspapers reveals that the media outlets provided readers with only a handful of Super Bowls stories from 1967 through the late 1980s. In the late 1980s Super Bowl coverage rapidly escalated, reaching a zenith in the early 2000s when the newspapers ran 60–70 stories on each Super Bowl. Since 2004 coverage has dropped off, but remains significant. Currently, the major newspapers generate 20–30 stories for each Super Bowl.

The *Nikkei, Asahi, Yomiuri,* and *Mainichi* newspapers represent the four major dailies in late twentieth-century and early twenty-first century Japan. All of them are national papers headquartered in Tokyo or Osaka with large average daily circulations of 4.15 million (*Nikkei*), 9 million (*Asahi*), 12.05 million (*Yomiuri*) and 4.2 million (*Mainichi*) during the first half of 2015.[24] Figure 1 shows the number of stories from these newspapers from 1967

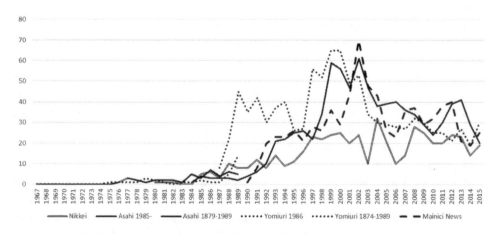

Figure 1. Frequency of newspaper stories' reference to the Super Bowl 1967–2015. Source: Nikkei Telecon 21, Kikuzo II Visual, Yomidasu Rekisikan, and Mainichi News Pack.

to 2015 that contained the term 'Super Bowl' in either the title or the body. Significantly, not a single Super Bowl story appeared in these Japanese dailies from 1967 to 1974. Super Bowl IX in 1975 marks the first time that these newspapers covered the spectacle. The frequency of reference to the Super Bowl has fluctuated considerably over the past 41 years, showing a changing Japanese attitude toward the Super Bowl (popular vs. less popular or more attention vs. less attention).[25]

Yomiuri and *Asahi* made the earliest reference to the Super Bowl, posting 15 January 1975 and 20 January 1976 stories, respectively. Among the four major dailies, *Yomiuri* recorded the highest number of references at 1,044 from 1975 to 2015. The dailies made 65 references in 1999 and 2000 but in 1982 totally ignored Super Bowl XVI, running not even one story about the game between the San Francisco 49ers and Cincinnati Bengals. *Asahi* had the second highest number of references at 899 from 1976 to 2015, with a high of 61 references made in 2002 but only a single reference in the years 1976, 1979, and 1983. *Mainichi* had 772 total references from 1990 to 2015, with 70 made in 2002 and only one made in 1990. *Nikkei* recorded the lowest number of references at 511 from 1980 to 2015, with 32 references made in 2004 but no references made in 1983 and 1984. The highest numbers of references by the four major dailies are concentrated between 1999 and 2004.[26]

The changes that the chart reveals can be grouped into three phases. In the first phase, only a few stories about the game appeared. This frequency remained stable at low levels through the first half of the 1980s, thus the period from 1967 to 1985 can be termed as the 'dawn' of Japanese interest in the Super Bowl. In the second phase, the frequency of reference rose gradually through the second half of the 1980s, reaching peaks at the turn of the twenty-first century. This period from 1986 to 2004 represents an era of increasing frequency, which can be termed as the 'peak'. The peak years included Japan's hosting of multiple American Bowls and two World Cup victories. In the third phase, from 2005 to 2016, the frequency of reference decreased to lower levels but it became more or less stabilized. The current period thus represents a 'plateau' in Japanese interest in the Super Bowl.[27]

Themes in Japanese Newspaper Coverage of Super Bowls

The four major dailies began to report on the Super Bowl in the mid-1970s, nearly a decade after the first Super Bowl (previously called the AFL-NFL World Championship Game) in January 1967.[28] The first *Yomiuri* story on the Super Bowl referred to Super Bowl IX between the Pittsburgh Steelers and Minnesota Vikings. The first story in *Asahi* mentioned Super Bowl X between the Steelers and the Dallas Cowboys.[29]

Yomiuri's 1975 reference was found in a story titled 'Short Wave Abroad' with the heading 'No Tackle, Please'. The story was accompanied by a photo of a glamorous woman wearing a bikini who is chased by a guard carrying a fur coat. The photo captured Sandra Sexton walking across the field skilfully shaking off the guard's tackles during half time. The column closes with a rather cynical comment: 'Many spectators must have enjoyed this better than the game itself'.[30]

Asahi's 1976 reference appeared in a more broad-spectrum story with a heading '85 Million Watched on TV'. The story contained observations on the Super Bowl that stressed the enormity of the spectacle. The report observed that '85 million Americans fixed their eyes on TV, an audience even larger than those of the Apollo astronaut's first step on the moon'. In another insight the story informed Japanese readers that in this bicentennial year of American independence, 'football is more popular than baseball [in the US]'. The reporter revealed that 'the festive mood went higher than usual' for this celebratory Super Bowl and that 'a regular ticket costs 20 dollars, but sells at the black market price of 300 dollars'. Through these descriptions, the reporter explained the grand scale of the game from several angles by making references to Apollo's moon landing, Japanese cultural preference for baseball, the historical context of Independence Day, and the fervour surrounding the spectacle.[31]

Nikkei's first Super Bowl mention was an announcement released on 5 March 1980 that TV Kanagawa and other companies would begin to broadcast the program titled 'Professional Football 80: The Super Bowl Series'.[32] That announcement heralded the arrival of the American extravaganza on Japanese television, ushering in a new era in which Japan could not only read about the Super Bowl in newspapers but actually watch the spectacle in their living rooms.

The angle and content of these three early newspapers stories on the Super Bowl reflect their editorial philosophy, focus, and policy. *Yomiuri* sensationalized the story by focusing on the scantily-clad woman. *Asahi* presented a more academic view by objectively narrating the event with certain descriptions that provided further understanding of the event. Nikkei's approach focused on the Super Bowl and Japan's broadcasting business – reflecting the newspaper's mission as an economic daily.

Meanwhile, the timing of the reports by the four major Japanese dailies reflected not only Japanese sensibilities but the evolution of the Super Bowl in the United States. According to Peter Hopsicker's and Mark Dyreson's 'Super Bowl Sunday' study, the Super Bowl made a rather meagre debut in 1967 and 1968, but remarkably grew in the beginning of the 1970s, to the extent that the NFL could enjoy the fruits of this celebration of 'conspicuous consumption'. Since Super Bowl VI in 1972, the television ratings have topped 40% and television share numbers have nearly reached 75%, making the Super Bowl show a mega-event in American culture.[33] The Japanese media began to pay attention to the Super Bowl as the game exploded into a 'national holiday' in the United States, appearing on the horizon of Japan's mass media in the mid-1970s as event that needed to be covered to explain the strange customs of the US to the Japanese public.

Those trends in coverage continued as the Super Bowl grew in popularity in the US. In 1996, a *Yomiuri* story stated that 'for a one-night event, the Super Bowl attracts the world's most concentrated attention'. This fact was substantiated by certain 'super topics' regarding 'the incomparable degree of the event's popularity'. As evidence of the Super Bowl's enormous attractions, the story cited evidence including 'TV ratings at more than 40% every time', 'the cost of a 30-second commercial message at $1.2 million', which was 'three times more than that of the NBA playoff finals, and four times more than that of the Major League World Series', and 'press cards issued to 2,356 people, compared with the 1,674 at the NBA playoff finals and 1,029 at the World Series'. The story concluded with NBA commissioner David Stern's envious admission that 'no comparable event exists in the US sporting world'. This story suggests that, by this time, the Japanese media had considered American football as part of the sport industry, with the Super Bowl as an index of dominion in US markets.[34]

A 1992 Asahi story explored another dimension of the Super Bowl's influence by referring to a Japanese media crew that was preparing for the American Bowl at the Tokyo Dome, an NFL pre-season game. The story stated that 'to create powerful images in the game's broadcasting, the Nippon TV crew has as many as 15 cameras in a similar manner as the set-up for the Super Bowl'. By this time, the Super Bowl had become a model for TV broadcasting crews not only in the US but in Japan.[35]

Another example from a 1998 story reveals that the Super Bowl had come to represent an ultimate goal for Japanese officials and players. IFAF President Sasada expressed his interest in the future IFAF World Championship games. He contended that 'we are much smaller than European players, but we have a tradition of more than 60 years with more than 200 university teams, and a playing population exceeding 20,000, which is the second largest only after the US'. He added, 'Therefore, ours is the team of a strong nation that should beat all the opponents but the Americans'[36] A number of veteran players such as Masato Itai, Masafumi Kawaguchi, Nachi Abe, and Tamon Nakamura had even higher ambitions. Each of them had played during the 1998 season in the European League and nurtured NFL dreams. Itai played for the Kansas City Chiefs against the Green Bay Packers in the 1998 American Bowl. When he knocked down a kick-off returner by a fierce tackle at the knee, he told a reporter that 'When I played in the Kyoto University Gangsters and the Kashima Deers, I led the team, but in Europe I played just as one player'. He added, 'Today I saw the real plays of the NFL's top professionals. I continue to strive for the top as long as my body works'.[37]

American Football and the Super Bowl in Japan's Near Future

While Japanese players continue to view the NFL and its Super Bowl as the mountaintop of their ambitions, the decline since 2004 of Japanese media coverage of the Super Bowl portends several problems for the continued spread of American football in the Japan. Recent trends in Japanese coverage of American football reveal important clues about the future of the game. Since 2010 publishers have produced 49 books in Japanese about American football, but only a handful provide real cultural insights into the game for Japan's readers.[38] Of the 49 publications, 24 appear under the category of 'American football', 20 under the heading of 'the NFL', and five under the 'Super Bowl' label. These books can be categorized into seven genres, namely, 'directory/season outlook', 'nonfiction/self-enlightenment', 'guidebook/introduction/rulebook', 'business/management', 'association/university memorial', 'academic/scholarly', and 'novels'. The numbers of books in each genre reveal where Japanese readers can derive information on America's most popular sport. (See Table 1)[39]

Most of these books focus on the 'directory/season outlook' genre (13), followed by the 'nonfiction/self-enlightenment' and guidebook/introduction/rulebook' genres (12). The number of available books in each genre reflects the area of readers' interest. Only one

Table 1. Genres of recent publications on NFL, Super Bowl and American football as topics.

	NFL	Super Bowl	American football	Total
Directory/season outlook	9		4	13
Nonfiction/self-enlightenment	5	2	5	12
Guidebook/introduction/rule book	2		10	12
Business/management	4	3		7
Association/University memorial			3	3
Academic/Scholarly			1	1
Novels			1	1
Total	20	5	24	49

Source: Webcat Plus by the National Institute of Informatics.

book, the Japanese version of Alan Tomlinson's *The World Atlas of Sport* (Maruzen, 2012), was categorized under 'academic/scholarly' genre. This book only assigns two pages for American football, which is one of 30 modern sports in the section titled 'Sports A to Z'. This section is intended to be an encyclopaedic guide on modern sports.[40]

Touchdown Corporation published Japan's oldest American football magazine. The publishing house's homepage shows that 13 books are recent publications.[41] Most of the books are introductions or guidebooks, except for *Iza Iza Iza* and Sadao Goto's *Common Sense of the NFL*. The former is a biographical documentary that traces the lives of Kwansai Gakuin University players, whereas the latter is a cultural study that includes a collection of the NFL's episodes in an effort to explain the US to Japanese readers.[42] At the beginning of Goto's book, he argues that 'a sport is a culture, and into American football, American culture is condensed'. Goto insists that 'Unless we understand the sport's philosophy and culture that underlie it, we can never diffuse its skills and rules accurately'[43]

Most of the other books published recently suggest that Japanese authorship on American football has not still met the standards set by Goto. The contents of the four dailies' news stories also suggest that reporters provide insufficient and inaccurate coverage of American football. The newspaper stories can be grouped into six genres. The first genre is 'trends of the season', which largely includes stories on the wins and losses of the games, strong and weak teams, and the chances of various teams for reaching the Super Bowl. The second genre is 'economic', which primarily covers stories such as materialistic tendencies, the importance of commercialism, high television ratings, and large consumptions of goods and food during the game, among other things. The third genre is 'racial', a category concerned with the rise of African Americans in football (especially quarterbacks and head coaches) and with the controversies over Native American mascots. The fourth genre is 'anecdotal', which includes stories ranging from betting clam chowders on the Super Bowl winner by Boston and New York mayors, to the seven wonders of the Green Bay Packers, to Janet Jackson's exposure of her breast while singing, to television viewers rushing to bathrooms during commercial message breaks and the resulting water shortages, to defeats raising mortality rates among losing fan-bases, to the winning of $400,000 in a bet, and to NFL players' visiting to a sumo house. The fifth category is 'individual' stories, with topics focusing on Japanese related to the Super Bowl such as players Noriaki Kinoshita, Soichiro Tsukuda, and Noriko Ogura, trainer Ariko Iso, cheerleaders Tomoko Kojima, Tomoko Mita, Minako Matsuzaki, and Emi Koike, and ground keeper Shoji Ikeda. The sixth category is 'critical' explorations, consisting mainly on criticism of the sport as too violent and dangerous.[44]

The six categories are not meant to be comprehensive, but provide a broad survey to highlight the claim that the media's attention to the cultural and historical aspects of the game remains limited. Such inadequate attention has prevented the public from understanding the sport deeply. The lack of understanding is further exacerbated by the relative lack of available published scholarly works. This inadequacy in information on American football poses a cultural obstacle in the course of Japan's dealing with American football.

The Linguistic Dilemma in Japanese Understandings of American Football

The availability of a game's fundamental terms in Japanese represents one important way to measure the intensity of a sport's rootedness in Japan and its culture. The American journalist and best-selling author Robert Whiting has conducted an insightful comparative analysis of

American 'baseball' and its Japanese equivalent 'yakyu'. Whiting observers that since Japan's Ministry of Education 'regards the American-born ball game as a useful tool to develop the Japanese national character' 'yakyu' developed into an utterly different game from the 'baseball' that Americans had played.[45] Whiting argues that when the Japanese translated the term 'baseball' into 'yakyu' and made it a part of Japanese culture they fundamentally transformed it. In contrast, American football has been called 'amerikan-futtobouru', which is the phonetically copied version of the English name in Japanese accent. Like baseball, the Japanese renamed American football with the Japanese term 'gaikyu' in 1940, implying a shift in cultural appropriation was underway, but that term only lasted briefly due to the Second World War.

The *Asahi* newspaper search engine 'Kikuzo II' contains a database of the newspaper's pocket edition from 1879 to 1999. Using this database, the frequency of the use of 'yakyu', 'besubouru' (baseball), 'gaikyu', and 'amerikan-futtobouru' in each of the four periods (1879–1926, 1927–1945, 1946–1989, and 1990–1999) was derived.[46] (See Table 2)

The word 'yakyu' was used throughout the four periods, indicating that 'yakyu' as a sport is deeply entrenched in Japanese culture with the term being widely used as part of the daily vocabulary. The word 'besubouru' was used more often in pre-war years. Its use declined significantly during the post-war years. In contrast, the word 'gaikyu' was used only during the second period, 1927–1944, which covered the years from the game's introduction in Japan to its prohibition by the imperial order. In the three other periods, this word never appeared in the newspaper. The word 'amerikan-futtobouru' was employed throughout the four periods, but with increasing frequency from five mentions in the first period to 380, 427, and 919 in the subsequent periods. Unlike baseball, American football was not translated consistently into a Japanese term.[47]

This comparative analysis on the English and Japanese names of the two major sports places baseball and American football in contrasting positions, as the data showed, respectively, decreasing and increasing use of their Japanese and English terms. If baseball is the sport deeply assimilated into Japanese culture, as Whiting suggests, American football must have resisted to such assimilation, as the linguistic analysis reveals.[48]

Beyond Language: Other Factors Limiting the Japanese Adoption of American Football

Compared with baseball, American football seems to have retained its 'American-ness' despite being played for over 80 years in Japan. Aside from being a foreign sport, China's economic rise and the current rugby boom have also contributed to its relative lack of popularity in Japan. Though China came onto the NFL's radar in the mid-1980s as a huge potential market,[49] the success of another American-invented game, basketball, inspired

Table 2. Frequency of use of major sports' English and Japanese names.

	1868–1926	1927–1945	1946–1989	1990–1999
Yakyu	5,845	15,667	98,083	41,875
Beisubouru (baseball)	137	44	7	14
Gaikyu	0	69	0	0
Amerikan-futtobouru (American football)	5	380	427	919

Source: The Asahi Newspaper 'Kikuzo II'.

renewed focus on the world's most populous nation. At the beginning of the twenty-first century, the National Basketball Association (NBA) was successful in recruiting Yao Ming, a Chinese star player in Houston Rockets who is seven feet six inches tall and played centre from 2002 to 2011.[50]

Inspired by the NBA's success, the NFL launched its own campaign to explore China's immense population for both fans and potential players soon after the turn of the century. China attracted the NFL with the potential promise of many talented athletes with a height of over two metres or six feet and eight inches.[51] The NFL started coaching programs for flag football, which is an introductory version of the American football, at Chinese junior high schools in Beijing, Shanghai, and Guangzhou. NFL Commissioner Paul Tagliabue announced in 2005 that he 'wanted to have two pre-season games immediately before the Beijing Olympics of 2008'.[52]

In 2005, the NFL closed the American Bowl, which Japan had hosted more often than any other major city in the world. It also disbanded NFL Europe in 2007, which suffered deficits that cost an average of $30 million per season.[53] Pre-season games in China were re-scheduled later to 2007, re-named as the 'China Bowl', and eventually cancelled for reasons never officially announced. NFL International Vice President Gordon Smeaton left a provocative but mysterious message when he admitted the league had 'confronted situations in China that they wouldn't in other countries, which took them too much time to deal with'.[54] The strategic shift to China, however, had given the NFL its first Chinese NFL player, Ed Wang, who joined the Buffalo Bills in 2010.[55]

In addition to the shift of the NFL's market strategy from China to Japan, a recent and unprecedented rugby boom has challenged Japanese interest in American football and raised concerns from Japan's American football community. American football boosters in Japan worry that the growing interest in rugby could potentially hamper the development of the American football. According to 2011 data on sports participation, rugby has 122,368 players in Japan compared with American football's roughly 19,000.[56] Moreover, a single game in the 2015 Rugby World Cup stirred Japanese fans' interest in the game. In this match Japan, ranked 13th in the world, upset two-time world champion South Africa, then ranked 3rd in the world, by a score of 34 to 32. The unexpected result marked Japan's first World Cup victory in 24 years, since a 1991 triumph over Zimbabwe. Although Japan failed to proceed to the final round of the tournament, the Japanese national rugby side succeeded in producing star players such as Ayumu Goromaru, further increasing the game's popularity through frequent media exposure.[57]

Rugby's popularity boom has continued. The Top League, which is Japan's highest-level corporate league, has enjoyed a remarkable increase of 39% in spectatorship. Japan's national rugby team has risen to 11th in the world as of 13 June 2016.[58] Japan will host the rugby World Cup in 2019, in all probability further increasing the popularity of the sport.[59] Rugby's enhanced popularity could lead to decreasing rates of participation in American football as students in high school and college students gravitate towards rugby during the recruitment process instead.

American Football's Enduring Organizational Strength and Human Resources

In spite of the challenges, several factors seem to guarantee the further development of Japan's American football culture. At the international level, Japan's American football community is remarkably well organized with its institutional networks spreading across every part of the population who could play the game. As mentioned earlier, IFAF's first president was Japanese, as a well-ordered Japanese-style of administration is highly esteemed among IAFA officials.[60] That solid administrative structure also shapes the national administration of American football in Japan. At the top of the national administrative hierarchy resides the Japan American Football Association (JAFA). The JAFA branches into three divisions, a National Football Association (X-League) for corporations, a Japan Collegiate American Football Association (JCAFA) for colleges, and a Japan High School American Football Federation for high schools.[61]

The X-League consists of 18 corporate teams, whereas the JCAFA has 8 regional branches, each of which is governed by an association. Of these 8, the largest is the Kanto branch or the Kanto Collegiate American Football Association, which consists of 96 college and university teams. It is followed by the Kansai branch with 53 teams (including five for six-player games). There are also Hokkaido, Tohoku, Tokai, Hokuriku, Chushikoku, and Kyushu branches. The total JCAFA enrolment is a remarkably robust 211 teams. This figure accounts for about 27% of the nation's 779 universities and colleges. Meanwhile, 138 Kanto schools and 45 Kansai schools or a total of 183 institutions are part of the High School Federation. This figure accounts for about 4.8% of the nation's 3,824 high schools.[62] To prepare an even younger population for future play, the association also teaches about 270,000 pupils flag football at roughly 2,300 elementary schools.

The human resources that fill these organizational networks are provided chiefly by old boys (OBs) of college and corporate teams, who are well connected with Japan's political and business leaders. Sadao Goto, the founder of *Touchdown*, Japan's oldest American football journal, represents an archetypical Japanese football booster. He was born in Tokyo in 1943, and played football at Keio High School and Keio University. He has been committed to writing about American football through his magazine and participating in Japanese television broadcasts of the sport. NFL Commissioner Roger Goodell had expressed his gratitude to Goto by naming him as the 'great ambassador' of the sport in Japan.[63] Photo Journalist Tak Makita is another example. He was a Seattle-born Japanese American, studied and played football at Kwansai Gakuin University, and provided first-hand information about the game to Japanese readers as a regular contributor to *Touchdown*.[64]

Other earnest devotees of the sport include Makoko Ohashi, a senior advisor to the Obic Seagulls. As the team's head coach in 2015, Ohashi immediately announced prior to the 5th IFAF World Championship his 'dream' of beating the US team. If Japan would beat the US team, Ohashi speculated, the conquest of that 'challenge will open the next door'. He proclaimed of American football, 'we will try again, again, again to make it bigger'.[65] The national team's head coach Mori Kiyoyuki agreed, saying that 'it won't happen right away, it might take five years, or 10 years, or even be 50 years away' to beat the Americans. The coach concluded that 'all we can do on the field is try to keep producing results'.[66]

The Super Bowl and American Football in Japanese Perspective

What is the Super Bowl for the Japanese? The answer to this question requires viewing the perspectives of two different groups. The first is the general public who see the Super Bowl as the convenient and useful medium through which they can learn about the American culture by tuning into the one-night mania of 'conspicuous consumption' that bedazzles the

United States. The second group comprises a more earnest set of devotees – the American football experts and enthusiasts, including 13,000 athletes and their OBs, coaches, trainers, and other staff members of the leagues and associations as well as the general sports fans. For this group, the Super Bowl is the apex of their favourite sport to which only a select and talented few have access. Goto, who belongs to the second group, summarizes his view of the Super Bowl as follows:

> The connotations of the term 'super bowl' are 'absentmindedly open', 'luxurious', 'comfortable', and 'comical'. They could also be easy, friendly, and thus truly American. They could also be cheerful, sincere, with a sense of justice, broad, large, funny, and rich. America is the world's single largest sport kingdom. The symbol of its sporting culture is American football, and the apex of football is the Super Bowl. Here, we find densely packaged elements of all the sports that have been polished in American culture.[67]

The analysis of the media content on the Super Bowl by major dailies suggests that American football in Japan has reached its plateau stage. Its declining football-playing population could even indicate the onset of a stagnant stage. However, Japan's well-organized human and institutional networks with their committed, competent, and industrious staff members hold out the hope that Japan's national team can someday beat its US counterpart in the IFAF World Championship. This success can bring about an unprecedented American football boom similar to that of rugby. If that happened, domestically, *amerikan-futtobouru* could win status as one of the nation's major sports, while Japan might lead the world as an American football power. Such a day may not belong to a distant future.

Notes

1. For generic sources on the Super Bowl's power in contemporary US culture, see Peter Hopsicker and Mark S. Dyreson, 'Super Bowl Sunday: An American Holiday?', in Len Travers (ed.), *Encyclopedia of American Holidays and National Days*, vol. 1 (Westport, CT: Greenwood Press, 2006); Michael Oriard, *Brand NFL: Making and Selling America's Favorite Sport* (Chapel Hill: University of North Carolina Press, 2007); and Bernice Kanner, *The Super Bowl of Advertising: How the Commercials Won the Game* (Princeton, NJ: Bloomberg Press, 2003).
2. 'Japan Aims to Earn Title, Respect at Worlds', *The Japan News*, 24 June 2015.
3. Hitoshi Kawaguchi, *Okabe Heita Shoden: Nihon de Saishono Amerikan Fottobouru Shokaisha* [A short biography of Okabe Heita: Japan's first introducer of American football] (Amagasaki: Kansai Fottobouru Kyokai, 2004), 6.
4. Ibid.
5. Ibid., 8.
6. Ibid., 15.
7. Ibid., 12–27. Also, Toshio Asami, et al. eds, *Gendai Taiiku Supotsu Taikei vol.25 Ragubi, Amerikan Futtobouru* [Contemporary physical education and sports vol. 25 Rugby, American football] (Tokyo: Kodansha, 1984), 170.
8. Tokuji Ogawa, 'Nihon Futtobouru no Chichitachi: Tanjo no Omoide' [Fathers of Japan's football: memories of its birth]; Japan American Football Association, *Kagirinaki Zenshin: Nihon Amerikan Futtobouru 50 Nenshi* [Limitless progress: fifty years of Japan's American football] (Tokyo: Japan American Football Association, 1984), 32–3. For details of Paul Rusch's career, also see Yamanashi Nichinichi Newspaper, *Kiyosato no Chichi Poru Rasshu Den – Do Your Best And It Must Be First Class* [Father of Kiyosato, biography of Paul Rusch – do your best and it must be first class] (Kofu: Yamanashi Nichinichi Newspaper, 2004).
9. Jun Hanaoka, 'Nihon Futtobouru Tanjo no Shiai: Showa 9 Nen 11 Gatsu 29 Nichi Jingu Gaien Kyogijo' [The birth game of Japan's football: November 29 of the 9th year of Showa at

Jingu Gaien Stadium]; and Japan American Football Association, *Kagirinaki Zenshin: Nihon Amerikan Futtobouru 50 Nenshi*, 34–5.

10. Ibid.
11. Motoyuki Inoue, 'Tanjo Chokugo no Nichibei Koryu: Zenbei Senbatsu Rainichi to Beikoku Ensei' [Japan-US exchange immediately after the birth: all-Americans' visit to Japan and all-Japan's US tour]; Japan American Football Association, *Kagirinaki Zenshin: Nihon Amerikan Futtobouru 50 Nenshi*, 36–7.
12. Ibid.
13. Kawaguchi, *Okabe Heita Shoden*, 23–8.
14. Ibid.
15. Tetuo Hamuro, 'Haisen kara Fukkatsu he: Koshien Bouru Tanjo' [From defeat to recovery: the birth of the Koshien Bowl]; and Japan American Football Association, *Kagirinaki Zenshin: Nihon Amerikan Futtobouru 50 Nenshi*, 40–1.
16. Ibid.
17. Shingo Hattori, 'Oorusutasen no Saikai: Kanto deno Fukkatsu' [The resumption of the all-star game: recovery in the Kanto area]; and Japan American Football Association, *Kagirinaki Zenshin: Nihon Amerikan Futtobouru 50 Nenshi*, 42–3.
18. Sadao Goto, *Common Sense of the NFL* (Tokyo: Touchdown, 2010), 192–4.
19. Kenji Yagura, '[Supotsu Maindo] Amerikan Fottobouru: Beikoku Igai niha Makerarenu' [[Sports Mind] American football no defeat except by US], *Mainichi Newspaper*, Osaka evening edition, 20 November 1998, 2.
20. Makoto Ohashi, *Yokuwakaru Amerikan Fottobouru* [Beginners' introduction to American football] (Tokyo: Jitsugyonotomo, 2011), 95.
21. Yagura, *Mainichi*, 2.
22. Kazuo Sakakibara, 'Dato Bei Buki ha Joho Ryoku Genchijin Tsukai Senryoku Bunseki Amefutto Sekaisenshuken 9nichi Kaimaku' [Beat America information as weapon strategy analysis with local human network American football world championship open on 9th], *Asahi Newspaper*, Evening edition, Sports section, 8 July 2015.
23. Ministry of Internal Affairs and Communications, 'Heisei 23nen Shakai Seikatsu Kihon Chosa (Seikatsu Koudou ni kansuru Kekka)' [2011 social life basic research (results on daily activities)], http://www.stat.go.jp/data/shakai/2011/gaiyou.htm (accessed 5 July 2016).
24. The search engines of the four dailies are as follows: For *Nikkei*, Nikkei Telecon 21, for *Asahi*, Kikuzo II Visual, for *Yomiuri*, Yomidasu Rekisikan [Museum of history], and for *Mainichi*, Mainichi News Pack. The circulation data are from the Japan Audit Bureau of Circulations. With these four engines, I have searched for stories that contain the term 'Super Bowl' in either the title or the body.
25. Ibid.
26. Ibid.
27. Ibid.
28. Nikkei Telecon 21 covers the years from 1975 to present, Kikuzo II Visual from 1879 to present, Yomidasu Rekishikan from 1874 to present, and Mainichi News Pack from 1989 to present. I could not find any stories between 1967 and 1974 from Kikuzo II Visual and Yomidasu Rekishikan, both of which cover these and much earlier years. It should be admitted that Nikkei Telecon 21 and Mainichi News Pack do not cover the whole period in which the Super Bowl has existed. Data was not available when I conducted this research, but I wish to supplement this shortage by later research.
29. Associated Press, 'Kaigai Tanpa: Takkuru wa Iyayo' [Short wave from abroad: no tackle, please], *Yomiuri Newspaper*, 15 January 1975, 3; and Special Correspondent Ariyoshi, '8500mannin ga Terebi Kansen: Supabouru Sutiirazu kaisho' [85 million watched TV: Steelers victorious in the Super Bowl], *Asahi Newspaper*, 20 January 1976, Sports Section.
30. Associated Press, 'Kaigai Tanpa: Takkuru wa Iyayo' [Short wave from abroad: no tackle, please], *Yomiuri Newspaper*, 15 January 1975, 3.
31. Special Correspondent Ariyoshi, '8500mannin ga Terebi Kansen: Supabouru Sutiirazu kaisho'.

32. 'Ukyoku Nettowaku Ugokidasu – Zenkoku 11sha Hatsuno Regura Bangumi wo 4gatsu kara Hoso' [U-Station network opens – 11 branches in nation, broadcasting first regular program from April], *Nikkei Sangyo Newspaper*, 5 March 1980, 4.

33. Hopsicker and Dyreson, 'Super Bowl Sunday', 39.

34. Atsushi Ihara, 'Asu NFL Supabouru Kauboizu vs. Sutirazu' [NFL Super Bowl tomorrow Cowboys vs. Steelers], *Yomiuri Newspaper*, 28 January 1996, Sports Section.

35. 'NFL Amerikan Bouru 92: Supa Bouru nami (Sandei Kansenseki)' [NFL American Bowl 92 just like the Super Bowl (Sunday watching seat)], *Asahi Newspaper*, Evening edition, 1 August 1992, Entertainment Section.

36. Yagura, *Mainichi*, 2.

37. 'Amerikan Futtobouru American Bouru 98 Encho de Pakkazu Sinsho' [American Football: American Bowl 98 packers narrowly won overtime], *Mainichi Newspaper*, 3 August 1998, Sports Section.

38. National Institute of Informatics, Webcat Plus, http://webcatplus.nii.ac.jp/ (accessed 6 July 2016). Table 1 presents the list containing entries from the searches conducted through Webcat Plus, a search engine run by the National Institute of Informatics. The search was conducted for books that have been published since 2010 with keywords 'NFL', 'Super Bowl', and 'American Football'.

39. This classification is my own but reference was made to Nippon Decimal Classification (NDC) and National Diet Library Classification (NDLC).

40. Alan Tomlinson, *The Atlas of Sport: Who Plays What, Where, and Why* (Brighton: Myriad Editions, 2011).

41. Books published by the Touchdown http://www.fujisan.co.jp/pub/4128/ (accessed 6 July 2016).

42. Kyoji Niwa, *Iza Iza Iza: Kangaku Amerikan no Nakama tachi* [Now Now Now: Teammates of the Kwansai Gakuin University American Football Team] (Tokyo: Touchdown, 2010); and Goto, *Common Sense*.

43. Goto, *Common Sense*, 4.

44. This classification into six genres is the result of my effort, based on the reading of *Nikkei Newspaper*'s 511 stories, *Asahi Newspaper*'s 899 stories, *Yomiuri Newspaper*'s 1044 stories, and *Mainichi Newspaper*'s 772 stories, discussed above, to classify frequently-mentioned topics.

45. Masayuki Tamaki and Robert Whiting, *Beisbouru to Yakyu do Nichibeikan no Gokai wo Shimesu 400 no Jijitu* [Baseball and the Way of Yakyu: 400 facts that reveal misunderstanding between Japan and America] (Tokyo: Kodansha, 1991), 4–5; and Robert Whiting, Midori Matsui (for translation), *Yakyu wa Beisbouru wo Koetanoka* [Has Yakyu transcended baseball?] (Tokyo: Chikuma, 2006), 43.

46. Asahi, Kikuzo II Visual. In the Japanese calendar, 1879 to 1926 covers the eras of Meiji and Taisho, 1927 to 1945 covers the pre-WWII era of Showa, 1946 to 1989 covers the post-WWII era of Showa, 1990 to 1999 covers the era of Heisei. The name of an era changes when a new Emperor succeeds the position.

47. Water polo shows a similar tendency to baseball, as its Japanese translation name 'suikyu' has come to circulate throughout the post-WWII years, while the original English name 'uotaporo [water polo]' has completely disappeared during the same period. On the other hand, hockey and ice hockey show similar tendencies to American football, as their Japanese translation names 'jokyu' and 'hyokyu' only circulated during the pre-WWII years only to disappear completely in the post-WWII years, while their original English names 'hokkei [hockey]' and 'aisu hokkei [ice hockey]' have become part of the daily vocabulary.

48. Admittedly, this is just an unverified hypothesis, which requires proof by further research, especially, by taking into account examples of water poll, hockey, ice hockey and others mentioned in the preceding paragraph.

49. See Mark Dyreson, in this issue. On the global marketing of the NFL see Oriard, *Brand NFL*.

50. Brook Larmer, *Operation Yao Ming: The Chinese Sports Empire, American Big Business, and the Making of an NBA Superstar* (New York: Gotham Books, 2005); and Guoqi Xu, *Olympic Dreams: China and Sports, 1895–2008* (Cambridge, MA: Harvard University Press, 2008).

51. Jun Ikushima, '(Yomi Toku Supotsu) Beikoku ga Chugoku ni Daisekkin' [Reading and explaining sports: America drastically approaches China], *Asahi Newspaper*, 17 February 2007, 2.
52. Hideaki Yuri, 'Bei Prosupotsu, Chugoku ni Shojun NFL to NBA' [American professional sports target China: NFL and NBA], *Asahi Newspaper*, 14 May 2005, Sports section.
53. Goto, *Common Sense*, 194.
54. Kiyoshi Miyata, '(Warudo Supotsu 2007) Beipuro Chugoku e Nesshisen Kyodai Shijo ni Shojun Ugoki Zokuzoku' [(World Sports 2007) American professional sports' eager look at China, targets at its large market with many new projects], *Asahi Newspaper*, 9 July 2007, Evening edition, Sports section.
55. '[Mega Chaina] Beichu Sinjidai (2) Kanji Kokoku wo Yobu Suta' [[Mega China] a new era of US-China relations (2) new stars for advertisement in Chinese], *Yomiuri Newspaper*, 18 August 2010, 1.
56. Information about rugby's playing population derives from the home page of the World Rugby, the global organization committed to the promotion of this sport, which was renamed in 2014 from the International Rugby Board at http://www.worldrugby.org/ (accessed 6 July 2016).
57. For Japan's recent rugby boom and its star player Ayumu Goromaru, see Kaori Araki, *Ragubi Nihon Daihyo wo Kaeta 'Kokoro no Kitae-kata'* ['Mental Coaching' that Changed Japan's National Rugby Team] (Tokyo: Kodansha, 2016).
58. For information about Japan's national team and Top League, see its home page at http://www.top-league.jp/ (accessed 6 July 2016).
59. On Japan's hosting of the 2019 World Cup, so many stories have been recently published, but for example, see 'Ragubi W-hai Koka wa 824 oku-en Tokyo-to' [The economic impact of the Rugby World Cup on the Tokyo Metropolis estimated at 82.4 billion yen], *Asahi Newspaper*, 30 January 2016, 37.
60. Yagura, *Mainichi*, 2.
61. For information about the organizational networks of Japan's American football, see the home page of the Japan American Football Association at http://www.top-league.jp/ (accessed 6 July 2016). Although not mentioned in the text, there are also organizations for junior high school teams in the Kanto (East) and Kansai (West) regions, which extend PR activities through the Facebook, the Chestnut League for even younger children, and the Japan Flag Football Organization for the promotion of this safer version of American football.
62. Counting the number of high school is not as easy as that of colleges, because there are several types of high schools by curriculums and courses, but the number shown here is for those of 2014 with the regular courses/curriculums (futsu-ka). See the home page of the Ministry of Education, Culture, Sports, Science and Technology at http://www.mext.go.jp/a_menu/shotou/shinkou/genjyo/021201.htm (accessed 6 July 2016).
63. Goto, *Common Sense*, 2–3. Goto has written numerous books. For one focusing on the Super Bowl, see his *Supa Bouru: Purofesshonaru Futtobouru Nyumon* [The Super Bowl: introduction to professional football] (Touchdown, 1991).
64. For the compilation of his essays, see Tak Makita, *Jibun Hitori no NFL Futtobouru* [NFL football only for myself] (Touchdown, 1991).
65. 'Japan aims to earn title', *The Japan News*, 24 June 2015. For a book supervised by Ohashi, see above-cited *Yokuwakaru Amerikan Fottobouru* [Beginners' introduction to American football].
66. Ibid. For a book supervised by Mori, see *Amerikan Fottobouru no Kisogijutu* [American football basics] (Touchdown, 2011).
67. Goto, *Common Sense*, 11.

Disclosure Statement

No potential conflict of interest was reported by the author.

The Super Bowl as a Television Spectacle: Global Designs, Glocal Niches, and Parochial Patterns

Mark Dyreson

ABSTRACT
In the contemporary US, the Super Bowl creates the largest 'shared experience' in the nation. More people tune into these spectacles than attend worship services, vote in elections, or celebrate traditional holidays. Super Bowls have become such powerful elements in US national culture that television corporations and the National Football League have sought to export them to the rest of the world. Indeed, executives in the television and football industries tout potential worldwide audiences in the billions and speculate that the Super Bowl might muscle its way into the realm of the Olympics and World Cup soccer tournaments as global mega-events. In spite of corporate bluster, the Super Bowl has not become a truly international event and has not garnered widespread international passion. American pundits have speculated ceaselessly about why the Super Bowl lags behind other US cultural products in terms of global influence and fretted about how the rest of the world sees the game. Their analyses reveal more about American perceptions of the world than they do about the world's views of the United States.

In February of 2016, Super Bowl 50 failed to meet the predictions of US media gurus. Not even the one-year hiatus from Roman numerals to an Arabic 'fifty' undertaken by the spectacle's marketing gurus could garner enough viewers to push the telecast over the top on the all-time charts of American television ratings.[1] The 'golden anniversary' game finished with a 'mere' 111.9 million viewers to earn a third-place ranking behind Super Bowl XLIX and Super Bowl XLVIII, which garnered 114.4 million and 112.2 million, respectively. Super Bowl 50's score still made it the third most-watched programme in the history of US television broadcasting, joining a score of other Super Bowls that rule American airwaves as the dominant programming in the history of that medium.[2]

Inside the United States the Super Bowl has become a cultural touchstone, the biggest shared event in the nation.[3] Some scholars have contended that Super Bowl Sunday has emerged as the nation's newest national holiday, a celebratory ritual that functions to crystalize American ideals and expectations on concepts ranging from affluence and patriotism to violence and excess.[4] Much of that sharing takes place through television, the medium that connects citizens to the season-ending spectacles. Indeed, in covering Super

Bowl VIII in 1974, the radical 'gonzo' journalist Hunter S. Thompson in one of his more sedate insights contended that

> if sporting historians ever look back on all this and try to explain it, there will be no avoiding the argument that pro football's meteoric success in the 1960's was directly attributable to its early marriage with network TV and a huge, coast-to-coast audience of armchair fans who 'grew up' – in terms of their personal relationship to The Game – with the idea that pro football was something that happened every Sunday on the tube.[5]

While in the next breath Thompson erratically, and in historical hindsight inaccurately, predicted that the national infatuation with the game would be over by 1984, his argument that the Super Bowl and television represented cultural forces that thrived when mated has proven prescient.[6]

The Super Bowl and Globalization

Television has propelled the Super Bowl into a national pandemic. Television has also exported the Super Bowl into international markets. American football stands as a uniquely parochial pastime that a miniscule number of the world's athletes play beyond the borders of the United States and Canada – where an alternative but very similar version has evolved – in the landscapes of contemporary global sporting culture.[7] Gridiron football, as the football snobs of the British Empire once dubbed the American football code, has garnered significant attention in other cultures almost entirely as a television programme. The power of the Super Bowl in US culture and its penetration into the world via television propel this mega-event into conversations about the broad Americanization of the globe. The game gets lumped with other forms of Americanization, including Disneyfication, McDonaldization, Walmartization, Hollywoodization, Nike-ization, Californication, and all the other 'ications' and 'izations' at the heart of the American imperial project.[8] Television itself, an industrial-cultural behemoth invented, designed, and perfected in the US, often comes under fire from anti-Americanization partisans. 'Super Bowlderization' seems an apt addition to any catalogue of the genus of *imperialis Americanus*, destined to join Disneyfication and the rest of the post-modern line-up of culture destroyers unleased on the world by the American empire.

As usual, however, history defies such oversimplification. McDonald's eaters and Walmart shoppers do indeed span the globe. Disney's kingdom and Hollywood's empire include a multitude of foreign subjects. California lifestyle products clothe and amuse billions beyond the US borders. Surveying foreign legions of Super Bowl fans reveals that the spectacle does not rank with these other truly global cultural powers. While the Super Bowl dominates television ratings in the US,[9] the global impact of the broadcast remains mysteriously murky. Solid numbers on global television ratings are peculiarly hard to come by, a shocking development in an industry that fetishizes market shares. Some observers make claims that the Super Bowl stands among the most-watched events on global television, but actual numbers are maddeningly difficult to locate. The National Football League (NFL) releases annual press blurbs that since the dawn of the twenty-first century have claimed global audiences of more than a billion viewers inhabiting as many as 200 nations. The NFL's propaganda, however, cites not historical data on the number of actual viewers beyond the US but rather 'potential' watchers with access to broadcasts – those who could tune in rather than those who actually do tune in.[10] Based on such hyperbole, American commentators routinely estimate in the twenty-first century that the Super Bowl draws upwards of a billion viewers.[11]

Media studies rarely tackle the actual global viewership of the Super Bowl. On the few occasions when they do, they reveal numbers considerably smaller than the NFL's tabulations of potential watchers. In 2005, a New York City research firm counted 93 million viewers outside of the United States. Fully 98% of those viewers were on the US border, in Canada and Mexico. Only two million people beyond North America actually tuned in to watch the New England Patriots beat the Philadelphia Eagles in Super Bowl XXXIX.[12] The researchers concluded that this tiny remnant consisted almost entirely of American expatriates residing overseas.[13] The lack of comparable studies stems, in large part, from the absence of accurate measurements of global audiences. Most rating systems, such as the Nielsen scores developed for the US market, only measure viewership within national boundaries. In addition, the quality and accuracy of ratings vary widely across national markets.[14] Those factors make the NFL's claims about 'potential' global spectators the only numbers available since precise measurements of international viewers are nearly impossible to construct.

Foreign commentators typically deride American football in general and the Super Bowl in particular, discounting any claims that the NFL makes about globalization. An editorial in the *Manchester Guardian* recently scoffed that

> Super Bowl Sunday is upon us, the day of the year when America unites in front of the TV to eat copious amounts of junk food and watch their fellow countrymen give each other brain damage through the medium of a contact sport.[15]

US observers of foreign affairs report similar dismissals of this great American holiday. Writing in the *Atlantic*, a veteran diplomatic correspondent admitted that 'Outside North America, many regard America's hallowed pro-football tradition the same way many Americans regard Mounties, Vegemite, and the vuvuzela – that is, with mild amusement, morbid curiosity, and perhaps a little squinting suspicion.'[16] An American expatriate in South Korea laments that in his global travels he has found it almost impossible to find a Super Bowl television feed to slake his desire to partake in America's national football holiday even though US television programmes appear regularly on South Korean airwaves.[17]

Still, the NFL and affiliated architects of American 'soft power' promote the idea that its championship game has a global reach. The official NFL website of Super Bowl 50 in 2016 noted that the spectacle was available in more than 170 nations, from Afghanistan to Yemen, and invited visitors to catch a feed directly in one of the six global languages, Spanish, Japanese, French, Portuguese, Mandarin Chinese, and German – and one less broadly diffused European tongue, Hungarian.[18] Scholars report that the Super Bowl has made inroads in a few important international markets, including Great Britain, Australia, Germany, and Japan.[19] The closest American neighbours, however, Canada and Mexico, account for the vast majority of foreign viewers. In fact, on a per capita basis, as the Canadian historian Craig Greenham reveals, a higher percentage of Canadians than Americans actually watches the Super Bowl.[20] Beyond neighbouring nations and a few niche markets overseas, the Super Bowl in the past half-century has struggled to garner attention in the global marketplace.

World Cups and other international association football matches as well as Olympic broadcasts regularly trounce the Super Bowl, even with the limited data on global television ratings.[21] *Washington Post* columnist Ishaan Tharoor, in contrasting the real audience for recent Super Bowls, noted that the 2014 World Cup final between Germany and Argentina as well as several recent cricket tests between India and Pakistan have drawn a number of eyeballs that dwarfs foreign audience of Super Bowl voyeurs.[22] Television industry publications pegged the audience for the 2016 Rio Olympics at half of the world's population, some 3.5 billion viewers.[23] That number dwarfs even the fantastical claims that the Super Bowl draws one billion oglers.

In some ways, measuring multiday events such as Olympics and World Cups against a one-day event such as the Super Bowl requires the comparison of 'apples and oranges'. Additionally, multi-national events such as the aforementioned global spectacles with many nations competing clearly enhance interest in many nations, as compared to a Super Bowl that pits two US franchises against one another. Reliable estimates of recent Olympic and World Cup viewership over the course of their multi-week calendars reveal that roughly half of the 7 billion people who inhabit the earth tune in for at least a snippet of these global mega-events. When calculating single-day audiences, things get more complicated. The International Olympic Committee estimated that 342 million people watched the 2016 Rio Olympics opening ceremony, about the same number as tuned into the 2012 London Olympics kick-off. The World Cup's organizing body, the Fédération Internationale de Football Association, claimed one billion watched the 2014 final from Rio.[24] To add another dimension to the comparison, one-day matches in cricket tests in recent India versus Pakistan contests have drawn a billion viewers around the world as well – as the *Washington Post*'s columnist observed.[25]

Clearly, in the twenty-first century, the one billion-viewer mark has become the gold standard for bragging rights, as the NFL's claim of a potential audience of that size underscores. World Cup finals and cricket tests between populous rivals Pakistan and India draw audiences that size, though the Olympics fall quite short when considered in one-day chunks. Indeed, the NFL's aspirations for an audience of one billion reveals that in spite of the differences, comparing Super Bowls to World Cups, Olympic spectacles, and cricket matches is quite fair. Television fuels the growth and expansion of each of these sporting events and they compete for advertising dollars in global as well as national markets. In addition, the NFL and its US television partners openly promote their aspirations to rank alongside the Olympics, international soccer, and big time cricket as a global mega-event. In its own press releases about reaching one billion global viewers, the NFL compares itself to its rivals. NFL commissioner Roger Goodell contends that American football 'absolutely' needs to be on the Olympic docket.[26] The NFL's branding savants perceive World Cup soccer as a major global rival as well.[27] In refusing to accept a parochial label and aspiring to global popularity, the Super Bowl's boosters have set the stage for these comparisons, in spite of some 'apples versus oranges' differences between the events.

These comparisons have not generally been kind to the Super Bowl. In a seminal article in 2001 entitled 'The Whole World Isn't Watching (But We Thought They Were)', the media scholars Christopher R. Martin and Jimmie L. Reeves wryly observed that claims the Super Bowl had become a global event were vastly overstated. Martin and Reeves argued post-cold war American triumphalism had led Americans to overestimate their power in global culture. They also contended that gridiron football in general and the Super Bowl in particular were too uniquely and distinctly parochial to become global passions, the way that association football or even the US-invented games of basketball and volleyball had become truly international pastimes by the dawn of the twenty-first century.[28]

Global, Parochial, and Glocal

The issue of why some team sports have become global passions while others have remained exclusively national pastimes remains one of the central puzzles of contemporary exploration into the history of sport. Clearly, all of team sports that dominate the athletic landscape of the twenty-first century world emerged from Anglo-American roots, from bat-and-ball games such as baseball and cricket to the progeny of the Young Men's Christian Association such as basketball and volleyball. Every football code is a product of English-speaking nations. Some have become truly global games – rugby has adherents in many parts of the world while the association version of football reigns as the most widespread sport on the planet. Others, not only the gridiron variants in the US and Canada but also the Australian rules game, have remained distinctly nationalistic. Enigmas remain as to why association football exploded into the world's game while American football remains almost entirely a parochial pastime connected to one particular national culture. Theories abound. Some scholars contrast the simplicities of the association code that made it easy to decipher and master in a wide variety of cultures to the complexities of the American rules that allegedly require a lifetime to decode. Others speculate about the supposedly collective and communal qualities of the association game that are more attuned to global sensibilities in comparison to the allegedly violent and individualistic tendencies of American football that attract only hyper-nationalistic Americans and repel the rest of the peace-loving denizens of the globe.[29]

Overly simplistic examinations of these issues tend to obscure more than they illuminate. Any serious analysis of football codes would have to wrestle with the reality that in any version of the game, the tensions between individual brilliance and cooperative teamwork reside at the core of the endeavour and that American football is in fact at the far communal end of the spectrum in terms of both essence and ethos.[30] Violence remains a fundamental part of not just the American variant but the Australian, Canadian, and rugby codes, and even the association game. Indeed, whether they intend it as a celebration or a condemnation, the undeniable ferocity of the American game is in many respects exaggerated by the multitude of believers, both domestic and foreign, in the concept of American exceptionalism.[31] In addition, strains of hyper-nationalism certainly exist beyond the United States.[32]

The gospel of American exceptionalism provides a partial explanation for why so many in the US uncritically accept the NFL's endless touts that Super Bowl broadcasts get beamed to global audiences of a billion or more, when from the meagre data available it appears that a couple of hundred million or thereabouts actually tune in to the spectacle. In fact, outside of Canada and Mexico, international viewership remains minimal. Given the actual numbers, the English comedian John Cleese's riff about the differences between the Americans and the British needs an adjustment. 'When we hold a World Championship for a particular sport, we invite teams from other countries to play, as well', Cleese famously observed.[33] When the British telecast a world championship or a royal wedding, people in other countries actually watch. In spite of the rhetoric by the NFL and pundits based in the US, the Super Bowl currently represents not a profoundly global event but rather a peculiarly parochial television moment that draws far fewer global gawkers than most Americans imagine.

Still, the Super Bowl does draw some 'glocal' audiences, particularly in Great Britain, Germany, Japan, Canada, and Mexico.[34] Glocalizaton represents the adaptation of global trends and products to local sensibilities, for instance, the creation of menus that suit local tastes by global fast-food chains or the marketing of local cultures to international tourists via the worldwide web. Foreign television viewers often tune in to sample the Super Bowl to experience the 'local' flavour of the spectacle. They also use the Super Bowl to create local niches within their own culture settings.[35] For instance, in Germany, beginning in the 1980s, a small but zealous band of German youth, disenchanted with their nation's adoration of association football and seeking alternative identities, went to great lengths to find broadcasts of the Super Bowl and to create clubs devoted to playing as well as watching American football.[36] Or, in another manifestation of glocal passion for American football, consider that the Dallas Cowboys have 1500 season-ticket holders in Monterrey, Mexico, who commute 500 miles, one way, to see 'America's team' (the famous nickname bestowed on the Cowboys during the 1970s and 1980s) play.[37] The Super Bowl, at least in the second decade of the twenty-first century, is not a global event but rather both a parochial and glocal spectacle.

Glocal Appetites in the American Borderlands

The history of international Super Bowl broadcasting remains as baffling as the global ratings while also revealing the parochial and glocal parameters of the televised spectacle. The Super Bowl has clearly not become a shared global experience. It remains primarily a national phenomenon limited to the United States – a parochial experience from an international perspective. Still, beyond the boundaries of the US, the Super Bowl has found a few glocal habitats where it flourishes – places where local conditions create receptive climates for a cultural production transmitted around the world from its parochial home in the United States. Interestingly, the history of Super Bowl broadcasting beyond US borders reveals that glocal patterns were there from the beginning – though the NFL and American television networks did not plan or design a global strategy and it emerged in a seemingly organic fashion.

Scholars have struggled to pinpoint the first international broadcast of the Super Bowl. Most date the development to some point in the 1980s.[38] However, a survey of the contemporaneous record in industry journals and the mass media reveals that the very first Super Bowl penetrated international markets. The early international telecasts from US stations that drifted across borders and into television sets in Canada and Mexico like a transnational smog were not a part of any scheme by the NFL and US broadcasters to Americanize the world but simply a reflection of the new medium's potential for blurring geopolitical boundaries. Sometimes, however, Canadian and Mexican networks partnered with US television corporations in this cross-border traffic. In these cases, the intent was precisely to export American culture into neighbouring nations.[39]

With 75% of its population clustered within 100 miles of the US border, Canada made a particularly rich target. While many Canadians could catch the Super Bowl on US stations that broadcast into Canadian territory, the NFL and its US television partners signed deals with Canadian stations to broadcast early Super Bowls with both English and French commentary. A total of 149 stations, including 36 French-language outlets, telecast Super Bowl I in Canada.[40] By 1971 that number had grown to 265 total stations, and by 1972 it reached 295.[41] By the late 1970s and 1980s, the Super Bowl had become a staple of Canadian television watching habits. Although, as Craig Greenham has documented, Canadians frequently watched the American spectacular through jaundiced lenses and held their own championship of Canadian professional football, the Grey Cup, as a far superior product that was emblematic of their distinctiveness from their neighbours to the south, they nevertheless tuned into the American carnival in huge numbers. Per capita, a larger percentage of Canada's population than US residents watched the Super Bowl.[42] Clearly, Canada has one of the largest glocal appetites for the Super Bowl in the world.

Mexico has provided another strong glocal market. The first record of a Super Bowl broadcast deal with a foreign nation predates the original game, when in December of 1966 the National Broadcasting Corporation (NBC) announced an agreement with a Mexican network to broadcast the very first game.[43] A year later, the Columbia Broadcasting System (CBS) made another Mexican deal.[44] Telecasts of the early Super Bowls built a solid niche market for American football in Mexico. By 1968, Telesisterna Mexicano was beaming not only the Super Bowl but regular season NFL and AFL games as well as intercollegiate games such as the Rose Bowl and the Sugar Bowl into Mexican homes.[45] As the Super Bowl became an ever-larger spectacle in the US, it grew in popularity in Mexico as well.[46] By the 1990s, Mexicans led the parade of foreign journalists who flocked to Super Bowls to cover American culture, outstripping Japanese, German, British, and even Canadian correspondents. So popular has the Super Bowl become that prognostications about an NFL expansion team settling south of the border are routine.[47]

When, in 2004, negotiations for Super Bowl broadcast rights broke down between the NFL and TV Azteca and Televisa, Mexican fans were solely disappointed. The failure to reach a deal marked the first time in 37 years, dating back to Super Bowl I, that a Mexican network did not offer a live telecast of the event. Many enterprising Mexican fans managed to garner Fox network feeds of the live US broadcast in order to circumvent the one-year embargo.[48] In Mexico City, enterprising nightclubs and cantinas found ways to access Super Bowl broadcasts for Mexican aficionados. Many wealthy Mexican fans purchased packages to watch the game live in Houston, a short flight from most major Mexican metropolises.[49] The one-year television blackout ended in 2005 as the NFL reconnected with the Mexican television market. A year later for Super XXXIX, NFL sources claimed a Mexican broadcast audience of 19 million households with 84 million viewers. Those numbers ranked the NFL's culminating gala fourth in sports programming on Mexican television, behind only telecasts of the nation's professional association football leagues, 'El Tri' (as the Mexican national soccer team is known), and the 2004 Athens Olympics.[50]

Television has guaranteed that since the first Super Bowl in 1966, American football has become an important dimension of interchanges between Mexico and the United States. Massive migration from Mexico to the US, as well as extensive repatriation of Mexican migrants to their homeland, has built fan bases that straddle the border. Nearly uninterrupted Super Bowl broadcasts across the border also whetted Mexican appetites for *fútbol Americano*, as the game is known in Mexican idiom. The Dallas Cowboys, located in the border state of Texas, have made an enduring and concerted effort to exploit the Mexican market. They began Spanish language radio broadcasts of Dallas games into Mexico (and in US markets) in the 1960s. In the 1970s they signed one of the first Mexican-born players to grow up in Mexico in NFL history, place-kicker Efrén Herrera, to provide color commentary on Spanish language broadcasts. Mexican fans routinely travel hundreds or thousands of miles to see the Cowboys play, as the aforementioned 1500 season-ticket holders from Monterrey reveal.[51] Mexican fan bases have also developed around other teams that dominated the league and flourished in the 1970s, 1980s, and 1990s when Mexicans built their Super Bowl holiday tradition, including the Pittsburgh Steelers, Oakland/Los Angeles Raiders, San Francisco 49ers, and the Miami Dolphins.[52]

The glocal power of American football comes into sharp relief in border towns, especially in Tijuana, across the line from San Diego, and Ciudad Juárez, across the river from El Paso. In those cities, the local economies respond to appetites on both sides of the border for American football. Indeed, a local Juárez merchant told a US correspondent visiting the city that on Super Bowl Sunday the street *mercados*, normally a staple of Sunday afternoon and evening culture, would be closed for one of the few 'holidays' that year since everyone in both Juárez and El Paso would be watching the game. 'On Sunday, there is no baseball, there is no football [soccer]', even in Mexico, the vendor observed. 'Only the Super Bowl'.[53]

Recently, for Super Bowl XLIX and Super Bowl 50, the cultural blends of the Mexican–US borderlands have surfaced in a new venue, in advertising for a popular transnational cuisine. Guacamole, an avocado-based dish that has long been a staple of Mexican gastronomy, has in the past few decades also become a cherished treat north of the border, securing a prominent place at American Super Bowl smorgasbords. Mexico leads the world in avocado production. In a novel campaign to expand its US market, Avocados from Mexico, the Mexican-based growers' consortium that promotes the fruit took the plunge into the most expensive advertising realm in the world and purchased television spots on US Super Bowl broadcasts. In the highly competitive 'ad bowl' competition that runs in tandem with the actual game on the gridiron, the hilarious 2015 spot entitled 'The First Draft Ever' astounded US audiences and ranked as one of the most innovative commercials in the Super Bowl XLIX line-up. A follow-up spot for Super Bowl 50, 'Avocados in Space', also garnered massive interest and spurred sales in the US market.[54]

Mexico's entry into the cultural production of Super Bowl spectacles through the marketing genius of Avocados from Mexico reveals that in tandem with Canada the two nations that border the United States have developed the most intense glocal markets for the Super Bowl in particular and for NFL football in general. Clearly, these are not global markets, nor do they threaten intense commitment to their cultures' own national pastimes. In neither Canada nor Mexico has American football supplanted the respective national pastimes of hockey or soccer. Nor has the NFL expanded in significant ways such as planting franchises and developing significant numbers of players from Canada or Mexico. Even if, as pundits frequently posit, Toronto or Mexico City represent prime sites for future NFL teams, it does not seem likely that American football would rise to national pastime status in Canada or Mexico. Canada remains patriotically committed to Canadian football as well as to hockey while Mexico remains wedded to the most popular global football code. American football remains a glocal product in Mexico and Canada, a popular import with a significant market niche that has adapted to local customs and outlooks. Given the intense historical intersections between Canada and the US and Mexico and the US, the emergence of thriving glocal Super Bowl markets in these two neighbouring states fits within the broader tradition of transnational sporting exchanges that have long characterized these two North American borderlands.[55]

Overseas Telecasts

Beyond the border regions, the Super Bowl has generated a few other glocal markets in scattered locales around the world. Super Bowl I and the succeeding instalments were also broadcast to Puerto Rico, making the broadcasts to that commonwealth and to the state of

Hawai'i literally the earliest 'overseas' Super Bowl broadcasts.[56] As early as Super Bowl III, the American Forces Network (AFN) beamed the game around the world to US military personnel in foreign posts in Europe, Asia, Africa, and other locations.[57] Arguably, the AFN's broadcasts were not 'international' in the true sense of the word as these Super Bowl telecasts were targeted at US military personnel stationed in foreign posts. However, local audiences near these posts would soon seek to tap into these telecasts. By the early 1970s, the Virgin Islands and Costa Rica, nations with close ties to the US, and Venezuela where the Spanish Independent Network that drew much of its programming from Mexican broadcasts sublet the games had joined the list of Super Bowl outlets.[58]

The first satellite transmission of a Super Bowl to an overseas location, beyond the AFN's endeavours, took place in January of 1981 when a British company called Viewsport broadcast Super Bowl XV live at the Odeon Theatre in London's Leicester Square.[59] The British entrepreneurs who sponsored the event pushed it as an authentic American-style extravaganza, complete with hot dogs and all the condiments, fresh popcorn, and flowing Budweiser. Gyrating cheerleaders and two British actors curiously dressed as New York City police officers, though neither the Jets nor the Giants were playing, rounded out the production 'razzmatazz'. Viewsport charged from $24 to $36 for tickets and sold out the 2000-seat movie theatre. The actor, box-office star, and international sportsman Omar Sharif attended. As he watched the Oakland Raiders thrash the Philadelphia Eagles, Sharif told a reporter covering the event that during his frequent sojourns in Hollywood he had become 'very keen on the sport'. The Egyptian-born movie star who made his home in London was the exception among the crowd – a gathering that was not comprised of throngs of curious Britons but consisted almost entirely of American expatriates. Texans working on North Sea oil platforms off the coast of Scotland came in droves, as did US servicemen and servicewomen stationed around the British Isles. US Embassy personnel also attended. The event was clearly an American patriotic rally, with a pregame moment of silence to give thanks for the safe return of the recently released US hostages from Iran, a raucous rendition of the 'Star Spangled Banner', and vying contingents of Raiders and Eagles fans. The reporter spied, in addition to Sharif, a small 'scattering of Britons and other foreigners in the audience'. The correspondent interviewed one Englishman who was mystified by the game itself but impressed by the camera work. Where commercials would appear during the US broadcast, the British feed went black – a development that irritated the US contingent who pined for a full Super Bowl experience.[60]

Europe's Glocal Market

Since 1981, when Sharif and the mostly American crowd of two thousand watched at the Odeon Theatre in London, the NFL's European broadcasts have expanded dramatically. In Great Britain during the 1980s and 1990s, as the historian Iain Adams has chronicled, NFL football found a market niche on a network that catered to tastes not satisfied by the mainstream programming on the British Broadcasting Corporation and quickly developed a strong niche following. Telecasts of the Super Bowl expanded the audience beyond the hardcore base and made once-a-year late Sunday night Super Bowl parties into mini-vacations for sampling the thrills of American culture for even those with the most casual acquaintance with gridiron football. These short sojourns were enough for most Britons, who happily returned to traditional British sports fare after their annual indulgence in

Super Bowl spectaculars. Once again, a glocal rather than a global market for American football developed in Britain.[61] The Super Bowl carved a similar niche in Germany. As the historian Lars Dzikus has demonstrated, the German glocal market developed initially through captured feeds from the American military's global network, AFN. As the local taste for football evolved, German broadcasters began to serve the niche market and a flourishing subculture emerged around the American football code.[62]

In both Germany and Britain as small but fervent communities of players as well as watchers emerged, American football remained an alternative pastime fed by a steady glocal stream of NFL-produced programmes. In an effort to spur participation rates and build a stronger fan base in Europe, the NFL planted a series of leagues with European franchises from the World League of American Football to NFL Europe to the Europa League. These leagues managed to survive for a couple of decades, from 1991 to 2007, before general European apathy for the gridiron code killed the endeavour. Franchises came and went at a dizzying pace, from the Berlin Thunder to the Cologne Centurions to the Frankfurt Galaxy to the Hamburg Sea Devils to the Rhein Fire in Germany, and from the London Monarchs (who also played games in Bristol and Birmingham) to the Scottish Claymores who at different times called Edinburgh and Glasgow home in Britain. American football leached across the English Channel into other parts of Europe as well, as the short lives of the Amsterdam Admirals and Barcelona Dragons reveal.[63]

Sometimes these teams played North American clubs, and sometimes they competed in all-European competition. These ventures mainly imported players from the US, but they did seek to cultivate indigenous talent as well. Ultimately, the experiment proved neither economically nor culturally sustainable. Association football faced no real threat from the American variant in the sporting passions of Europe. Still, the NFL's efforts managed to make gridiron football a niche sport beyond Great Britain and Germany. In France, Italy, Holland, Spain, and other nations, small but devoted groups of players continue to create their own clubs and leagues.[64] These new regions offered potential glocal markets for the expansion of Super Bowl broadcasts. The NFL regularly plays exhibitions and even regular season contests in the most lucrative of these glocal marketplaces, especially in London. Occasional rumours about exploiting these niches appear in NFL propaganda about planting a franchise in London or Berlin in an effort to expand glocal tastes into a more global system.[65]

Grander Global Designs

In the midst of the turn-of-the-century efforts to export American football to Europe, nations such as Japan and Australia, where small but devoted pockets of American football aficionados had longer histories, collaborated with Germany and other European nations and with Mexico to found the International Federation of American Football (IFAF) to foster the game internationally. The IFAF, headquartered in Paris, France, stages a quadrennial American Football World Cup, lobbies to gain a spot for gridiron football on the Olympic docket, and claims 71 member nations and 23 million amateur players.[66] Underscoring the still glocal nature of the game around the world, Football Canada belongs to the IFAF but promotes the Canadian version of gridiron football.[67]

During the 1980s, as the historian Kohei Kawashima has detailed, the Super Bowl first began to draw interest in Japan. Over the next two decades, a solid glocal market developed as many Japanese became fascinated with the game as a symbol of the national values of Japan's rival and ally along the Pacific Rim. American football, or 'armour-ball' as the Japanese sometimes called it, had an older history in Japan. With help from an American missionary, the game began in the 1920s and 1930s in elite Japanese universities and prep schools. A small but ardent population of players have through the beginning of the twenty-first century continued to dedicate themselves to playing the game. The mainstream public, meanwhile, samples gridiron football on occasions such as the Super Bowl, curious to discover what the United States finds so fascinating about the spectacle but hardly eager to abandon their own traditions and national pastimes to embrace the American craze.[68]

During the 1980s and 1990s, as the NFL pondered expansion, Japan seemed an obvious target. Japan had a small but thriving American football subculture. As in Europe, the NFL used exhibition games to test the Japanese waters.[69] However, another Asian market, potentially more lucrative but lacking even a hint of interest in American football, beckoned. Besotted by the globe's largest cache of potential consumer, the NFL tried to garner a beachhead in China by extending Super Bowl telecasts into the 'Middle Kingdom'. In 1986, the NFL made its first broadcast to China, Super Bowl XX between the Chicago Bears and New England Patriots.[70] This innovation led the NFL's chief operative for overseas exports, director of broadcasting Val Pinchbeck, to gloat that 'we won't have to hear any more about the 100 million Chinese who don't care about the Super Bowl'.[71]

Pinchbeck's exultations about opening a China market owed more to serendipity than to the NFL's business acumen. The NFL initially had little interest in a China broadcast. It took the foresight of international marketing executive, native Chicagoan, and devoted Bears fan Lyric Hughes of TLI International to make the deal. Hughes made a bet with Jim Bukata, an old friend who was an NFL marketing representative, that if the Bears won the Super Bowl she would get the rebroadcast rights to beam the game to China. When the Bears crushed the Patriots, she got the telecast rights for a paltry $200. Hughes packaged the game into a 90-minute format that included selected advertisements and broadcast the show on government-run Central China Television (CCTV) one day after the live event. Hughes claimed that Chinese officials estimated that 300 million watched the broadcast. She and the NFL had apparently struck the motherlode.[72]

As other observers of the China market for Super Bowls noted, however, that figure of 300 million came from Lyric Hughes and her firm rather that from verifiable Chinese ratings. Like most NFL claims of vast foreign audiences for Super Bowls, the numbers signalled potential rather than reality. Still, business analysts dreamed of enormous profits. A year later, as the NFL again prepared to beam the Super Bowl to China, a *Wall Street Journal* reporter contended: 'Even if the Chinese audience is smaller than TLI [and Hughes] advertises to its advertisers, it is big league by any standard, and reinforces the status of the Super Bowl as the U.S.'s premier sporting export'. The analyst asserted that including China, '[p]eople in no less than 60 countries will watch Sunday's clash in Pasadena between the New York Giants and Denver Broncos'. The expert predicted that '[t]heir numbers will far exceed the 100 million or so Americans who are expected to tune in'. The newly opened portal to China market led the NFL's Pinchbeck to speculate: 'Who knows? Maybe one day we'll top World Cup soccer's audience'.[73]

Nearly 30 years after Pinchbeck's prediction that one day the Super Bowl would top the World Cup in global television ratings, gridiron football remains nowhere near unseating association football in the world's imaginations. The last three Super Bowls in 2014, 2015, and 2016 drew approximately 150 million viewers around the world while the 2014 World

Cup final drew more than one billion.[74] In the China market, even after three decades of Super Bowl shows, most viewers remain mystified by the American brand of football. A proprietor at a Beijing hotspot setting up for a Super Bowl breakfast party a few years ago admitted that 98% of his patrons for the broadcast would be US expatriates. Chinese 'person-on-the-street interviews' revealed the world's biggest consumer market remained dumbfounded by the Super Bowl. As one Chinese informant stated: 'Wear a helmet and run around? Oh, yeah! Yeah, I've seen that before. I often watch sports programs on TV'.[75]

Parochial and Glocal Realities amidst Enduring Global Dreams

In many other realms, American-made television programmes represent the contemporary global dominion of US culture.[76] The global spread of *Baywatch* seems to underscore that phenomenon – providing an ironic capstone to the architecture of American soft power.[77] In football, as the sport scholars Simon Kuper and Stefan Syzmanski have trenchantly observed, Great Britain still remains supreme: 'Long after the sun set on the British Empire, it is achieving a posthumous victory in sports'.[78] The 'beautiful game's' enormous lead over American football persists, in spite of the constantly recycled rhetoric about the Super Bowl's growing global reach that pops up in the oddest places, such as a recent story in the pages of *China Daily*, the ruling Communist Party's English language organ, heralding gridiron football's tremendous spurt in popularity in the People's Republic of China.[79]

Seeing NFL propaganda fit so neatly into communist Chinese party lines is not only disconcerting but underscores the frustration that many Americans feel that around the world American football has so far only managed to carve glocal markets. American angst that the skeletal remains of British Empire exert greater cultural influence than the US variant of football remains palpable, as the NFL's continuing releases of the worldwide number of potential viewers rather than the number of actual viewers reveal – and as the American media's consistent acquiescence to this ruse betray. This torment even generates overwrought prophecies about how someday soon Americans will abandon their historic attachments to the gridiron game and gravitate en masse to association football.[80] Incidents such as the 2012 announcement that General Motors (GM) was punting its Super Bowl patronage in favour of the cheaper and more global branding opportunity to sponsor Manchester United's brand of football fuel jeremiads about the United States descending into football Armageddon.[81]

As the great twentieth century homily crafted by GM chief executive officer Charles Wilson about what is good for General Motors being good for America goes, GM's exile of the Super Bowl to the sidelines of its advertising strategy seemed a trenchant omen. In fact, GM could not even maintain that threat for a single Super Bowl. It bought several spots for its Chevrolet division at the next spectacle, Super Bowl XXXXVI in 2013. One hilarious spot featured a rugged American individualist driving out of a post-apocalyptic landscape, as predicted for the end of the year 2012 by the ancient Mayan calendar, in his Chevrolet pick-up to the strains of the pop-singer Barry Manilow's 'Look Likes We Made It'. His friend, who drove a Ford, was not so fortunate.[82]

In spite of wild prognostications that Americans are quickly moving to embrace the world's version of football and equally outrageous divinations that the world will soon embrace American football, neither proclamation seems to fit the current data. Perhaps for imperial games to become truly global pastimes a setting sun serves as a crucial prerequisite.

Or, perhaps, in both cases, the still pungent ideology of American exceptionalism remains the crucial variable. As the *Atlanta Journal-Constitution*'s sports columnist Jeff Schultz remarked in 2009 the whole point of American football in general and the Super Bowl in particular is to provide platforms for parochial celebrations of American exceptionalism. Sure, Americans will let the rest of the world watch if they want, but 'we don't want cricket, warm beer or the Arsenal-Manchester United game as compensation' Schultz fulminated.[83] In spite of global designs and glocal niches, the Super Bowl endures after its first half-century as a beacon of American nationalism.

Notes

1. Darren Rovell, 'NFL: It's Super Bowl 50, not L', *ESPN.COM*, 5 June 2014, https://www.espn.com/nfl/story/_/id/11031941/nfl-take-one-year-hiatus-roman-numerals-super-bowl-50 (accessed 5 June 2016).

2. https://variety.com/2016/tv/news/super-bowl-50-ratings-cbs-third-largest-audience-on-record-1201699814/ (accessed 23 May 2016). Interestingly, the NFL claimed the golden anniversary broadcast was the most watched programme in US television history. Andie Hagemann, 'Super Bowl 50 Most-watched Program in TV History', *NFL.com*, 8 February 2016, https://www.nfl.com/news/story/0ap3000000634876/article/super-bowl-50-mostwatched-program-in-tv-history (accessed 15 September 2016).

3. Richard C. Crepeau, *NFL Football: A History of America's New National Pastime* (Urbana: University of Illinois Press, 2010); Mark Dyreson and Jaime L. Schultz, *American National Pastimes – A History* (London: Routledge, 2015).

4. Peter Hopsicker and Mark Dyreson, 'Super Bowl Sunday', in Len Travers (ed.), *The Historical Dictionary of American Holidays*, Vol. I (Westport, CT: Greenwood Press, 2006), 30–55. For other insights into the Super Bowl see Crepeau, *NFL Football*; Don Weiss with Chuck Day, *The Making of the Super Bowl: The Inside Story of the World's Greatest Sporting Event* (Chicago, IL: Contemporary Books, 2003); Craig Coenen, *From Sandlots to the Super Bowl: The National Football League, 1920–1967* (Knoxville: The University of Tennessee Press, 2005); Michael MacCambridge, *America's Game: The Epic Story of How Pro Football Captured a Nation* (New York: Anchor Books Random House, 2005); Michael Oriard, *Brand NFL: Making and Selling America's Favorite Sport* (Chapel Hill: The University of North Carolina Press, 2007); Thomas Patrick Oates and Zack Furness (eds), *The NFL: Critical and Cultural Perspectives* (Philadelphia, PA: Temple University Press, 2014).

5. Hunter S. Thompson, 'Fear and Loathing at the Super Bowl', *Rolling Stone*, 28 February 1974, https://www.rollingstone.com/sports/features/fear-and-loathing-at-the-super-bowl-19740228 (accessed 22 May 2016).

6. For more on Thompson and the role of the Super Bowl in American popular culture see, Peter Hopsicker, '"Superbowling": Using the Super Bowl's Yearly Commentary to Explore the Evolution of a Sporting Spectacle in the American Consciousness', *The International Journal of the History of Sport* (2017), (this issue).

7. Tony Collins has argued fiercely and convincingly that from the nineteenth-century origins of the various football codes through the First World War, the myriad games were far more similar than different. Tony Collins, 'Unexceptional Exceptionalism: The Origins of American football in a Transnational Context', *Journal of Global History*, 8, no. 2 (July 2013), 209–30. However, as the codes matured through the twentieth century, American (and Canadian) football diverged substantially and became far more distant cousins.

8. Pierre Bourdieu, *The Field of Cultural Production* (Cambridge: Polity, 1993); Pierre Bourdieu, *Outline of a Theory of Practice* (Cambridge: Cambridge University Press, 1972); Anthony Giddens, *The Constitution of Society* (Berkeley: University of California Press, 1984); Alan Bryman, 'The Disneyization of Society', *Sociological Review*, 47 (1999), 25–47; Steven Watts, *The Magic Kingdom: Walt Disney and the American Way of Life* (Columbia: University of

Missouri Press, 1997); George Ritzer, *The MacDonaldization of Society* (Thousand Oaks, CA: Pine Forge, 1993); Steven Mintz and Randy Roberts, *Hollywood's America: Twentieth-Century America through Film* (Malden, MA: Wiley-Blackwell, 2010); Stanley D. Brunn, *Wal-Mart World: The World's Biggest Corporation in the Global Economy* (London: Routledge, 2006); Matthew Futterman, *Players: The Story of Sports and Money, and the Visionaries Who Fought to Create a Revolution* (New York: Simon & Schuster, 2016); Mark Dyreson, 'The Republic of Consumption at the Olympic Games: Globalization, Americanization, and Californization', *Journal of Global History* 8, no. 2 (July 2013), 256–78; Hopsicker and Dyreson, 'Super Bowl Sunday', 30–55.

9. List of most watched television broadcasts in the United States, https://en.wikipedia.org/wiki/List_of_most_watched_television_broadcasts_in_the_United_States#Super_Bowl (accessed 23 May 2016).

10. 'Super Bowl XLI broadcast in 232 countries', NFL press release, 3 February 2007, https://www.nfl.com/news/story/09000d5d80022760/article/super-bowl-xli-broadcast-in-232-countries (accessed 10 January 2016).

11. Steve Rushin, 'A Billion People Can Be Wrong', *Sports Illustrated*, 6 February 2006, 19; Steve Schy, 'Super Bowl XL to Attract Close to 1 Billion Viewers Worldwide', *Voice of America*, 3 February 2006, https://www.51voa.com/VOA_Standard_English/VOA_Standard_5023.html (accessed 10 May 2016).

12. Rushin, 'A Billion People Can Be Wrong', 19.

13. Eliot C. McLaughlin, 'Super Bowl is King at Home but Struggles on World Stage', CNN news service, 5 February 2010, https://www.cnn.com/2010/US/02/05/super.bowl.viewers.profit/ (accessed 23 May 2016).

14. Jérôme Bourdon and Cécil Méadel, *Television Audiences across the World: Deconstructing the Ratings Machine* (Basingstoke, UK: Palgrave Macmillan, 2014); and Helen Wheatley, *Re-viewing Television History: Critical Issues in Television Historiography* (New York: I.B. Tauris, 2007).

15. Joe Ware, 'From a UK Perspective, American Football and the Super Bowl Look Downright Socialist', *Manchester Guardian*, 1 February 2014, https://www.theguardian.com/commentisfree/2014/feb/01/super-bowl-socialist-game-nfl, (accessed 20 June 2016).

16. Ashley Fetters, 'Was Ist das Super Bowl? What Other Countries Say About the Big Game', *Atlantic*, February 2013, https://www.theatlantic.com/entertainment/archive/2013/02/was-ist-das-super-bowl-what-other-countries-say-about-the-big-game/272786/ (accessed 20 March 2016).

17. Michael L. McManus, 'Super Bowl, the World and Korea', *Korea Times*, 6 February 2013, LexisNexis® Academic.

18. https://www.nfl.com/superbowl/50/live/foreign-language-broadcasts (accessed 23 May 2016).

19. Craig Greenham, '"Super Bore": The Canadian Media and the Grey Cup-Super Bowl Comparison', *The International Journal of the History of Sport* (2017), (this issue); Lars Dzikus, 'Amerika: The Super Bowl and German Imagination', *The International Journal of the History of Sport* (2017), (this issue); Iain Adams, 'A Century of British Readings of America through American Football: From the Fin de Siècle to the Super Bowl', *The International Journal of the History of Sport* (2017), (this issue); Kohei Kawashima, '"We Will Try Again, Again, Again to Make It Bigger": Japan, American Football, and the Super Bowl – Past, Present, and Future', *The International Journal of the History of Sport* (2017), (this issue).

20. Greenham, 'Super Bore'.

21. Andrew Both, 'Super Bowl has Ways to Go in Captivating Global Audience', Reuters news service, 24 January 2015, https://www.reuters.com/article/us-nfl-international-idUSKBN0KX0KK20150124 (accessed 23 May 2016); Greg Price, 'How Many Countries Will Watch the Super Bowl?', *International Business Times*, 29 January 2015, https://www.ibtimes.com/how-many-countries-will-watch-super-bowl-1799734 (accessed 23 May 2016); John McDuling, 'Deglobalization: Why Everybody in the US and Nobody Outside it Watches the Super Bowl', *Quartz*, 28 January 2014, https://qz.com/171174/putting-the-global-perspective-

into-the-superbowls-massive-tv-audience/ (accessed 23 May 2016); McLaughlin, 'Super Bowl is King at Home but Struggles on World Stage'.

22. Ishaan Tharoor, 'WorldViews: These Global Sporting Events Totally Dwarf the Super Bowl', *Washington Post*, 5 February 2016, https://www.washingtonpost.com/news/worldviews/wp/2016/02/05/these-global-sporting-events-totally-dwarf-the-super-bowl/ (accessed 23 May 2016).

23. Scott Roxborough, 'Rio Olympics Worldwide Audience to Top 3.5 Billion, IOC Estimates', *Hollywood Reporter*, 18 August 2016, https://www.hollywoodreporter.com/news/rio-olympics-worldwide-audience-top-920526 (accessed 22 October 2016).

24. '2014 FIFA World Cup™ Reached 3.2 Billion Viewers, One Billion Watched Final, 16 December 2015, https://www.fifa.com/worldcup/news/y=2015/m=12/news=2014-fifa-world-cuptm-reached-3-2-billion-viewers-one-billion-watched--2745519.html (accessed 10 June 2016); and Roxborough, 'Rio Olympics Worldwide Audience to Top 3.5 Billion, IOC Estimates.'

25. Daffydd Bynon, 'Cricket World Cup: India v Pakistan Watched by a Billion People', *Manchester Guardian*, 15 February 2015, https://www.theguardian.com/sport/gallery/2015/feb/15/cricket-world-cup-india-v-pakistan-watched-by-a-billion-people-in-pictures (accessed 5 July 2016).

26. Will Brinson, 'Roger Godell: American Football Should 'Absolutely be an Olympic Sport', *CBS Sports*, 3 August 2012, https://www.cbssports.com/nfl/blog/eye-on-football/19719275/roger-goodell-american-football-should-absolutely-be-an-olympic-sport (accessed 10 March 2013); Albert Breer, 'Football in Olympics is a Dream that Could Become a Reality', 26 July 2012, https://www.nfl.com/news/story/09000d5d82acf42b/article/football-in-olympics-is-a-dream-that-could-become-a-reality (accessed 22 July 2016).

27. Oriard, *Brand NFL*; and Crepeau, *NFL Football*.

28. Christopher R. Martin and Jimmie L. Reeves, 'The Whole World Isn't Watching (But We Thought They Were): The Super Bowl and United States Solipsism', *Culture, Sport, Society* 4, no. 2 (June 2001), 213–36.

29. For various perspectives on globalization and sport see, Allen Guttmann, *Games and Empires: Modern Sports and Cultural Imperialism* (New York: Columbia University Press, 1994); Richard Giulianotti and Roland Robertson, *Globalization and Sport* (Oxford: Blackwell, 2007); Walter LaFeber, *Michael Jordan and the New Global Capitalism* (New York: W.W. Norton, 1999); Barbara J. Keys, *Globalizing Sport: National Rivalry and International Community in the 1930s* (Cambridge, MA: Harvard University Press, 2006); and Joseph Maguire, *Global Sport: Identities, Societies, Civilizations* (Cambridge: Polity Press, 1999).

30. Allen Guttmann, *A Whole New Ball Game: An Interpretation of American Sports* (Chapel Hill: University of North Carolina Press, 1988).

31. Tony Collins, *Oval World: A Global History of Rugby* (London: Bloomsbury, 2015); David Goldblatt, *The Ball is Round: A Global History of Football* (New York: Viking, 2006); Andrei Markovits and Steven L. Hellerman, *Offside: Soccer and American Exceptionalism* (Princeton, NJ: Princeton University Press, 2001).

32. On resurgent nationalism in the global era see the 19–25 November issue of *The Economist* on 'The New Nationalism'. The classic studies on the history of nationalism note caution about optimistic claims that it might wither away in the near future. See, for instance, Benedict Anderson, *Imagined Communities: Reflections on the Origin and Spread of Nationalism*, Rev. ed. (London: Verso, 1991); E.J. Hobsbawm, *Nations and Nationalism since 1780: Programme, Myth, Reality*, 2nd ed. (Cambridge: Cambridge University Press, 1992); Robert H. Wiebe, *Who We Are: A History of Popular Nationalism* (Princeton, NJ: Princeton University Press, 2002); and Samuel P. Huntington, *The Clash of Civilizations and the Remaking of World Order* (New York: Simon & Schuster, 1996).

33. Cleese's entire riff reads:

   The three differences between American and British people: We speak English and you don't.

   When we hold a World Championship for a particular sport, we invite teams from other countries to play, as well.

When you meet the head of state in Great Britain, you only have to go down on one knee. https://en.wikiquote.org/wiki/Talk:John_Cleese (accessed 23 May 2016).

34. Greenham, 'Super Bore'; Dzikus, 'Amerika'; Adams, 'A Century of British Readings of America through American Football'; and Kawashima, 'We Will Try Again, Again, Again to Make It Bigger'.

35. For a primer on glocalization see Victor Roudometof, *Glocalization: A Critical Introduction* (London: Routledge, 2016).

36. Dzikus, 'Amerika'; and Grant Wahl, 'Football vs. Fútbol', *Sports Illustrated*, 5 July 2004, 68–75.

37. L. Jon Wertheim, 'The Whole World is Watching', *Sports Illustrated*, 14 June 2004, 72–86.

38. Martin and Reeves, 'The Whole World Isn't Watching', 13–236.

39. George Strickler, 'Day of Decision! Packers vs. Chiefs: First Super Bowl Boasts Highest Stakes in Sports', *Chicago Tribune*, 15 January 1967, sec. B, 1; 'Super Bowl Gate Down, TV Draws 60 Million', *Chicago Daily Defender*, 17 January 1967, 24; 'NBC-I's Super-Dooper Bowl for Mex vs. CBS', *Variety*, 28 December 1966, 22; 'Radio-Television: 76 Share for CBS Super Bowl Solo', *Variety*, 17 January 1968, 27; 'Futbol en Mexico', *Broadcasting*, 29 April 1968, 53; 'Special Report: Step-up in Worldwide Networking', *Broadcasting*, 25 August 1969, 32–5.

40. Strickler, 'Day of Decision!'

41. Clarence Petersen, 'TV Throws Carpet over Super Bowl', *Chicago Tribune*, 14 January 1971, sec. D, 15; 'At Deadline: Certainly is Super Bowl', *Broadcasting*, 10 January 1972, 8.

42. Greenham, 'Super Bore'.

43. 'NBC-I's Super-Dooper Bowl for Mex vs. CBS', 22.

44. Jack Pitman, 'Radio-Television: U.S. Sports Girdling Globe', *Variety*, 11 October 1967, 69, 88.

45. 'Futbol en Mexico', 53.

46. George Strickler, 'Colts, Jets Meet Today in Super Bowl', *Chicago Tribune*, 12 January 1969, sec. B, 1; Petersen, 'TV Throws Carpet over Super Bowl'; 'At Deadline: Certainly is Super Bowl', *Broadcasting*, 10 January 1972, 8; William N. Wallace, 'Dolphins Choice over Vikings in Today's Super Showdown: How Super Bowl Rivals Match Up Facts on Super Bowl', *New York Times*, 13 January 1974, sec. A, 1; 'TV Game Plan Is Simple: Lots More of Everything', *New York Times*, 13 January 1974, sec. A, 3; and 'CBS-TV Says Super Bowl was an All-Timer for Sports', *Broadcasting*, 23 January 1978, 48.

47. Larry Weisman, 'Game-day Coverage Offers Proof of Worldwide Appeal', *USA Today*, 29 January 1996, sec. C, 6; and Larry Weisman, 'NFL Has Whole Wide World in its Hands on Super Sunday', *USA Today*, 26 January 1998, sec. C, 4.

48. Ken Bensinger, 'Mexico Might Miss B'cast of Super Bowl', *Daily Variety*, 27 January 2004, 10.

49. Dudley Althaus, 'Mexicans Hyped for Super Bowl Fiestas', *Houston Chronicle*, 27 January 2004, https://www.chron.com/sports/article/Mexicans-hyped-for-Super-Bowl-fiestas-1976629.php (accessed 22 November 2016).

50. Anthony Cotton, 'NFL Is Making a Big Play for Mexican Fan Base', *Denver Post*, 2 October 2005, sec. A, 1.

51. Donald E. Chipman, Randolph Campbell, and Robert Calvert, *The Dallas Cowboys and the NFL* (Norman: University of Oklahoma Press, 1970); Joe Nick Patoski, *The Dallas Cowboys: The Outrageous History of the Biggest, Loudest, Most Hated, Best Loved Football Team in America* (New York: Little, Brown and Company, 2012); Robert Fleishman and Robert McKenzie, 'How the National Football League (NFL) Has Strategically Managed the 1961 Sports Broadcasting Act (SBA) to Gain Market Supremacy in the USA and a Dominant Market Niche in Mexico', *Derecho Comparado de la Información* 20 (2012), 61–71.

52. Sara Miller Llana, 'Super Bowl: Why Mexico City is Chock Full of Pittsburgh Steelers Fans', *Christian Science Monitor*, 6 February 2011, LexisNexis®Academic; Dudley Althaus, 'Mexicans Hyped for Super Bowl Fiestas', *Houston Chronicle*, 27 January 2004, https://www.chron.com/sports/article/Mexicans-hyped-for-Super-Bowl-fiestas-1976629.php (accessed 13 October 2016); Daniel Brown, 'In Mexico, NFL has Untapped Market', *San Jose Mercury News*, 28 September 2005, sec. A, 1; Tom Weir, 'Futbol-Mad Mexico Ready for Football', *USA Today*, 30 September 2005, sec. C, 1; Kevin Baxter, 'Football in Mexico: Viva! Football', *Los Angeles*

Times, 7 November 2008, sec. D, 1; and Kevin Baxter, 'NFL's Wide Borders: Mexico is Home to Millions of the League's Fans', *Los Angeles Times*, 29 January 2010, sec. C, 1.

53. Paul Oberjuerge, 'Big Game Means Much South of the Border', San Bernardino (California) *Sun*, 1 February 2005, LexisNexis® Academic.

54. Andrew MacMains, 'The Story Behind Avocado's from Mexico Surprise Super Bowl Hit', *Adweek*, 10 February 2015, https://www.adweek.com/news/advertising-branding/story-behind-avocados-mexicos-surprise-super-bowl-hit-162864 (accessed 10 July 2016); Sydney Ember, 'Second-year Super Bowl Advertisers Face Their Own Pressures to Succeed', *New York Times*, 25 January 2016, sec. B, 1; 'Super Bowl XLIX 2015 Commercial – Avocados From Mexico #FirstDraftEver', *YouTube*, https://www.youtube.com/watch?v=xt4pED6XDV8 (accessed 10 July 2016); '#AvosInSpace | Avocados From Mexico 2016 Big Game Commercial', *YouTube*, https://www.youtube.com/watch?v=1ndPEQCoSzk (accessed 10 July 2016).

55. Colin Howell's delightful essay on the Canadian–US borderlands remains the crucial text for anyone pondering the importance of such regions in the history of sport. Colin D. Howell, 'Borderlands, Baselines and Bearhunters: Conceptualizing the Northeast as a Sporting Region in the Interwar Period', *Journal of Sport History* 29 (Summer 2002), 250–70.

56. 'Super Bowl Gate Down, TV Draws 60 Million', 24; 'NBC-I's Super-Dooper Bowl for Mex vs. CBS', 22; 'Radio-Television: 76 Share for CBS Super Bowl Solo', 27; 'Futbol en Mexico', 53; 'Special Report: Step-up in Worldwide Networking', 32–5; Petersen, 'TV Throws Carpet over Super Bowl', 15; 'At Deadline: Certainly is Super Bowl', 8; Wallace, 'Dolphins Choice over Vikings in Today's Super Showdown', 1; 'TV Game Plan is Simple', 3.

57. 'Special Report: Step-up in Worldwide Networking', 32–5; Strickler, 'Colts, Jets Meet Today in Super Bowl', 1; and Petersen, 'TV Throws Carpet Over Super Bowl', 15.

58. Petersen, 'TV Throws Carpet Over Super Bowl', 15; 'At Deadline: Certainly is Super Bowl', 8; Wallace, 'Dolphins Choice Over Vikings in Today's Super Showdown', 1; 'TV Game Plan Is Simple', 3; and 'As SIN Goes Satellite, it Aims to Be a Network', *Variety*, 19 April 1978, 61.

59. 'Radio-Television: Super Bowl in London', *Variety*, 21 January 1981, 61; 'English Will Get Super Bowl TV', *New York Times*, 13 January 1981, sec. C, 13. One source claimed that in 1980 the British broadcast the Super Bowl to sites in Birmingham and Soho. Gerald Eskenazi, 'Pro Leagues in America Eye the Globe: Pro Sports U.S. Leagues Eye the World', *New York Times*, 9 April 1989, sec. Sports, 1. However, I could find no confirmation of that claim.

60. William Borders, 'Super Premiere Plays for London Fans: Super Bowl Premier in London, Omar Sharif in Crowd, Cheerleaders on Stage', *New York Times*, 27 January 1981, sec. B, 15–16.

61. Adams, 'A Century of British Readings of America through American Football'.

62. Dzikus, 'Amerika'.

63. World League of American Football website, https://www.worldleagueofamericanfootball.com/ (accessed 10 September 2016); and Crepeau, *NFL Football*.

64. These efforts have gone almost entirely unnoticed by scholars save for a couple of journal articles, a couple of dissertations, and one confessional from a European convert. Joe Maguire, 'The Media-sport Production Complex: The Case of American Football in Western European Societies', *European Journal of Communication* 6, no. 3 (September 1991), 315–35; Maarten van Bottenburg, 'Thrown for a Loss? (American) Football and the European Sport Space', *American Behavioral Scientist* 46, no. 11 (July 2003), 1550–62; Carlton Hartsell Bryan, 'An Analysis of Selected Attendance Factors in the World League of American Football' (PhD diss., University of Oregon, 1993); Lars Dzikus, 'From Violence to Party: A History of the Presentation of American Football in England and Germany' (PhD diss., Ohio State University, 2005); and Lars Anderson, *The Proving Ground: A Season on the Fringe in NFL Europe* (New York: St Martin's Press, 2001).

65. Roger Thurow and A. Craig Copetas, 'NFL Goes Long in Its Attempt to Sell World League in Europe', *Wall Street Journal*, 28 March 1997, sec. B, 7; Phil Sheridan, 'NFL Lags in Global Race', *Philadelphia Inquirer*, 6 May 2009, sec. D, 1; Wahl, 'Football vs. Fútbol', 68–75; and Bryan Gardiner, 'London Calling', *Sports Illustrated*, 11 January 2016, https://www.si.com/vault/2016/02/11/london-calling# (accessed 12 September 2016).

66. Website of the International Federation of American Football, https://ifaf.org/ (accessed 22 May 2016).

67. Website of Football Canada, https://footballcanada.com/ (accessed 22 May 2016).

68. Kawashima, 'We Will Try Again, Again, Again to Make It Bigger'.

69. Peter King, 'How Long Will Dallas Reign', *Sports Illustrated*, 6 September 1993, 44–53; and Wahl, 'Football vs. Fútbol', 68–75.

70. Jack Pitman, 'O'seas Interest in Super Bowl Pulls Huge Audience', *Variety*, 29 January 1986, 1, 92. Television experts noted that with a nightly audience of a little over 111 million, the one network equaled the entire American market for football. Paul Nicholson, 'Programme Sales: China Prizes', *Broadcast*, 24 July 1987, 19.

71. Steve Daley, 'Super Bowl: A Case Study in Capitalism', *Chicago Tribune*, 26 January 1986, sec. B, 1.

72. Hal Plotkin, 'Multi-National Start-up', *Inc* (Fall 1988), 15–17.

73. Frederick C. Klein, 'On Sports: Gridiron Broadcasts Behind the Great Wall', *Wall Street Journal*, 20 January 1987, sec. A, 1.

74. '2014 FIFA World Cup™ Reached 3.2 Billion Viewers, One Billion Watched Final', FIFA press release, 16 December 2015; https://www.fifa.com/worldcup/news/y=2015/m=12/news=2014-fifa-world-cuptm-reached-3-2-billion-viewers-one-billion-watched--2745519.html (accessed 20 June 2016).

75. Fetters, 'Was Ist das Super Bowl?'

76. Jean K. Chalaby, *Transnational Television Worldwide: Towards a New Media Order* (London: I.B. Tauris, 2005); William Marling, *How 'American' is Globalization?* (Baltimore: Johns Hopkins University Press, 2006); and Matthew Fraser, *Weapons of Mass Distraction: Soft Power and American Empire* (New York: Thomas Dunne, 2005).

77. Brendan Baber and Eric Spitznagel, *Planet Baywatch: The Unofficial Guide to the New World Order* (New York: St. Martin's Griffin, 1996).

78. Simon Kuper and Stefan Syzmanski, *Soccernomics* (New York: Nation Books, 2014), 215.

79. 'Gridiron Racking up Global Gains', *China Daily*, 31 January 2015, LexisNexis®Academic.

80. For a brilliant corrective to these wild predications as well as insights into the 'culture wars' over soccer in the US, see Franklin Foer, *How Soccer Explains the World: An Unlikely Theory of Globalization* (New York: HarperCollins, 2004).

81. 'Super Bowl Out, Manchester United In', *Toronto Star*, 1 June 2012, sec. B, 1; 'Soccer Bigger Bang for GM Buck than Super Bowl', *Sports Business News*, 3 June 2012, https://www.sportsbusinessnews.com/node/1973 (accessed 12 September 2016); 'GM Trades Super Bowl for Soccer, Sponsors Manchester United', *Advertising Age*, 31 May 2012, https://adage.com/article/media/gm-trades-super-bowl-soccer-sponsors-manchester-united/235054/ (accessed 30 August 2016).

82. Chevy Super Bowl Commercial for 2013, 'End of the World', *YouTube video*, https://www.youtube.com/watch?v=uyOu_yfcpFo (accessed 11 September 2016).

83. Jeff Schultz, 'Please, No More NFL in England', *Atlanta Journal-Constitution*, 14 May 2009, sec. C, 1.

Disclosure Statement

No potential conflict of interest was reported by the author.

Index

Page numbers in **bold** denote tables